AMERICAN RACE RELATIONS THEORY

A Review of Four Models

Hermon George, Jr.

LANHAM • NEW YORK • LONDON

University Press of America,™ Inc.

4720 Boston Way
Lanham, MD 20706

3 Henrietta Street
London WC2E 8LU England

Printed in the United States of America

Library of Congress Cataloging in Publication Data

George, Hermon.
American race relations theory.

Bibliography: p.
Includes index.
1. United States—Race relations—Historiography.
I. Title.
E185.615.G46 1984 305.8'00973 83-27360
ISBN 0-8191-3813-4 (alk. paper)
ISBN 0-8191-3814-2 (pbk. : alk. paper)

All University Press of America books are produced on acid-free paper which exceeds the minimum standards set by the National Historical Publications and Records Commission.

This book is dedicated to the activists,
theoreticians, and supporters of the Black
liberation movement and
to my wife,
Susan,
to my parents,
Henrene and Hermon George, Sr.,
to my sister, Ina,
to the memory of my daughter,
Aimee Patrice,
and to my son,
Dahren Malcolm,
who is the future.

Acknowledgments

I wish to thank the American Sociological Association for granting permission to quote from Beverly Duncan and Otis Dudley Duncan, "Minorities and the Process of Stratification," American Sociological Review 33 (1968), pp. 360, 363.

A slightly different version of Chapter 1 appeared as Afro-Scholar Working Paper #12, "The Ethnic Group Model of American Race Relations," published in March 1983 by the Afro-American Studies and Research Program of the University of Illinois, Urbana.

The typing of this manuscript at various stages in its gestation was done by Jeannette Groff, Dorothy Tucci, Eve Mahoney, and -- in this version -- by Susan Davison; a special debt of gratitude is owed to them all.

Thanks also to the following people: Joe Jorgensen, Marvin Jackson, Greg Pitts, Andrea Hedgley, Wayne Byrd, Walter Robinson, Michele Davis, Roberto Rodriguez, and Susan George.

Table of Contents

Introduction

Format and Methods of the Study

The aim here is to review and judge various statements on U.S. black/white race relations to determine their utility and veracity in the hope that inaccurate and misleading views will be challenged and superseded. The statements chosen have been grouped together into four distinct sets which are represented as "models."(1)

The statements are models in the sense that they contain correlated propositions by which policy can be guided; further, they are models because they provide simplification and greater determinateness of real social relations about which, using the model and its propositions, deductions can be made.(2) Some of the models do not fulfill these requirements, but this informal definition provides a starting point. And while some statements more than others descend from a coherent social theory or tradition in social theory whose assumptions can be examined, it is perhaps wiser to concede that the statements reviewed are "verbal 'image(s) of society'" which offer "perspective(s)" or "orientation(s)."(3) Nonetheless, a rigorous examination of these statements, such as that attempted below, may reveal the adequacy of these "perspectives" on race relations, and thus aid in securing reliable knowledge about this important aspect of the social world.(4)

Furthermore, the models may be inspected from the point of view of the assumptions which they contain. These assumptions, which principally supply the writer's or social scientist's value orientation and value judgments about the social world, are significant influences on the form and content of his statement.(5) In what follows, I have attempted to uncover the most significant assumptions contained in each of the works examined. And, in so doing, I have grouped the statements into recognizable clusters, each identifiable by the sharing of certain assumptions.(6) It is the groupings of assumptions and propositions embedded in these clusters, then, which I have termed models.

My efforts to group the assumptions contained in the race relations literature have derived much of their substance from the application of a six-fold framework. This conceptual scheme stems in large part from my reading of the seminal work of Oliver C. Cox.(7) The six concepts are: _group definition_, _power_, _conflict_, _exclusion_, _exploitation_, and _historical situation_. A major premise of this study is that all statements on U.S. black/white race relations may be judged by their abilities to successfully define, give substance to, and interrelate these six fundamental concepts. After presenting definitions for each of these concepts, my study renders such judgments.

Another organizing principle followed here directs attention to the political outlooks in each model. In simplest form, the political views that underlie race relations models can be dichotomized with liberal on one side and radical (i.e., Marxist and other critical points of view) on the other. Deeper analysis, of course, suggests a continuum of models, distinguishing polar cases from more intermediate positions.

A continuum of four types of models comprises the general format for the study. Following an introduction to the definitions of the concepts we will analyze, the models are discussed seriatim. The _ethnic group model_ (Ch. 1) constitutes one polar type, is the most visible viewpoint on race relations, and is rooted primarily in liberal social and political philosophy. Sharing a similar political outlook, but offering somewhat different propositions to account for race relations, is the _caste model_ (Ch. 2). The _colonial model_ (Ch. 3), whose social and political philosophy is critical of liberal social theory, represents a variant of radical critical social theory. The other polar type is the _Marxist model_ (Ch. 4), whose propositions and political outlook draw upon a tradition that is highly critical of liberalism: it sustains a polemical alternative vision of social reality. A model's position on this continuum of types suggests its frequency of use, and its acceptability as conventional social wisdom. The family of studies that we have classified as belonging to the _ethnic group model_ far outnumbers the studies of

American race relations conducted in a Marxist mode.

In each chapter, a specific format has been followed. First, the central propositions of the model are outlined. This is followed by a critical discussion of selected explanations made by researchers in the mode. The statements that we analyze are not necessarily representative or typical, but on the basis of my reading and impressions, they seem to be representative of each type as I have defined them. A summary of the discussion concludes each chapter.

The concluding chapter (Ch. 5) provides a summation of the substantive criticism offered in the four main chapters, and a set of criteria by which some of the central difficulties noted may be resolved. Though a synthesis is not advanced, I argue that certain lines of analysis can be combined so as to stimulate clarity and promote useful research in the investigation and explanation of relations between Black people and Euro-Americans in the United States.

Finally, a note on the selection of the research and the researchers that I have analyzed within each type. Four criteria have guided the selection process. First, I have tried, for the most part, to concentrate on the work of authors who enjoy some degree of influence and visibility. Second, the statements chosen tend to carry rather explicit theoretical structures. Third, with the exception of Chapter 1, some of the works included in each chapter have been chosen in order to convey a sense of the historical development of the model. And, fourth, I have decided to study statements whose ideological disposition can readily be ascertained.

The Basic Concepts Used

Six concepts comprise the framework used here to typologize, and analyze, the statements on race relations presented in the four main chapters of this study.(8) They are: group definition, power, conflict, exclusion, exploitation, and historical situation. Let me explain how these concepts are employed.

Two concepts are of particular importance, (1) group definition and (2) historical situation. The latter is associated with prediction in race relations. Group definition, on the other hand, is the principal salient differentiator of statements on race relations.

Group definition is the social definition (used by group members and interested parties alike) of the groups which interact in race relations. It provides a major clue to their putative sociological and political orientation. Hence, groups in race relations are variously defined as "ethnic groups," "castes," "colonized and colonizer," and "super exploited segments of the working class," among others. Moreover, this concept subsumes two important aspects of the groups interacting: their position in the socioracial hierarchy (i.e., the pattern of subordination and superordination established in a racist, ethnically heterogeneous society) and the mode of consciousness (the most common among racial or ethnic groups are assimilationism, pluralism, and nationalism) which tends to characterize that group.(9)

Power may be defined as "the capacity of some men to produce intended effects on other men."(10) To this statement of the actual dimension of power, another dimension, that of potential, must be added. The actual dimension of power expresses a zero-sum game: the amount of power within the social order is limited, and any taking of it by one party involves its diminution for another. In this sense, the actual dimension of power, and the power relations which it establishes, are hydraulic. Those relations, moreover, tend to be hierarchial, ranging from the relatively powerful to the relatively powerless, and asymmetrical, assigning unequal degrees of power to subordinates and dominators. By contrast, the potential dimension of power expresses its latency, i.e., the possibility for change which is present in the power relations established by its actual dimension. Since the potential dimension of power is often, under certain conditions, capable of modifying or supplanting existing power relations, this dimension of power is generative, or capable of developing new kinds of power relations not given within the context of actual power relations.

The two dimensions of power continually interact, and their interaction produces certain unintended consequences. Depending on the type of unintended consequences produced, it may be possible to say something about the relative proportion of the actual to the potential in power relations at a specified point and thus about the likelihood of change in those relations from actual to potential. Finally, though many additional aspects of power could be discussed (e.g., its intentionality, its scope, its asymmetry, etc.), for our purposes we add only one more distinction: types of power -- principally economic, social, and political -- to which also correspond characteristic modes of expression.(11)

Conflict may be defined as a special case of social interaction between individuals and groups who are in contact and communication and who possess divergent projects (i.e., aspirations, goals, means, ends, values, etc.). Conflict may be a conscious or unconscious social activity and tends to be intermittent, though its intensity may vary.(12) For this study, the most important aspects of conflict concern its group manifestations, in addition to some judgment about the homeostatic or disjunctive nature of conflict. These two aspects of conflict commonly interpenetrate, but in any given social situation a tendency toward the domination of one or the other may be discerned. Depending on the nature of conflict, then, the relationship of conflict to social change -- generally to be understood as change which remains within the established social order or that which transcends it -- may be posited.

As with power, the basis of conflict, and characteristic modes of its expression, may be identified as economic, political, and social or cultural. Special attention should be devoted to the manner, if any, in which the unintended consequences of power promote the use or creation of specific modes of conflict expression. In this regard, race relations theory often takes up the question of conflict attitudes, their latency, the conditions of their expression, and the meaning of outbreaks of sporadic interracial violence as evidence of conflict. Also, one particular base of conflict, and its accompanying mode of expression, often receive special attention in race relations theory, viz., the social or cultural base of conflict and the determination of its singularity (racial conflict based within a single, unifying consensual, assimilative cultural field) or duality (racial conflict based on competing, partially exclusive cultural fields, usually with one predominating).(13)

Exclusion (also designated by cognate terms such as "segregation," "separation") refers to a regularized social relationship which establishes and maintains social distance (which subsumes physical distance) and limits contact and communication. The basis for exclusion must be ascertained together with the positive or negative social effects which it produces. Race relations theory most often seeks this basis in ethnicity, phenotypical difference or cultural difference, and judges the effect of exclusion to be either integrative of group traditions and norms (positive) or disintegrative of them (negative). Exclusion may be thought of as producing a negative effect in another sense, viz., in its relation to creating and sustaining subordination. When patterns of subordination are partially maintained by exclusion, it becomes necessary to situate them socially at the structural level. Institutional racism may then be understood as a pattern of subordination, partially caused by exclusion, in which a set of stable, regular, expected social relations based on perceived racial distinctions operates to produce an invidious socioracial hierarchy (i.e., a pattern of subordination and superordination among racially heterogeneous groups) that is supported by interacting social spheres. These spheres are principally three: the subjective, in which prejudicial attitudes (prejudice) are usually expressed as hostile conflict attitudes commonly directed against racial subordinates; the objective, in which regularly expected and obtained differential outcomes (discrimination) in social institutions perpetuate and enforce the socioracial hierarchy; and the cultural, here taken to mean those normative and aesthetic patterns which ensure injurious comparison of subordinate and superordinate groups in the socioracial hierarchy.

Paradoxically, though it is often argued that exclusion minimizes conflict by limiting contact, the opposite effect must also be taken into account. Exclusion may serve to aid in the development and maintenance of group traditions and norms, i.e., culture, which serve as bases from which conflict in opposition to exclusion may derive.

Exclusion can only serve as a partial explanation of subordination because it is not only necessary to explain the "outside" position of disfavored groups but their "down" position, too. Here, the next concept assumes importance.

Exploitation, in one sense, may be defined as unequal exchange between two parties in an economic relation. The nature of this economic relation may vary (say, as between peasant and landlord, or capitalist and wage earner) and with it the degree of exploitation.(14) Since economic relations often shape the arena in which social action occurs, exploitative economic relations are of special interest. Such relations generally entail a division of society (e.g., the division of labor), the principal of hierarchy which includes domination and superordination as its opposite poles, and the unequal distribution of power and its contingent attributes (i.e., ownership of capital represents power, but the exercise of parliamentary decision-making is clearly contingent but not directly identical to that ownership).

As regards race relations theory, the nature and degree of exploitation are important factors which may influence the other concepts put forward: hierarchical power relations predicated on exploitation may serve to erect and maintain exclusionary social barriers which enforce subordination, and this type of exclusion (i.e., negative, or restricting) may allow certain kinds of conflict (e.g., racial) while attempting to diffuse others (e.g., class). However, the precise role played by exploitation in race relations must always be based on an assessment of its nature and degree, and the reciprocal effect of other forces on it (e.g., type of power, type of conflict, etc.).

In another sense, the term exploitation is often used to connote a set of injurious social relations -- sometimes including, but not restricted to, the economic -- which beset a particular social group. This second meaning, though more common than the first, is less precise. It calls attention to those features of race relations situations that are here discussed under concepts such as group definition, power, conflict, and exclusion. Thus, analysis of this term in the following statements will concentrate on the first meaning outlined above.

Finally, the exact nature of all of the concepts so far elaborated will be greatly conditioned by the last concept to be presented, the <u>historical situation</u>. The concepts advanced must all be given a specific content which derives from the particular society at a particular point in historical time to which they are applied. It matters very much whether the relations between distinct groups are set within the perspective of a feudal society, a capitalist society, or a hunting and gathering society. Differences in those relations should be expected in each of the different contexts and it might be shown that certain kinds of group relations are typical of certain kinds of societies. Indeed, a demonstration of the changes in group relations as they move from context to context, diachronically, might be undertaken. For race relations theory, it is most important to establish the social context in historical time, i.e., the historical situation, in which "races" and their interaction are viewed. The ability to accurately depict this historical situation and its constituent elements may lead to an assessment of its tendencies and toward prediction, both of the changes in the historical situation and the attendant changes in subsequent race relations. Conversely, failure to define adequately the historical situation can only promise to plague any analysis with ambiguity and questionable methods.

With this evaluative conceptual framework at hand, its application to the statements selected may be undertaken. We turn first to the ethnic group model.

H. G., Jr.
New York, 1983

Notes

1. The quotation marks here are meant to indicate that I recognize the exactness with which natural science generally endows this word, and that I do not use it, throughout this essay, with the same standards in mind. As footnotes 2, 3, and 4 below make clear, I think social science derives this term from somewhat different standards, but with equal validity. Therefore, throughout this essay, the term will appear without quotation marks to mean the type of model that I am defining in this Introduction.

2. Gellner outlines the properties of a model which must concern us here: simplification, greater determinateness, and deductive ability. See E. A. Gellner, "Model (Theoretical Model)," A Dictionary of the Social Sciences, ed. by Julius Gould and William L. Kolb (New York: Crowell-Collier Publishing Co., 1964), p. 435.

3. These phrases are taken from Jonathan H. Turner, The Structure of Sociological Theory (Homewood, Illinois: The Dorsey Press, 1974), p. 9. Turner describes the main components of theory as concepts, variables, theoretical statements expressing the two, and a logically consistent format which organizes the preceding three. Judged by these standards, which Turner has derived essentially from natural science, none of the statements here examined possesses a "scientific" theory (Ibid., pp. 1-12).

However, the appropriateness of such standards for social science is open to question.

4. As the above footnote intimates, I am not a partisan of the notion that social science and natural science are, or should be, identical kinds of endeavors. The value question and the inability to permanently suppress subject-object identity are sound reasons for taking this approach. However, social science is a science but it is a human science. This debate cannot be settled here, but its existence must be noted, as are my

preferences. The defense of social science as a different kind (i.e., humanistic) of science -- but science, nonetheless -- is very ably presented by two scholars, themselves historians: See E. H. Carr, What is History? (New York: Random House, 1961), esp. Ch. 3; and Howard Zinn, The Politics of History (Boston: Beacon Press, 1970), esp. Chs. 1-3. A narrow technocrat's defense, heavily influenced by natural science, is given by Ernest Nagel, "The Logic of Historical Analysis," in Hans Meyerhoff, ed., The Philosophy of History in Our Time (Garden City, New York: Doubleday and Co., 1959), pp. 203-215. Finally, various attempts at infusing physical science tradition into the corpus of social science are labeled "abstracted empiricism" and convincingly rejected by C. Wright Mills, The Sociological Imagination (New York: Oxford University Press, 1959), esp. Chs. 3 and 6.

5. These value orientations have been identified by Alvin Gouldner as "domain assumptions" which, whether explicit or not, act to affect the whole of the social scientist's work, from theorizing to actual research. See Alvin W. Gouldner, The Coming Crisis of Western Sociology (New York: Basic Books, Inc., 1970), pp. 29-35.

6. Thomas S. Kuhn has suggested that a scientific community shares a set of beliefs, techniques, and values which may be called a "paradigm." Later, for conceptual clarity, he designates this entity a "disciplinary matrix." See Thomas S. Kuhn, The Structure of Scientific Revolutions, 2nd ed., enl. (Chicago: University of Chicago Press, 1970), pp. 175-187. At any rate, Kuhn's notion is directly analogous to a consensual social scientific community united by its members' adherence to certain assumptions.

7. The work referred to is Caste, Class, and Race (New York: Monthly Review Press, 1948). The framework does not appear, but Dr. Cox's treatment of the subject matter readily suggests it.

8. It should be made clear that the term "race" is used throughout this essay to denote perceived

phenotypical differences that have social consequences. This is a social definition of race, and persons so defined constitute a social race. The concept of "social race" is outlined by Marvin Harris in his article, "Race," International Encyclopedia of the Social Sciences, 1968 ed., vol. 13, pp. 263-269, esp. pp. 263-264. Indeed, the rudimentary and unsatisfactory scientific status of the term "race" has long been noted; see Ashley Montagu, Man's Most Dangerous Myth: The Fallacy of Race, 5th ed. (New York: Oxford University Press, 1974), and Jacques Barzun, Race: A Study in Superstition, rev. ed. (New York: Harper and Row Publishers, 1965).

9. As used in this study, the word "racist" denotes psychological and structural social patterns which regularly assign invidious differential outcomes to individuals and broad groups distinguished by putative phenotypical differences. From this central usage, the two principal modes of racism -- its subjective sphere (often referred to as prejudice) and its objective sphere (commonly known as discrimination, but here more frequently treated as exclusion, subordination, and institutional racism) -- are given extended treatment at various points throughout.

10. Dennis Wrong, Skeptical Sociology (New York: Columbia University Press, 1976), p. 165.

11. In the work cited above, Wrong (op. cit., pp. 163-82) sets forth some of these other aspects. Dahl provides an informative, though biased toward liberal premises, discussion of power in Robert A. Dahl, "Power," International Encyclopedia of the Social Sciences, 1968 ed., vol. 12, pp. 405-415. In demarcating three principal types of power, the convention of Weber has been used, though it will become apparent that his conclusions are not shared; see H. H. Gerth and C. Wright Mills, eds., From Max Weber: Essays in Sociology (New York: Oxford University Press, 1946), pp. 47, 50, 180-252.

12. This part of my definition of conflict is a modification of the views expressed in R. E. Park and E. W. Burgess, Introduction to the Science of Sociology,

ed. by Morris Janowitz, 3rd ed. rev. (Chicago: University of Chicago Press, 1969), p. 574.

13. The question of the interpretation of conflict in this particular aspect becomes especially important when one considers the subject of Black nationalism in the United States. Though it is possible to see this phenomenon as just another in a series of "ethnic dualisms" that have characterized ethnic groups as they encounter difficulties on their journey of assimilation (i.e., ethnic or racial conflict occurs within a singular cultural field), it is also possible to argue that this ideology makes manifest deep cleavages in moral and social vision, and thus sustains conflict (i.e., it is symptomatic of racial conflict which occurs in a dual cultural field) over basic issues about the society itself. An excellent statement of this difference of opinion is John H. Bracey, Jr., August Meier, and Elliott Rudwick, eds., Black Nationalism in America (New York: Bobbs-Merrill, 1970), pp. lii-lx: The editors disagree on the proper interpretation of their subject matter, with Meier and Rudwick defending the "ethnic dualism" position while Bracey argues that Black nationalism has a more profound significance. When synopses of the four models are presented below, I will return to this question.

14. The discussion in this section is grounded in Marx's presentation of this term. See Karl Marx, Capital, vol. 1, trans. by S. Moore and E. Aveling, ed. by F. Engels (New York: Charles H. Kerr and Co., 1906), pp. 240-241.

> Prefabricated Negroes are sketched on sheets of paper and superimposed upon the Negro community; then when someone thrusts his head through the page and yells, 'Watch out there, Jack, there're people living under here,' they are shocked and indignant.
>
> Ralph Ellison,
> Shadow and Act,
> 1964, p. 123.

Chapter 1
The Ethnic Group Model

Introduction

A great deal of the literature of social science and social pundits dealing with U.S. race relations casts them in the framework of relations between distinct ethnic groups. This focus results from a persistent attempt to read the experience of nineteenth century Europe and European immigrants into the history of U.S. race relations between blacks and whites.(1)

But this mistaken notion does not enjoy its persistence through oversight. Rather, it is essentially the reflection, in sociological perspectives on race relations, of the dominant (but increasingly challenged, by critics and by its own failings) neo-classically liberal view of the American social order. In economics, neo-classical liberalism has produced Keynesianism and its variants. In politics, it supports theories of pluralism and the elite/mass concept of democracy; and, in the sociological approach to race relations, it fosters assimilationism and variations on this theme, the most notable being cultural pluralism.(2)

This last field is the focal point of this chapter, and a summary comment on just how the assimilation process is supposed to work, according to its proponents, is in order. Talcott Parsons maintains that "the process of inclusion" is similar to the supply and demand process of economics.(3) The inclusion (this is Parsons' word for assimilation) process acts hierarchically and temporally through three levels: the civil or legal as lowest; the political as intermediate; and, the social as highest. The speed of the ethnic group in gaining each level is determined by the demands for inclusion, both from within and outside of the group, and by the supply of positions ("slots," as Parsons calls them) in the receiving society. Inclusion (assimilation) is complete when the ethnic group has entered all three levels. At bottom, the entire process rests on the social consensus, i.e., "the ultimate social grounding of the demand for inclusion lies in commitment to the values [the social consensus] which legitimize it."(4)

Assimilation, so conceived, is fundamentally dependent on the command of resources, financial, political, and social.(5) And, it is not accidental that those who occupy the commanding heights of the American resources structure are most concerned to define assimilation in their own interests.(6) These interests most often coincide with a social philosophy which enshrines gradualism and an ethical viewpoint based on liberal individualism. But the statements on race relations which this liberal view supports tend to misunderstand or ignore the collective features of these situations, to slight or deny the existence of institutional racism, and to picture the culture of racial subordinates as pathological. These statements will be treated, for analytic purposes, as exemplifying the ethnic group model.

We shall argue, in essence, that this model of U.S. race relations does not comprehend the significance of the patterns of separate, ethnic group interaction which it uncovers and glorifies. This interaction can most realistically be seen as a subordination process based on socially significant phenotypical distinctions, and not as an all-inclusive assimilation process. Further, institutional racism (i.e., the ubiquitous process of assigning systematically unequal inputs and outcomes to racial subordinates in all spheres of social life), is a central expression of this subordination and is almost universally ignored or belittled by proponents of this model; instead, the subject of cultural pathology is used to avoid any serious critical examination of the structural aspects of American capitalist democracy and its effects on the groups which interact. And this avoidance is itself a product of the model's adherence to liberal social theory in its presentation of fundamental concepts such as power, interest, consensus, and economic relations. Only a break with liberal theory is likely to enable us to develop a theoretical perspective more in line with the realities of the subordination process. But before such a break can be attempted, orthodox notions must be challenged, skewered, and rejected. It is to this task that, armed with the six evaluative concepts outlined in the Introduction, we devote the remainder of this chapter.

Central Propositions of the Model

There is much variety in the writings of the adherents of this model (7), but at least five central propositions appear with enough regularity to allow one to see tendencies toward these interpretations.

First, there is the assumption that society is divided into separate groups, varying in size and strength, each possessing a cultural tradition, a set of primary contact institutions, and a history peculiar to it. The group may or may not be defined by socially significant phenotypic characteristics.(8)

Second, these groups interact in a society in which the most powerful social force is that of assimilation: a sort of "escalator assimilation" is at work carrying original immigrant groups from their entry-level lowly status to positions of security and influence several generations later.(9)

Third, this assimilation itself is predicated on a

social equilibrium maintained by value consensus, a normative framework to which all members of the social order subscribe and whose existence is said to explain the fact that conflict occurs only on the basis of the social distribution of valued attributes, and not over the very question of the attributes and the organization of society itself.(10)

Fourth, a pluralist dispersed power model of social, economic, and especially political power is used to expound on the manner in which conflict does occur. The chief vehicle of analysis is the interest group, and typically, the ethnic group is equated with the interest group.

And fifth, those social factors which are held to operate outside the sphere of ethnicity itself, such as education, income level, patterns of consumption, and occupational status, but which are admitted to influence the course of the assimilation of the ethnic group, are usually brought into the analysis of the school via a stratificational assessment of social classes.

Sub-groups of the Model

The above five propositions sketch a general foundation for the ethnic group model. Moreover, the works examined in this chapter can be arranged into sub-groups of the model, each of which tends to emphasize one or more of the central propositions while implicitly subscribing to those which remain.

Three sub-groups may be outlined: the quantitative, the political empowerment, and the assimilationist/pluralist, this last being fundamentally a summation and extension of the first two. The first examines or collects statistical and empirical data which reveal some portion of the experience of selected ethnic groups; this sub-group centers its analysis on variables (such as residential patterns, educational attainment, etc.) in the assimilation process which reveal stratified inequality (the fifth proposition). The second sub-group makes arguments about the routes to political empowerment which ethnic groups traditionally have or have not followed; its writing is guided by neo-classical liberal political theory (the fourth proposition). The third sub-group is most concerned to address the ethical, social, and cultural aspects of race relations ("ethnic group relations") from an assimilationist or pluralist point of view; its work tends to emphasize ethnic history, unilinear assimilation, and the consensual nature of American society (i.e., the first, second, and third propositions).

The Quantitative Sub-group

The first sub-group to be examined, as pointed out, deals in quantitative analysis of the ethnic experience. Aspects of this experience which, as assimilation variables, are most commonly studied include income patterns, mobility rates, residential dispersion or segregation, social distance attitudes, political participation, the effects of social stratification, and the like.

Two of these variables, residential patterns and the effects of social stratification, will be singled out for attention. The first confronts the problem of exclusion while the second approaches the nature of the American social order itself. But, in neither case do the authors' efforts produce satisfactory discussions.

In what follows, it should be made clear that the selected statements are not being scrutinized methodologically, as concerns their empirical techniques and procedures. Rather, the critique offered is intended to reveal the serious errors and shortcomings in the normative and conceptual frameworks used to direct this kind of research. We turn to the subject of residential segregation.

The problem of exclusion as a barrier to the residential dispersion and assimilation of Black folk is discussed by Karl and Alma Taeuber.(11) In this article, they are particularly concerned to scrutinize the validity of comparisons between the socioeconomic advance of European immigrants and their descendants, and those of Afro-Americans.

For their purposes, assimilation is taken to mean the net intergenerational changes in socioeconomic and residential status such that substantial gains are registered on various socioeconomic attributes (e.g., years of schooling as measured by percent high school graduates, income, etc.) and on a measure of residential segregation. As assimilation increases, it should be reflected by gains in socioeconomic status and a concomitant decline in residential segregation, i.e., a breaking-up of "ethnic colonies" and an increase in "residential dispersion."(12)

The authors find that, although various white ethnic groups studied have made significant gains in the attributes studied and their residential segregation indices have dropped, Black people continue to suffer an extremely high residential segregation index even though they have posted the necessary socioeconomic gains (principally in education, white collar job-holding, and home ownership) to be expected according to the traditional pattern of assimilation.(13)

This finding creates considerable doubt about the utility of Black-white analogies based on the experience of European immigrants since, explicitly citing Myrdal's work, the Taeubers argue that, historically, the improvement of the ethnic group's socioeconomic status has always been accompanied by its decreasing residential segregation.(14) Further, neither the rate of Black population increase nor the level of Black acculturation to city life show promising routes toward an explanation of continuing Black exclusion.(15) In fact, it can even be shown, the authors argue, that other "newer" immigrant groups, principally from Latin American countries (specifically, Mexico and Puerto Rico), though not making socioeconomic gains as quickly, are, however, not subject to the same rigid segregation.(16)

Finally, in an attempt to sort out the influence

of socioeconomic status factors and racial factors as causes of Black residential segregation, the Taeubers employ the indirect standardization of census data for income by community area in the city of Chicago as an example. A comparison between expected frequencies and obtained frequencies of residential locations of whites and Black people by income distribution, when contrasted with actual indices of residential segregation, leads the authors to conclude that income differentials can account for only a small part of the actual reported indices for 1950 and 1960. Add to this, the authors argue, the fact that Black people are "apparently" blocked out of competition for housing for which they economically qualify and it becomes clear that some other factor must be cited in their continuing, high residential exclusion.(17)

But the Taeubers, aside from denying the validity of the immigrant analogy, do not offer any insight as to what this other factor could be; they are content to rest their criticism on the sparseness of the known data regarding assimilation processes.(18) That consistently wide quantitative differences in the residential segregation indices of Black people vis-a-vis whites as compared with whites vis-a-vis other whites could translate as an important qualitative difference between these two situations never occurs to them. Like many authors of this school, they refuse to broach the subject of institutional racism though, here, their own data confirm its existence. They prefer, instead, a middle course; to admit the uniqueness of the Black predicament whereby Black people make some socioeconomic advances but are still subjected to extreme residential exclusion unlike European immigrant groups, but also, simultaneously, to avoid or close off any discussion of those structural considerations which under a racist, capitalist social system demand the existence of that exclusion.

While the Taeubers entertained a rather narrow statistical discussion of residential segregation, the next statement broadens its statistical presentation to include several other facets of the assimilation process as reflected in social stratification. But, the liberal assimilationist presuppositions of the school impose themselves so that fundamental social and cultural realities, e.g., the preferential treatment accorded European ancestry groups in this country, and the concomitant devaluation of Third World peoples and cultures, are obscured or distorted.

In an article written for the United States Government (Office of Education) and based on census data, many of the primary characteristics of this school are visible, especially the role of stratification.(19) The Duncans hold that the process of social stratification is propelled by certain "distributive processes" which differentially affect the social position of the various groups in society, said groups being defined by "ascribed characteristics," or attributes.(20) The authors propose to examine census data in order to determine the effect of national origin (i.e., ethnicity) on vertical mobility as measured by educational attainment and job status.

Armed with statistical techniques such as partial regression analysis, the authors construct intergenerational comparisons for thirteen ethnic groups. They conclude that a "melting pot" phenomenon is observable, since the amount of variance between groups due to national origin in attainment of formal schooling has declined from 11% to 3%.(21) They do admit, however, that membership in certain groups can constitute either a plus or a minus. And similarly, the Duncans find that occupational achievement variance between the groups due to national origin narrowed from 4% to 1%, with the same caveat.(22)

In the end, the authors proclaim: "(t)he notion of equal opportunity irrespective of national origin is a near reality...."(23) Such a proclamation is possible, in part, only because the authors consistently seek to minimize the role of discrimination in ethnic group attainment and mobility. Witness:

> Membership in a particular national-origin group can rather clearly constitute a substantial 'handicap' or 'bonus' in the stratification process, although

> the relative numbers of individuals holding such membership may be too small for the nationality factor to make a major contribution to variation in the total population.(24)

And:

> Loosely speaking, the indirect effect of the nationality factor [i.e., membership in a particular ethnic group] on occupational success reflects inequalities in the distribution of education *above and beyond* those based on social origin. The direct effect reflects inequalities in the distribution of job opportunities *above and beyond* those based on formal educational qualifications and social origin. A national-origin group can suffer discrimination or enjoy preferential treatment in either distributive process (emphasis added).(25)

This peroration, especially in its last part, conjures up the image of a great roulette game-in-the-sky by which "national-origin groups" fatalistically discover whether or not their particular nationality will be a hindrance or a help in meeting the additional obstacles ("inequalities") to favorable life chances put there, together with the judgment on the desirability of their ethnicity, by something unknown and unexplained.

This inability to explain comes across very clearly in this passage:

> *Whatever* mechanism one wishes to adduce as causative, there can be little doubt that a 'melting pot' phenomenon obtains in America... (emphasis added).(26)

In fact, astounding as it may seem, the Duncans are at a loss as to how to explain the apparent preference for the most well-known ethnic group in this country:

> Among the national-origin groups separately identified here, there occurs but one instance of distinctly preferential position with respect to competition for jobs. The group is a rough approximation to the Anglo-Saxon Protestants.... There is no evidence that they are over-achievers in the American school system, but their occupational success is greater than that of other Americans with similar social origin and educational qualification (emphasis added).(27)

Indeed, the obfuscation that the Duncans construct in this article is a consequence of minimizing any discussion of discrimination (i.e., exclusion), and of completely denying, in the specious fashion of academic pundits, the existence of institutional racism. This last point is clearly illustrated here:

> Let us suppose that the process of stratification operates in an identical fashion for men in the so-called majority and in the several minorities, i.e., that the respective net effects of head's education and occupation and the number of siblings on educational achievement are constant over national-origin groups.(28)

Writing in a period of U.S. history which experienced the greatest degree of urban upheaval, dissent, and turmoil that was racially based, the Duncans attempt to deny its reality. Their belated, brief admission that the Black Experience causes them to wonder about the evenhandedness of distributive processes does little to buttress the house-of-cards they build in the article with academic code-words and numbers which hide more than they reveal.(29)

Their central failing is that they cling to an outmoded liberal position that time and events have simply left behind. The persistence of depression-level rates of Black unemployment, the devaluation and distortion of Black culture and society, the waxing and waning but ever present tension associated with race relations, and the reluctant involvement of government in remedial legislation all convincingly reject the "melting pot" idea which is at the core of the Duncans' theoretical assumptions about social stratification.(30) Handicapped and yet made to feel cheerful by this notion, they completely fail to come to grips with white racism, its history and contemporary pervasiveness in American society, and its possible causes.

In sum, the Duncans' article must be judged a piece of liberal, scholarly jactitation in which the need to vindicate "the system" by presenting a celebratory view of stratification and its implied end, assimilation, outweighs the need to confront reality. It is a fine piece of self-deception, an exercise in "abstracted empiricism."(31)

The Political Empowerment Sub-group

The second discernible tendency in the broad outlines of the ethnic group model has as its typical theme politics, specifically the routes to political empowerment that ethnic groups use. There is some disagreement over the question of exclusion. Its importance, as institutional racism, is alternately accepted or rejected as regards the political process, but what unites these statements is their coherence with established liberal political axioms. However, within this liberal purview, there is also disagreement as to how the ethnic group should proceed: traditional approaches tend to stress cooperation with established political parties and sanctioned orderly political styles; non-traditional approaches are usually hostile to the two-party system and more likely to endorse political styles which are not sanctioned and are not necessarily orderly. An example of the traditional approach follows.

A case study of Black political involvement in Los Angeles seems to conform to all the adages about ethnic groups "making it" in society by closing ranks.(32) Traditional routes to political empowerment for ethnic groups emphasize bloc-voting, political machines, and nepotism. The ethnic group, it is argued, sticks together because of its common national origin and culture, plays by the rules of the game, and finally, perhaps after a generation or two, achieves political power for itself.(33) The political system into which the ethnic groups enter is not monopolized by one group, open to fluid combinations of interest, and capable of being influenced by a wide array of resources, not necessarily or primarily economic in nature; the system into which they enter, to quote Robert Dahl, is one in which:

> Nearly every group has enough potential influence to mitigate harsh injustice to its members, though not necessarily enough influence to attain a full measure of justice. The system thus tends to be self-corrective, at least in a limited fashion. If equality and justice are rarely attained, harsh and persistent oppression is almost always avoided. To this extent, the system attains one of the important ends of political equality without the means. It is, in a word, a pluralistic system.(34)

But this optimistic view of the political system usually overlooks the fact that the cities, traditional bases for earlier ethnic political machines, have entered into a period of decline. Suburbanization, declining tax bases, increasing subjection to external financial and juridical authority (usually federal), and the imbalance between small-capital and corporate-capital sectors of the national economy, have all drastically lessened the ability of cities to serve this traditional function. Thus, the proposed traditional route to empowerment simply does not reckon with changed, unfavorable circumstances.(35)

Patterson, however, states that "American

minorities" (i.e., ethnic groups) have long sought recognition in a number of different ways, "political recognition" being chief among them. This political recognition, in turn, may be secured through traditional means such as tokenism, patronage and bloc-voting, or the more direct routes of referendum, initiative, and recall. Often, as happened in the case under review, an ad hoc group of citizens must coalesce in order to express a specific community interest, here, the election of one of its own number to municipal office.(36)

Since the politics of Los Angeles are "decentralized and pluralistic," the author implies that the group has a reasonable chance of seeing its demands met; and, after pointing to the hazards to Black political representation that gerrymandering and large districts represent, this successful resolution is exactly what he notes.(37) Primarily responsible for this welcomed outcome, viz., the increase in Black representation on the city council during 1961-63 from zero to three, are an initially unsuccessful recall drive and bloc-voting.(38)

Thus, a traditional "avenue" to recognition, the electoral process, stands vindicated as obtaining for Black people in Los Angeles some measure of political empowerment. Patterson's analysis does not say how this successful process of securing representation relates to the more ominous and soul-desiccating processes which in two short years from the time of his study (1960 to 1963) would culminate in one of the bloodiest, explosive Black rebellions of the '60s, i.e., Watts, August, 1965. Nor is he helpful in explaining why, assuming the dispersed nature of power in Los Angeles politics as he does, the political outcomes of bloc-voting and other traditional political maneuvers have not had the same results for Afro-Americans as for the European groups who employed them earlier. Finally, the author fails to take into account the quality of the representation newly secured, since the pursuit of old policies and practices by new "ethnic" faces only serves to perpetuate under new guise the deleterious effects of the past.

Other writers in this sub-group of the ethnic group

model are not unwilling to explore non-traditional routes to political empowerment. In fact, several Black authors of note have pursued an ethnic group analysis of U.S. race relations even though they have often been concerned to present their formulations in striking, unconventional ways. That they do so is most likely attributable to their inability to dismiss the legacy of exclusion, subordination, and relative powerlessness which have been the general hallmarks of the Black Experience in the political arena.(39) However, the recognition of these contradictory phenomena does not push these writers to abandon liberal political theory, especially its assumptions about interest group action.

Stokely Carmichael and Charles V. Hamilton make arguments and take positions that are not often encountered in the writings of this school.(40) Their rejection of assimilation or "integration" is not typical. Nor is their examination of the political, economic, and cultural oppression to which Black people are subjected. And their defense of Black culture and history, and the right of Black people to self-definition and self-determination marks a qualitative distinction between them and the vast majority of those who write in this tradition. Further, an even more important qualitative distinction between the work of Carmichael and Hamilton and that of the ethnic group school is their insistent focus on a subject generally neglected, minimized or denied by practitioners of ethnic group analysis, namely, institutional racism.

The authors staunchly advocate the need for independent Black power bases and support this contention by debunking the myths of alliance-building and providing illustrative case studies containing the appropriate lessons.(41) But, their ultimate formula for the achievement of those power bases reduces to one of the oldest canards of ethnic group analysts: "...[*b*]*efore a group can enter the open society, it must first close ranks*" (emphasis in the original).(42)

In fact, in formulating the ideological terrain that the new political concept of "Black Power" must stake out, the authors never move beyond bourgeois, liberal political theory. The group (i.e., Black people) must close ranks so that it can achieve "a bargaining position of strength in a pluralistic society" (emphasis added). This is so because the American political system rests on an ethnic basis; further, quoting Hans Morgenthau, the authors aver that it is a system in which political power may be defined as "...the psychological control over the minds of men...," a definition which entirely overlooks structural sources of power. Though institutional racism is deemed a form of "colonialism," and its creation and maintenance tied to "a combination of oppressive forces and special interests in the white community," when the project for self-determination is depicted its chief enemy is considered to be the white middle class, with no thought given to the white working class or the white ruling class. And, as for the coalitions with white liberals, poor whites, or organized labor, though the authors initially see a monolithic white populace united in its racism, they eventually, in a self-contradicting manner, adopt the standard of self-interest resting on the assumption of human inertia combatted only by the inescapable necessity to avoid loss and secure gain; the standard of human potentiality and spontaneity remains unarticulated.(43) Thus, by their equation of "Black Power" with group power in the sense that it was traditionally held by previous European immigrant groups, by their definition of enlightened self-interest based on rational calculation as being at the heart of desirable coalitions, and by their contradictory acceptance of the pluralistic nature of the American political order, the authors' liberal political assumptions may be confirmed.(44)

The conclusions must be that their search for new forms of Black political enfranchisement and mobilization, with which they close the book, is destined to be frustrated, defeated, or co-opted because they have failed to take into account both racial and structural, political-economic factors which make up the necessary ingredients for the "politics of liberation in America." Had structural aspects of the problem been considered, Carmichael and Hamilton might have felt constrained to offer a more thorough program for social change.

The Assimilationist/Pluralist Sub-group

The discussions of quantitative analysis and routes to political empowerment which we have noted are complemented by another salient perspective within the ethnic group model. This last sub-group (which may be designated assimilationist/pluralist) undertakes to discover the features of the process of assimilation itself, and the resources and obstacles which characterize it. Another version of the assimilative process, cultural pluralism (often simply stated as "pluralism"), is also common to this sub-group's outlook. Not only is the process of assimilation (pluralism) spelled out, but the consensual moral precepts which sustain it, commonly referred to as the American Creed, are presumed to be primary determinants of this process. The American Creed, as understood by these writers, is taken to mean a value-complex that is chiefly the heritage of Anglo-Saxon political traditions. These traditions, it is asserted, form the basis of liberal social and political theory, and it is this theory which characterizes the modern democratic state. Modern society is not only shaped by these traditions, but the corresponding normative injunctions must be understood as the ultimate determinants of the individual's behavior. Those whose behavior does not measure up to these standards must be counted incompletely socialized, deviant or pathological, or otherwise lacking in the proper motivation.

The specific elements of the value-complex are typically given as follows: individual initiative (individualism), industriousness (free enterprise and private property), thrift (capital accumulation), and asceticism or deferred gratification, especially sensual.(45) In the critical review which follows, this consensual or creedal view will be challenged because it typically lacks recognition of the structural features (e.g., the maldistribution of power and resultant relative powerlessness of certain groups, the active social force of institutional racism, etc.) of modern American capitalist democracy which strongly inhibit the realization of such a consensus. Instead, such problems of the efficacy of the Creed as are admitted tend to be attributed to a failure on the part of the group in question, whose behavior and culture are derogated as pathological or products of a suspect "culture of poverty." But, this response to the failure of the Creed simply manifests the unwillingness of its proponents to investigate structural constraints, and their profound arrogance toward, and ignorance of, cultural styles developed beyond the Veil.

Two views of the assimilation process have been especially influential among ethnic group analysts. Both attempt to show how American society invests the ethnic group with a special role. We will consider Gordon first.

Milton M. Gordon, in <u>Assimilation in American Life</u>, approaches the role of the ethnic group by examining social stratification.(46) Preliminarily, assimilation is defined as a complementary process. Seven variables, which may be thought of as steps, comprise assimilation: in order, from lowest to highest, cultural (or behavioral), structural, marital, identificational, attitude receptional, behavioral receptional, and civic.(47) All ethnic groups most easily attain cultural assimilation (also called "acculturation," he notes), though some may become indefinitely stuck at that level.(48)

"The nature of group life itself," he maintains, is such that, in an industrial, urban, democratic, modern society, two basic relationships condition its existence and its direction: those of the ethnic group provide primary-group (family, marriage, social clique, religion, etc.) contact and support to its members, and through its interaction with the social structure develops its own "subculture" and "subsociety"; each of the latter, in turn, bear the stamp of the particular refraction of the national culture through the heritage of each ethnic group.(49)

For Gordon, the social structure consists of social classes, which, in addition to the ethnic group, form the other major source of group identification in American life. Social classes are based on "social-psychological constructs or categories in people's minds," do not have impermeable boundaries, and may be hierarchically typologized, following Warner, into six categories. Moreover, again like the ethnic group, the social class creates its own primary group relations, institutional activities and cultural patterns, i.e., its own subsociety with a distinct subculture.(50)

The intersection of ethnic group stratification and social class stratification creates a social unit which Gordon christens "the ethclass." Ethnic group stratification is vertical while social class stratification is horizontal, and in the case of ethnic group stratification we are never told just how the vertical ranking of ethnic groups was decided. At any rate, the "ethclass" is held to be "the essential form of the subsociety in America."(51)

With this elaborate theoretical framework constructed, Gordon now concentrates on the avowed central concern of the book, i.e., the reduction and elimination of ethnic prejudice and discrimination, and the manageability of value conflict between ethnic groups.(52) This will not be an easy task since the author's investigations lead him to believe that the United States is a "multiple melting pot" that has managed to accomplish the acculturation of all immigrant groups, thereby lessening most value conflict, but in which the separation of groups at the primary level -- what Gordon calls "structural pluralism," on the basis of race and religion -- is the dominant sociological fact-of-life.(53)

The Jewish group, the Catholic group, and the white Protestant group have all been overwhelmingly acculturated. However, value conflicts do exist between these groups, with varying degrees of severity depending on position in the respective social class structures of the groups. And, the most accurate reflection of the distance which remains between them is the low rates of intermarriage which they exhibit.(54)

When Gordon discusses the Black group, it is

apparent that his "theory" has not advanced beyond stereotypes. The Black lower class is characterized by a "way of life" that does not value ambition, is prone to violence, illegitimacy, and delinquency, and family instability which is promoted by wandering male partners.(55) The Black upper and middle classes have largely assimilated to the standards of the "core society" -- middle class white Protestants -- a process made less difficult by the fact that Black folk do not have distinctive religious values to preserve.(56)

Moreover, though Gordon admits that prejudice and discrimination bear a great deal of the responsibility for the social degradation of the numerically large Black lower class, the genesis and maintenance of these exclusionary systems is only obliquely explained.(57) Apparently these systems arise out of the ethnic group's ability to rationally assess the extrinsic and intrinsic traits and institutional life of another group's subsociety and subculture, and then to make invidious comparisons designed to buttress its own status.(58) Legal precepts, whether of the segregationist variety of the South or those of a racially-neutral flavor as in the North, do not significantly alter this process.(59) In other words, in the tradition of pluralist welfare liberalism, Gordon has ascribed those characteristics formerly attributed by classical liberalism to the individual to the group: ambition, independence, and rational calculation.(60)

The problem of "structural pluralism" or "structural separation" (terms which the author uses interchangeably), then, can only be approached once it is realized that it is legitimated by "American democratic ideals." Structural pluralism is, in fact, the basis for some degree of cultural pluralism.(61) Those difficulties which remain for specific ethnic groups should be alleviated by a combination of public governmental action and the civic statesmanship of ethnic group leaders: the (federal) government must get "out of the business of supporting racial discrimination."(62) It must achieve desegregation, but not by imposing quotas or integration; and, the ethnic group itself must act to deal responsibly with the "behavioral problems" of the group.(63) Of course, Gordon means these strictures to apply most directly to Black folk, and he singles out "Negro communal leaders" as having a definite "responsibility" (or, more diplomatically, an "opportunity") to curb the anti-social acts prevalent in the Black lower class.(64) Praising the Black community for its efforts to defeat discrimination, at the same time he assures whites that the end of discrimination will not mean instant intermarriage.(65) Cultural pluralism, based on structural pluralism, can only be achieved, the author finally decides, if "ethnic communality" can be kept within its proper bounds and not be allowed to threaten the "basic good will" needed for interethnic harmony and the successful operation of a "democratically pluralist society" in secondary relations and functional activities.(66)

At bottom, Gordon's book is a moral sermon. Gordon's structural-functional analysis is suffused with the moralistics of value consensus, i.e., the belief in the efficacious social power of Judeo-Christian ideals and moral norms throughout the whole of American society.(67) Though he once mentions that crime and delinquency are "the products of general sociological and psychological forces," he does not explain these forces but, instead, returns time and again to emphasize the choices, essentially moral in nature, which confront the ethnic group, its leaders, and its individual members.(68) And, ever since the time of Gunnar Myrdal's classic study, An American Dilemma, the choice which moral consensualists writing on race matters have chosen to enshrine is that of marriage partner.(69) Matters relating to housing, employment, job discrimination, public transportation, and education are unaddressed or left at a low level of theoretical treatment.(70)

With a structural accounting of racial and cultural oppression, exploitation, and exclusion thus precluded, or minimized, the discussion and analysis is free to roam the purview of the Judeo-Christian religio-ethical tradition.(71) Institutional racism disappears from the analysis. This also explains why Gordon is unable or unwilling to discuss the origins of the vertical ranking of ethnic groups: to do so would bring him squarely to the subject of racism.(72)

Further, Gordon's use of social stratification analysis reveals several of the problematic aspects of this analytic and conceptual mode. First, there is the whole question of just how many social classes there are. Those who write in a quite different tradition have also scrutinized this issue, and have disagreed as to its resolution.(73) Though Gordon is aware of this problem, since he speaks of the possibility of "one vast hierarchical continuum" and acknowledges the "imprecise nature of class boundaries in American life," he nevertheless adheres to Warner's six-fold typology.(74) It becomes apparent, then, that the line between social classes is one arbitrarily drawn by the social scientist.(75) Therefore, comprehension of those systemic variables which account for the genesis and maintenance of the social class system may or may not figure into the analytic conventions of the social scientist who uses social stratification analysis. And since the disposition of most work done via this mode is to arrive at a description of the attributional aspects of an arbitrary aggregate of individuals rather than an explanation of those structural forces which promote a certain type of historically-conditioned social inequality, the results of such work are not likely to cast light on the processes responsible for social inequality or its elimination.(76) That Gordon intends no illumination here is evidenced by his failure to go beyond mere mention of such topics as industrialization and urbanization.(77) Thus, without a consideration of capitalism and with a socio-psychological definition of the existence and permanence of social classes, Gordon's work tends to empty the concept of social inequality of its specific historical content and thereby impart an air of its universality and inescapability.(78)

The remaining two statements included in this subgroup attempt to portray not only the moral but also the structural (economic, political, and social) components which give form and substance to the assimilation process. As noted earlier, this process is usually pictured as dependent upon particular resources (e.g., a strong family structure, small business institutions, political skill, etc.) which the assimilating group must control in order to succeed. Those groups which do not succeed are judged to be lacking in these resources, usually because of their internal weaknesses (e.g., a weak family structure). Two versions of this internal weakness argument are possible: a harsh view and a mild view. As specifically regards Black people, the two views aver the following: in the first, the "tangle of pathology" of Black culture and social norms is not amenable to state action, while in the second, such action may be deemed necessary.

But, as the critique below will attempt to demonstrate, neither view comprehends the structural restraints on the assimilation process inherent in modern American capitalist democracy. Actual power in American society is monopolized and hierarchical, and its social and political expression tend to resonate closely with its economic base.(79) In fact, the real process involving Black people in America is not an assimilation process at all; it is a subordination process. The chief characteristic of this subordination and exclusion is its institutionally racist nature, which talk of cultural pathology and internal weakness merely serve to disguise. Moreover, there is actually reason to believe that when Black people resist the illicit racial consensus which consigns them to subordinate roles, they shake off some of the signs of "pathology" often attributed to them.(80)

However, the subject of pathology is much in evidence in the statements below. We take up first the harsh view. In fact, probably one of the gloomiest pictures to emerge in recent years of U.S. race relations based on ethnic group analysis is Edward C. Banfield's The Unheavenly City Revisited, a revision of an earlier work similarly titled.(81)

Banfield studies the problem of today's cities. He contends that two major causes are responsible for the blight and despair: the peculiar culture of American social classes especially the lower class, and the social, moral, legal, political, and economic impedimenta which hamper the effectiveness of competition in a capitalist society.

As he regards the first major causal area, Banfield offers a definition of social classes and their cultures based on a time horizon concept. There are four such classes with attendant cultures: _the upper class_, most future-oriented, able to defer gratification, independent, creative, civic-minded, self-confident, and self-sufficient; _the middle class_, less future-oriented, strongly upwardly mobile, less concerned with self-expression, and community responsibility, and also able to defer gratification; _the working class_, little future orientation, less able to defer gratification, often authoritarian and violent, little concern for self-expression, privacy, or upward mobility, and a tenuous sense of community involvement; and, _the lower class_, extremely present-oriented, lives from "moment to moment," governed by impulse and bodily needs, hostile and resentful of authority, low self-concept, no sense of community attachment, disdains or does not value work, and family household relations are unstable and usually dominated by women. Banfield labels lower class culture "pathological" and the other cultures "normal."(82) It is this pathological lower class culture, then, which the author finds to be at work creating many of today's urban ills. The slum, to Banfield, is merely the reified cultural norms of the lower class.(83)

Banfield asserts that the ethnic content of these four social classes, visible in America's earliest cities, has varied. But, in line with one of the major assumptions of this school, he sees all immigrant groups as assimilating, though admittedly at different speeds, to the "Old Stock American future-oriented ideal."(84)

When Banfield finally gets around to discussing Black people, he turns to the second major causal area -- the mechanics of competition under capitalism. However, first he "demonstrates," as much by constant repetition as by statistical legerdemain (as when census data are manipulated to show that black/white differentials in education, income, occupational prestige may be controlled by social class _without_ admitting that all of these factors were and continue to be influenced by institutional racism), that racial discrimination is not a significant factor in ethnic group relations and that it is rapidly declining.(85) Next, he asserts that one must separate "historical cause" from "presently operating cause" in order to understand the plight of the Black lower class; thus, Banfield is able to minimize his consideration of racial discrimination (in its "historical" form, as slavery and de jure segregation) by claiming that as a cause it has been largely displaced by social class prejudice, a "presently operating," and non-racial, cause.(86) The Black lower class, then, suffers from its own twisted culture, which dooms many measures intended to aid these persons,(87) as much as from a sense of poverty, "relative deprivation," rooted in perception, that is ultimately ineradicable because it is based on status feelings and not materially ascertainable fact.(88) The "rising expectations" of the urban poor are often intensified by self-interested, irresponsible leaders who do not represent fairly the progress which has been made.(89) But often these Black leaders themselves are part of a rapidly-growing Black bourgeoisie which attests to, on the one hand, the general upward improvement of social classes which Banfield dubs "middle-class-ification" and on the other hand, the inexorability, also true of all other ethnic groups, of "the Negro's" move up the social class ladder.(90)

So, with these distinctions made and preliminaries offered, the author's view of the problem of the Black lower class is this: that its labor power is overpriced. Remove all restrictions, such as minimum wage laws, credentialed job qualifications, and relative inability to relocate, that stand in the way of a decline in the market price of this labor power and employers will eagerly purchase it.(91) The laws of supply and demand in the market place must be unimpeded and free to operate.(92) If some lower class workers still do not make a living wage, subsidization by public agencies may be considered.(93)

Banfield's use of social stratification analysis, a characteristic of this school mentioned at the beginning of this chapter, allows him to deny the validity and importance of exclusion (as racial discrimination, segregation, etc.), minimizing and ignoring it, while claiming that other non-racial factors (e.g., income level, years of schooling, family size, etc.) and the culture of the Black lower class constitute the crux of Black social degradation.(94) And, his view of American capitalism, long since superannuated by events after 1900, places him squarely in the tradition of that branch of liberal social philosophy, rooted in Benthamite utilitarianism and Millean libertarianism, which holds a laissez-faire conception of the social world.(95)

That is, Bentham's unyielding insistence that "the greatest good for the greatest number" could only be insured by the individual's constant, rational, egoistic strivings to maximize pleasure and to avoid pain and to do only those things which were useful (utility) toward this end and J. S. Mill's utilitarian defense of the individual's right to liberty according to which social life is divided into two spheres -- the inner life of the individual; and the external public life of other-regarding actions, governmental interference being absolutely banned in the former and relatively proscribed in the latter -- constituted important ideological positions on which intellectual support for early, competitive capitalism could be built. Banfield's social vision of race relations merely amounts to his elaboration of these classic positions.

And this elaboration allows him to argue, in so many words, that the Black lower class simply is not competitive enough; and, in a very competitive world, it suffers a predictable fate. Banfield's dire assessment of this fate is further bolstered and given an unpleasantly insidious tone by his unsavory depiction of Black lower class culture, a feat which, by itself, relegates the book to modern-day annals of racism and social Darwinism.(96) The doctrine of the survival of the fittest coupled with a belief in the progress of society through evolution characterizes social Darwinist thought. Typically, less evolved peoples do not make progress and cannot be remedially assisted. Their difficulties are merely a reflection of their own inefficiency, and not a result of their subordinate incorporation into modern industrial society.

Thus, as with most writers of this school, Banfield presents no conception of exploitation or oppression, and his discussion of exclusion is broached only to show its impotency and near-demise. In fact, the good professor assures us that, if only "the poor" (that bloodlessly euphemistic academic code word for undesirables) can be managed, the end of poverty is in sight -- in 2040 A.D.!(97)

We turn now to the mild view of the assimilation process which may be commonly associated with proponents of the welfare state. No less judgmental or inspired by the American Creed than the harsh view, nonetheless, these writers usually endorse state actions designed to promote social stability.(98) Rather than entertain the social dislocations which would result from unbridled competitive activity, they are willing to entertain reforms within the limits of the status quo of American capitalist democracy.

Though Moynihan and Glazer, in the next statement, do not dwell on welfare proposals, this element is clearly present in their treatment of the assimilation process. Here, they are more concerned to elaborate the specific workings of that process.

In _Beyond the Melting Pot_, the authors see the history of the U.S. city (here, New York) and by extension, of U.S. society itself, as the complex interaction of "major, fairly well-defined [ethnic] groups."(99) The major social force at work is assimilation, though a sort of "sliding scale" (the term is mine) of assimilation is operative as evidenced by the relatively high ethnic consciousness of a group like Afro-Americans and the comparatively low ethnic consciousness of a virtually completely assimilated group, i.e., German-Americans.(100)

Power, say the authors, is a function of interest groups, which they equate with ethnic groups. It is hierarchical and diffused, much like the old Irish political machine. By "an almost mechanical process" groups in power tend to fractionate; this suggests that no one group is able to monopolize, or have unfair access to, power.(101)

The small businessman tradition is crucial to the acquisition of power by the ethnic group. The small businessman promotes community cohesion through his patronage, has access to the world of credit and finance, and, hence to great potential wealth, and through his search for influence in local politics he becomes privy to important issues which he may affect in the interest of benefiting the entire ethnic community.(102)

The problem of exclusion, according to the authors, is not that it works systematically as a selective barrier against the mobility of certain groups, but that rather its effect on ethnic groups depends on the relative strength or weakness of the internal structures (e.g., family, civic groups, fraternal associations, the small businessman tradition, etc.) of the group. In varying degree, this last area, _viz._, the weakness of group internal structures, is the problem facing Black people and Puerto Ricans. In any case, exclusion is interpreted positively by the authors to mean the sense of fellow-feeling of the ethnic group which it cultivates in order to protect and preserve its culture and tradition; completely neglected and specifically denied are the negative effects of exclusion which, when viewed historically, lead to the premise of a stable, institutionalized set of relations which center around racial distinctions.(103)

Moynihan and Glazer's denial of institutional racism, a formidable obstacle to the assimilation process (but a key feature of the maintenance of subordination), is rooted in a conception of ethnic group life that is very similar to Gordon's: groups inspect one another, test one another, and then make invidious comparisons, from which self-segregation and ethnic preservation apparently result. Moreover, according to them, the nature of American society itself is such that the ethnic group has persisted even while being transformed into new guises by the all-pervasive social force of assimilation; not all cultural styles have survived the second generation nor have all groups melted to a common core, hence, beyond the melting pot....(104)

But the view of ethnic group life which Moynihan and Glazer present is really a rather superficial, one-sided look at the process of interaction between racial and ethnic groups and the American social order. Separate and persistent ethnic groups and their traditions and the relations of these groups with each other do constitute a palpable reality, but their existence and interaction occur within a capitalist democratic framework which generates hierarchy, power imbalance, and dominance combined with a long social history of racist thought and practice. The subject of exploitation, if seriously considered (the authors mention it only twice in the entire treatise: once as a past phenomenon under slavery, and again in a passing reference to Black and Puerto Rican workers) would open up entire vistas of analysis which are closed off in their statement.(105)

An examination of this subject would also lead to a reckoning of the interests of ethnic groups in the putative social value consensus. If the objective, i.e., systematically structurally-determined, interests of such groups could be distinguished from their subjective, i.e., psychologically-held, interests, the existence and strength of this alleged consensus could be determined. But Moynihan and Glazer do not explore this problem. Their various pronouncements on the matter -- e.g., that ethnic group conflict typically involves a mix of rational economic interests and irrational non-economic attitudes, that ethnicity and religion are real objective and subjective bases for difference and conflict, and that social class issues routinely become ethnic issues in the political arena -- may all be taken as an indication that no serious consideration of the problematic nature of interests and consensus is intended.(106) One could certainly not argue, based on their historical experience in America, that Black people have any consensual interest in maintaining racial domination or the defense of private property (as distinct from industriousness and work), yet the converse is certainly disputable for American capitalist society as a whole. Moynihan and Glazer are no help here.

Moreover, their conception of conflict reinforces the difficulties noted. Since salient points in the social order (e.g., religious outlook, the political process, job level, etc.) are taken as given, the account of their origin (e.g., how do certain political patronage slots get to be "Negro" jobs?) is neglected. But, without a clear sense of the emergence and development of these points of conflict, no accurate declaration can be made as to the homeostatic or disjunctive quality of the arguments between ethnic groups over these attributes of the social system. Moynihan and Glazer's equation of the ethnic group with the interest group, having failed to clarify the concept of interest, only compounds the inadequacies of their discussion of conflict. Their use of a dichotomous model of U.S. race relations, i.e., the North and the South are treated separately with the latter society defending strict, violence-prone racial norms while the former is guided in such matters by organized, routine competition via a political process steeped in a consensual mold, is further evidence of this failure.(107)

In sum, Moynihan and Glazer's entire work amounts to a monumental evasion. The facts of society-wide (not just in New York) racial subordination are plainly visible. In 1974, just four short years after the second edition of their book was issued, the U.S. Government found, in part, that: Black family median income was 58% of white; more than three times as many Black persons had low income (below $5,038, nonfarm) as white; a 2 to 1 black-to-white unemployment ratio has held in effect <u>since the Korean War</u>; Black federal employees are still concentrated in lower grades; year-round full-time Black male employees earned only 68% of comparable white workers; Black life expectancy at birth was 61.9 vs 68.4 (black to white, males; 70.1 vs 76.1, females) years; and, Black people, whether owners or renters, were more than twice as likely to occupy dwellings lacking some or all plumbing facilities as were white persons.(108) Another government study four years later (1978) confirmed, in substance, many of these findings (especially those relating to employment and income).(109) And as for Black business providing employment: in 1977, the top 100 Black firms in the United States employed 8,356 people while Black unemployment in November of that year stood at 1,599,000 persons; and this despite the fact that there was a dramatic increase in Black firms, to 195,000 as of 1972.(110) So much for the small business tradition which Moynihan and Glazer ballyhoo.

And, their evasion of practical realities is matched by their evasion of their own theoretical dilemmas. Clearly, as pluralists, they (like Gordon) have been forced to confer sociopolitical apotheosis on the group, and not the individual, by the highly socialized and interdependent nature of production in a technologically-advanced capitalist state. But to openly and genuinely admit this, and face up to its implications for social theory and policy, is more than our good professors can manage. So, they are content to wander into the safe vicissitudes of unexposed contradictions, fatalism, and irrationality: the place of ethnic groups in the social hierarchy was determined by "the American mind"; "It may be that society needs unpopular groups around"; a sort of Freudian hydraulic impulse explains the unquenchability of the entrepreneurial itch; "...all good things are scarce, and involve conflicts..."; and, the processes by which the American national character is formed are "mysterious."(111)

This last opaque conclusion rests on many stereotypical, and hence racist, views of the ethnic groups studied: even Jewish criminals are brainy, not brawny; Italians have a genious for making cities liveable and their amoral, individualistic, xenophobic moral code disposes them to organized crime; Puerto Rican people are gentle and gay; the Irish are contradictorily conformists and fantasizers, plodding routine-keepers and adventurers, tough and defiantly democratic at the same time that they are afflicted with alcoholism; and, Black people are anti-Semitic because it makes them feel more American, have a weak business tradition, show little clannishness, and have a weak family structure.(112) So, here too, our white liberal authors' patina of urbanity and cosmopolitan <u>angst</u> is not caked thick enough to hide a surprisingly deep arrogance toward, and ignorance of, Third World peoples, and an unmistakable theoretical barrenness.

The foregoing critique hopefully has prepared the reader for the judgment that Moynihan and Glazer do not really comprehend their subject matter. To understand the subordination process would require them to dispense with most of their theoretical scaffolding, certainly an even not likely to occur.

Conclusion

Likewise, a similar judgment may be rendered of all the statements reviewed. Whether quantitative, political empowerment, or assimilationist/pluralist, they all share basic assumptions which create theoretical impotence and corresponding inadequacies; and this despite the fact that their empirical findings are often valuable and usable. The first sub-group (quantitative) tends to view race relations disconnectedly as "assimilation variables" that cannot account for a systemic pattern of invidious racial outcomes whose existence its own data often confirms; the second sub-group (political empowerment) is unable to explain how either traditional or non-traditional routes to political power can succeed, given the analysts' failure to examine closely the contours of American capitalist democracy and its regnant liberal political theory; and the last sub-group (assimilationist/pluralist), whose work tends to incorporate the errors of the first two, presents a consensually-inspired version of the assimilation process which can account for the failure of this process on certain occasions only by reference to the supposed internal deficiencies of the group(s) involved, thereby closing off a critical examination of the social order and its interaction with all groups. We have attempted to demonstrate that all of these failings on the part of the ethnic group model (and its identified sub-groups) stem from its adherence to the five central assumptions (or propositions) outlined at the outset of this chapter: the assumption that the ethnic group is <u>the</u> primary American social reality; the belief that assimilation is society's most powerful social force; that this process is founded on social equilibrium and value consensus; the assertion that political power is dispersed and unmonopolized in the social order; and, that factors essentially extraneous to ethnicity may be "added in" as secondary considerations.

The ethnic group model misperceives the reality which it examines: the existence of separate ethnic groups in America is not the basis for an assimilation process but rather an expression, viewed racially, of a subordination process especially as regards Black people (and other Third World groups). The ethnic group model cannot gauge this process accurately since it refuses to investigate institutional racism (negative exclusion) as a key referrent of subordination and chooses instead to indulge racist notions (polite or vulgar) of the assumed cultural pathology of racial subordinates. But most important, it refuses to break with liberal theory as to its conceptions of power, interest, consensus, deviance, and economic reality in American capitalist democracy. Given this basic posture, it is understandable that its treatment of the six basic concepts is unable to explain racial subordination and neglects key structural concepts such as exploitation.

Indeed, most characteristic of this school is its generally celebratory treatment of assimilation. The preceding exposition and review, while not exhaustive, is certainly suggestive of some of the principal features of analysis which characterize many of the writings of the ethnic group model.

What is needed in order to explain the racial subordination which characterizes American society is a break with liberal theory. Such is the aim of two other models to be considered: the colonial model and the Marxist model. But first, we turn our attention to a theoretical position on U.S. race relations whose main assumptions reveal remarkable continuity with those of the ethnic group analysts, i.e., the caste model.

Notes

1. Nathan Hare, "The Sociological Study of Racial Conflict," Phylon, 33 (1972), pp. 27-32.

2. The roots of Keynesianism (which generally denotes the manipulation of the fiscal policies of the state so as to affect positively chances for investment) and its variants (such as Galbraith's "countervailing power," and Berle and Means' "managerial revolution") -- see J. K. Galbraith, American Capitalism, the Concept of Countervailing Power (1956); and A. A. Berle and G. C. Means, The Modern Corporation and Private Property (1932) -- are sketched in E. K. Hunt, Property and Prophets: The Evolution of Economic Institutions and Ideologies (New York: Harper and Row Publishers, 1972).

The contemporary liberal theory of democracy as based on elite consensus, an elite/mass leadership system, and the inadequacy of the average citizen, as appears in the works of Seymour Martin Lipset (Political Man, 1960), Robert Dahl, (Who Governs, 1961), Nelson Polsby (Community Power and Political Theory, 1963), David Truman, ("The American System in Crisis," Political Science Quarterly, 1959), and others, is critically reviewed in Peter Bachrach, "Elite Consensus and Democracy," Journal of Politics, 24:3 (August 1962), pp. 439-452; and Jack L. Walker, "A Critique of the Elitist Theory of Democracy," The American Political Science Review, 60:2 (June 1966), pp. 285-295.

As for the liberal view on race relations, the essay attempts to present and critique it.

3. Talcott Parsons, "Full Citizenship for the Negro American?" in T. Parsons and K. Clark, eds., The Negro American (Boston: Beacon Press, 1966), pp. 709-754.

4. Parsons, "Full Citizenship for the Negro American?," p. 722.

5. Ibid., p. 718. On this page, Parsons speaks of

two basic kinds of resources necessary to the inclusion process: financial ones, and those which represent "the underlying capacity of the units [i.e., ethnic groups]" such as its health and educational attainment level.

6. The most notable example of the scholar whose professional views resonate with the needs of the powerful is Daniel P. Moynihan. Serving in the Nixon Administration (as Assistant for Urban Affairs and Cabinet member, 1969-70) and later elected Senator (D) from New York (1977), Moynihan's opinions have continued to exert wide influence. Similarly, Edward C. Banfield, Talcott Parsons, and Otis D. Duncan all enjoy wide followings, and are all essentially liberals of one kind or another. Parsons was recently the president of the American Academy of Arts and Sciences (1967-71), and was past president of the American Sociological Society (1949), and the Eastern Sociological Society (1941-42). Banfield held the prestigious posts of Henry Lee Shattuck Professor of Urban Government at Harvard (1959-72), and Kenan Professor of Public Policy and Political Science at the University of Pennsylvania, 1973-76. Duncan was associate director of the University of Chicago's Population Research and Training Center (1951-62), and has served on various federal commissions (e.g., Census Advisory Committee on Population Statistics, Commission on Population Growth and the American Future, both 1975-77). See _Who's Who in America_, 40th ed., 1978-79, pp. 161, 902, 2330.

7. A rudimentary working definition of "model" is given by E. A. Gellner, "Model (Theoretical Model)," ed. by Julius Gould and William L. Kolb, _A Dictionary of the Social Sciences_ (New York: Crowell-Collier Publishing, 1964, p. 435).

8. There is some confusion here among the proponents of the school themselves. See, for example, Moynihan and Glazer's insistence that Black people in the United States are an ethnic group even though, unlike other ethnic groups, it is their skin color which identifies them as group members and bearers of a particular "cultural style." See Daniel P. Moynihan and Nathan Glazer, _Beyond the Melting Pot: The Negroes, Puerto_

Ricans, Jews, Italians, and Irish of New York City, 2nd ed. (Cambridge: M.I.T. Press, 1970), pp. xiii, xxxvi, xxxix. Subsequent reference in this chapter to this book will be as Moynihan and Glazer, Beyond the Melting Pot, 2nd ed.

9. Assimilation, a term subject to protean manipulation, may be defined for purposes of this essay, following Park and Burgess, as the "process of interpenetration and fusion in which persons and groups acquire the memories, sentiments, and attitudes of other persons or groups, and, by sharing their experience and history, are incorporated with them in a common cultural life." See Robert E. Park and Ernest W. Burgess, Introduction to the Science of Sociology (Chicago: University of Chicago Press, 1921), p. 735. The profusion of definitions for assimilation and its related term, acculturation, is clearly visible in the first three essays of Deward E. Walker, Jr., ed., The Emergent Native Americans: A Reader in Culture Contact (Boston: Little, Brown, 1972), pp. 6-50. Of course, the authors reviewed in this chapter often settle on their own definitions of assimilation, and this will be noted when appropriate below.

10. In liberal social theory, when the term "social equilibrium" is used, the definition of Talcott Parsons is most often cited. Parsons, speaking grandly of society, has said: "Beyond the most general meaning of the concept of equilibrium, the meaning which is most directly applicable here is that applying to what we have called a 'boundary-maintaining' system..."; T. Parsons, The Social System (Glencoe, Illinois: The Free Press, 1951), p. 481. Furthermore, "The definition of a system as boundary-maintaining is a way of saying that, relative to its environment, that is to fluctuations in the factors of the environment, it maintains certain constancies of pattern, whether this constancy be static or moving..."; Parsons, op. cit., p. 482, emphasis in the original. Typically, the pattern whose constancy Parsons is most concerned to assert theoretically is the normative framework, or value consensus; all components of the social system contribute to its maintenance; ibid., pp. 36n, 297-298. A critical reply to Parsons

on this subject is found in David Lockwood, "Some Remarks on 'The Social System,'" British Journal of Sociology, 7 (1956), pp. 134-146.

11. Karl E. and Alma F. Taeuber, "The Negro as an Immigrant Group: Recent Trends in Racial and Ethnic Segregation in Chicago," American Journal of Sociology, 69 (1963-64), pp. 374-382.

12. Taeuber and Taeuber, p. 375.

13. Taeuber and Taeuber, pp. 375-378.

14. Taeuber and Taeuber, pp. 375, 378, 382.

15. Taeuber and Taeuber, pp. 378, 379-380; this second proposition, the "failure-to-acculturate" thesis, is advanced by Philip M. Hauser in "The Challenge of Metropolitan Growth," Urban Land, 17 (December 1958). It is also rebutted by Charles Silberman in Crisis in Black and White (New York: Random House, 1964), Ch. 3, pp. 36-57.

16. Taeuber and Taeuber, pp. 376 (Table I), 380.

17. Taeuber and Taeuber, pp. 381-382.

18. Taeuber and Taeuber, p. 382.

19. Beverly Duncan and Otis Dudley Duncan, "Minorities and the Process of Stratification," American Sociological Review, 33 (1968), pp. 356-364.

20. Duncan and Duncan; this synopsis of the Duncans' view of stratification is pulled together from various places in the article; the quotes appear on pp. 358, 363.

21. Duncan and Duncan, p. 360.

22. Duncan and Duncan, pp. 361-362.

23. Duncan and Duncan, pp. 363-364.

24. Duncan and Duncan, p. 360.

25. Duncan and Duncan, p. 363.

26. Duncan and Duncan, p. 360.

27. Duncan and Duncan, p. 363.

28. Duncan and Duncan, p. 359.

29. Duncan and Duncan, p. 364.

30. Bart Landry, "The Economic Position of Black Americans," in H. R. Kaplan, ed., American Minorities and Economic Opportunity (Itasca, Illinois: F. E. Peacock, 1977), pp. 50-108; and H. R. Kaplan, "The Road Ahead: Prospects for Equality in the World of Work," ibid., pp. 279-318, esp. pp. 297-311.

31. The phrase and the spirit of criticism of quantitative work for its failure to grasp the structural and theoretical essence of social issues that it embodies are borrowed from C. Wright Mills, The Sociological Imagination (New York: Oxford University Press, 1959), Ch. 3, pp. 50-75.

32. Beeman C. Patterson, "Political Action of Negroes in Los Angeles: A Case Study in the Attainment of Councilmanic Representation," Phylon, 30 (1969), pp. 170-183.

33. These essentials of the ethnic group model's typical arguments about traditional routes to political power used by ethnic groups are briefly sketched in Raymond S. Franklin and Solomon Resnik, The Political Economy of Racism (New York: Holt, Rinehart, and Winston, 1973), pp. 133-134.

34. Dahl's very influential views on the political system and its pluralistic nature are summarized in Richard Gillam, ed., Power in Postwar America (Boston: Little, Brown, 1971), pp. 23-31; the quote from Dahl's work appears on p. 31. Another prominent ethnic group analyst, the historian Oscar Handlin, also sees no

crucial differences between the situation of Black people and other ethnic groups in American politics; Oscar Handlin, "The Goals of Integration," in T. Parsons and K. Clark, eds., The Negro American (Boston: Beacon Press, 1966), pp. 659-677, esp. pp. 668-669.

35. These features of the urban scene are presented in Ira Katznelson and Mark Kesselman, The Politics of Power (New York: Harcourt, Brace, Jovanovich, 1975), pp. 402-428. Many of the problems, particularly with regard to the cities as bases for "Black Power," have been noted earlier; see Frances Fox Piven and Richard A. Cloward, "What Chance for Black Power?" The New Republic, 158:13 (March 30, 1968), pp. 19-23.

36. Patterson, pp. 170-171.

37. Patterson, pp. 170-171, 183; the quoted phrase is found on p. 170.

38. Patterson, pp. 172-174, 177, 180, 183.

39. This experience is briefly recounted, as concerns the modern era (e.g., post World War II) by James Q. Wilson, "The Negro in Politics," in T. Parsons and K. Clark, eds., op. cit., pp. 423-427.

40. Stokely Carmichael and Charles V. Hamilton, Black Power: The Politics of Liberation in America (New York: Random House, 1967).

41. Carmichael and Hamilton, Chs. 2-6.

42. Carmichael and Hamilton, p. 44.

43. Carmichael and Hamilton, pp. 5, 22, 35, 40-41, 47, 75. The quotes, in order of appearance, may be found on pp. 47, 35, 5, and 22.

44. Carmichael and Hamilton, pp. 48-51, 75, 79-80. Girvetz' discussion of classical liberalism's "psychological creed" illuminates their presentation of interest group coalition strategy; see Harry K. Girvetz, From Wealth to Welfare: The Evolution of Liberalism (Stanford,

California: Stanford University Press, 1950), Ch. 1. Also, Carmichael and Hamilton's discussion of pluralism is contradictory because, after initially labeling white people a monolithic bloc that precludes pluralism on issues of race, they later insist that Black Power must recognize the ethnic basis (i.e., pluralist quality) of American politics (ibid., pp. 7, 9-10, 44, 47).

45. Weber's well-known treatise sets forth these points; see Max Weber, *The Protestantic Ethnic and the Spirit of Capitalism*, trans. by T. Parsons (New York: Charles Scribner's Sons, 1958). An excellent secondary treatment is available in Anthony Giddens, *Capitalism and Modern Social Theory* (New York: Cambridge University Press, 1971), pp. 119-132. Another presentation of this value-complex, with especial reference to its applicability to certain Third World peoples in the United States is H. R. Kaplan, ed., *American Minorities and Economic Opportunity*, pp. 1-9.

46. Milton M. Gordon, *Assimilation in American Life: The Role of Race, Religion, and National Origins* (New York: Oxford University Press, 1964).

47. Gordon, p. 71.

48. Gordon, p. 77.

49. Gordon, pp. 3, 31-32, 34, 38.

50. Gordon, pp. 41, 46.

51. Gordon, pp. 47, 51, 58. The statements which may be adduced in the text just *assume* a vertical order, they do not explain its genesis. The quoted words and phrases are from p. 51.

52. Gordon, p. 159.

53. Gordon, pp. 234-235.

54. Gordon, pp. 181, 191-194, 205, 215-217, 221-224.

55. Gordon, p. 45.

56. Gordon, pp. 14-15, 171, 173.

57. Gordon, p. 173.

58. Gordon, pp. 81-82, 237-239; the three points of evaluation of ethnic group comparability as to assimilation -- extrinsic traits (behavior), intrinsic traits (values), and the nature of institutional life -- are given on pp. 171-172.

59. Gordon, pp. 164-165.

60. Robert Paul Wolff elaborates this critique in "The End of Ideology?" in Richard Gillam, ed., Power in Postwar America, pp. 184-190, esp. p. 188.

61. Gordon, p. 239.

62. Gordon, p. 249; Gordon does not seem to know how the government got "in" this business. Discrimination apparently has only a moral history, not a legal and political one. One look at how the government got "in" this business is provided by Wolgemuth's discussion of the deliberate institutionally racist policies of the Wilson Administration; see Karen Wolgemuth, "Woodrow Wilson and Federal Segregation," Journal of Negro History, 44 (1959), pp. 158-173. Additional evidence appears in A. Meier and E. Rudwick, "The Rise of Segregation in the Federal Bureaucracy, 1900-1930," Phylon, 28 (1967), pp. 174-184.

63. Gordon, pp. 257-261.

64. Gordon, pp. 260-261.

65. Gordon, pp. 247, 261. Another writer, published twenty years earlier and writing in a different field, had sought to give the general white population the same reassurance about the probable result of the end of discrimination: he argues that the one-way sexual process (white male - black female) and a phenomenon of marrying up the color scale in the Black community

would eventually bleach the group out of existence. See Franz Boas, Race and Democratic Society (New York: J. J. Augustin, 1945), pp. 70-95.

66. Gordon, p. 264.

67. Gouldner skillfully explicates this belief and its action on social theory deriving from the functionalist tradition: the status quo is sanctioned as a good and powerful social order produced by centuries-old Christian traditions and values; see Alvin W. Gouldner, The Coming Crisis of Western Sociology (New York: Basic Books, 1970), pp. 247-257.

68. Gordon, pp. 236-237, 240, 246-247, 249, 259. The quoted phrase is from p. 259.

69. Gordon, pp. 165-166, 246-248, 254.

70. Significantly, in Gordon's "programs" chapter (Ch. 8), on two occasions when he deals at length with the moral choices the group (and the individual) must make, one of which deals with amalgamation, the subject of jobs, housing, etc., appears as a minimal addendum in both (ibid., pp. 247-248, 261-262).

71. My critique of structural-functionalism draws heavily from Gouldner, The Coming Crisis of Western Sociology, passim.

72. At one point, Gordon even denies that one of the theories of assimilation, Anglo-Conformity, which he examines before settling on cultural pluralism as the preferred vehicle, can be equated with racism (ibid., pp. 103-104).

73. The tradition of Marx begins with his own writings referenced in Karl Marx, "On Class" in Celia S. Heller, ed., Social Inequality (New York: MacMillan, 1969), pp. 14-23. Modern exponents take views as divergent as Bottomore's assertion that modern industrial societies -- capitalist and socialist alike -- are all coming under the sway of bureaucratic elites to Wright's contention that basic class realities (i.e., the

contradiction of capital and labor) have not dissipated but have been complexly augmented by "contradictory class locations"; see T. Bottomore, Classes in Modern Society, American ed. (New York: Pantheon Books, 1966) and Erik Olin Wright, "On Class Boundaries in Advanced Capitalist Societies," Studies on the Left (1976), pp. 3-42. In spite of these divergences, it remains true to say, with Stolzman and Gamberg, that the Marxist tradition sees class as a central analytic category of the capitalist system, inextricably bound up with its fate and the class struggle; James Stolzman and Herbert Gamberg, "Marxist Class Analysis versus Stratification Analysis as General Approaches to Social Inequality," Berkeley Journal of Sociology, 18 (1973-74), pp. 104-127. It is precisely these points which Gordon's analysis does not and cannot admit.

74. Gordon, pp. 41, 171.

75. An illustration of the arbitrariness of social stratification analysis in arriving at the number of "strata" is found in St. Clair Drake and Horace R. Cayton, Black Metropolis, rev. and enl. ed. (New York: Harper and Row, 1962), vol. 2, fns 1, 2, 3, pp. 787-792 where the authors unconvincingly described how they arrived at the social class breakdown they present of the Black community.

76. See Stolzman and Gamberg, "Marxist Class Analysis."

77. These two words appear on p. 3 of the book and the adjective forms are sprinkled throughout.

78. Stolzman and Gamberg ("Marxist Class Analysis," p. 110) make this criticism as does Paul M. Sweezy in The Theory of Capitalist Development (New York: Monthly Review Press, 1942), pp. 5-7, Sweezy referring specifically to some of the central concepts of economic theory.

79. The phenomenon of interlocking, ruling groups in American economic and state affairs has been documented by Katznelson and Kesselman, The Politics of

Power, pp. 35-68; and Ferdinand Lundberg, The Rich and the Super Rich (New York: Lyle Stuart, 1968), pp. 531-678. A particularly careful study done on foreign policy matters is Gabriel Kolko, The Roots of American Foreign Policy (Boston: Beacon Press, 1969), esp. pp. 3-26.

80. A preliminary survey of aggravated assaults and direct action non-violent protest in Southern Black communities concluded that there is reason to believe that crimes of violence in these communities decreased as direct action activities increased; see F. Solomon, M.D. et al., "Civil Rights Activity and Reduction in Crime Among Negroes," Archives of General Psychiatry, 12:3 (March 1965), pp. 227-236.

81. Edward C. Banfield, The Unheavenly City Revisited (Boston: Little, Brown, 1974). The earlier work (1968) was titled The Unheavenly City: The Nature and Future of Our Urban Crisis, same publisher.

82. Banfield, The Unheavenly City Revisited, pp. 54-63. Banfield's time horizon arguments about the poor are essentially comparable to Lipset's puerilization argument about the supposed authoritarian tendencies of the working class; see S. M. Lipset, Political Man: The Social Bases of Politics (Garden City, New York: Doubleday and Co., 1960), Ch. 4, "Working-Class Authoritarianism," pp. 87-126.

In addition, it should be pointed out that Banfield's description of the Black lower classes finds resonance in the work of influential Black social scientists: e.g., the discussion of this class in Drake and Cayton, Black Metropolis, vol. 1, pp. 121-122, 202; vol. 2, pp. 581-610. Charles A. Valentine in Culture and Poverty (Chicago: University of Chicago Press, 1968), refers to a "Frazierian tradition" of pathological views in this regard, citing Frazier's familiar work on Black social structure; on this same point, see also Valentine, "Black Studies and Anthropology: Scholarly and Political Interests in Afro-American Culture," McCaleb Module Series, No. 15 (Reading, Massachusetts: Addison-Wesley Publishing Co., 1972), pp. 7-14.

83. Banfield, The Unheavenly City Revisited, p. 71.

84. Banfield, The Unheavenly City Revisited, pp. 63-67.

85. Banfield employs the statistical technique of "factoring out" the amount of difference that is attributable to racial discrimination as regards black/white socioeconomic status on a specific variable, e.g., income. His presentation occurs, in The Unheavenly City Revisited, pp. 80-82. The Taeubers, in the article cited above, also use a version of this technique; see n 75 above. The standard work in this method of addressing racial discrimination is considered to be Gary Becker, The Economics of Discrimination (Chicago: University of Chicago Press, 1957).

Banfield's numerous assertions about the greatly lessened impact of racial discrimination may be found in The Unheavenly City Revisited, pp. 21, 114, 227-228, 282, 284. Here, Banfield anticipates the position elaborated so unconvincingly by William J. Wilson in The Declining Significance of Race: Blacks and Changing American Institutions (Chicago: The University of Chicago Press, 1978). My assessment of Wilson's work appears in "The Latest Scam in 'Ethnic Group Analysis,'" The Journal of Ethnic Studies, 7:4 (Winter 1980), pp. 93-98; other evaluations are contained in Charles V. Willie, ed., The Caste and Class Controversy (Bayside, New York: General Hall, 1979).

86. Another example of the displacement causal strategy is Stanley Lieberson and Glenn V. Fuguitt, "Negro-White Occupational Differences in the Absence of Discrimination," American Journal of Sociology, 73 (1967-68), pp. 188-200. Banfield's use of the strategy is in The Unheavenly City Revisited, pp. 80, 87-91.

87. Transfer payments (e.g., welfare income), job training programs, compensatory education, curbs to gratuitous violence and sex are all, according to the author, not very workable remedies for the affliction of Black lower class culture; Banfield, The Unheavenly

City Revisited, pp. 121, 123, 139, 143, 151, 166, 185, 196, 265-266.

88. The insatiability of humankind has been, historically, a favored theme of conservative social philosophy; see Gouldner, The Coming Crisis of Western Sociology, pp. 430-432.

Banfield gives his version as four kinds of poverty -- destitution, hardship, want, and relative deprivation -- the last being the most common among the poor, and essentially a matter of status deprivation, not material deprivation (The Unheavenly City Revisited, pp. 141-143, 261-262).

89. Banfield, The Unheavenly City Revisited, pp. 22, 222, 228. A sharp rebuttal to Banfield's contention is H. J. Bryce, "Are Most Blacks in the Middle Class?," The Black Scholar, 5 (February 1974), pp. 32-36.

90. Banfield, The Unheavenly City Revisited, pp. 74-75, 96.

91. Banfield, The Unheavenly City Revisited, pp. 107-109, 111, 115, 118, 120.

92. Banfield, The Unheavenly City Revisited, pp. 102, 275.

93. Banfield, The Unheavenly City Revisited, p. 118; the "working poor," then, may have to be shepherded into a state of more-or-less continuous dependency. A similar prospect is recommended by James S. Coleman in "Race Relations and Social Change," in Irwin Katz and Patricia Gurin, eds., Race and the Social Sciences (New York: Basic Books, 1969), p. 307.

94. My concern with the problem of exclusion, as with other concepts delimited, focuses primarily on its application to Black folk in the United States. Banfield, however, makes it clear that the social class prejudice he describes operates evenhandedly for Black people and whites (The Unheavenly City Revisited, p. 87).

95. The branch of social philosophy alluded to is today known as conservatism. Wolff maintains, with great cogency, that both today's welfare liberalism and (political and economic) conservatism share common origin in the different facets of classical liberalism, especially the work of Jeremy Bentham and J. S. Mill; see Robert Paul Wolff, The Poverty of Liberalism (Boston: Beacon Press, 1968), Ch. 1; and Girvetz, From Wealth to Welfare, pp. 7-27.

The obsolescence of Banfield's view of small-scale competition today under capitalism may be gauged in Ferdinand Lundberg, The Rich and the Super Rich, pp. 1-34, 295-326; Paul A. Baran and Paul M. Sweezy, Monopoly Capital (New York: Monthly Review Press, 1966), pp. 14-51, 137-171, 218-248; John M. Blair, Economic Concentration (New York: Harcourt, Brace and Jovanovich, 1972), pp. 255-550; and V. I. Lenin, Imperialism, The Highest Stage of Capitalism (Peking: Foreign Languages Press, 1970), pp. 11-30.

96. The "culture of poverty" thesis which Banfield pursues is criticized in William Ryan, Blaming the Victim, rev. ed. (New York: Random House, 1976), pp. 3-141; and Charles A. Valentine, Culture and Poverty (Chicago: University of Chicago Press, 1968), pp. 18-47, 78-97, 141-153.

Banfield's social Darwinist tendencies may be put into perspective by consulting Richard Hofstadter, Social Darwinism in American Thought, rev. ed. (Boston: Beacon Press, 1967). Banfield's opposition to minimum wage laws may be compared directly with Spencer's opposition to public charity and poor laws; see Hofstadter, p. 41.

97. Banfield, The Unheavenly City Revisited, pp. 281-282. This is a "program" book and the author dutifully lays out his prescriptions in Ch. 11.

98. The welfare state, and its social programs designed to harmonize the interests of the state and the corporate and small-capital sectors of the economy, is detailed in Katznelson and Kesselman, The Politics of

Power, pp. 429-457.

99. Moynihan and Glazer, Beyond the Melting Pot, 2nd ed., pp. xxxi, 2. The quote is from p. xxxi.

100. Moynihan and Glazer, pp. 12, 30, 311-312.

101. Moynihan and Glazer, pp. lviii, lxxxiii, 17, 227.

102. Moynihan and Glazer, p. 31.

103. Moynihan and Glazer, pp. xxxix, lxxix, lxix, 14, 139, 291, 49, 79.

104. Moynihan and Glazer, pp. 12-16.

105. Moynihan and Glazer, pp. lxxxiv, 299.

106. Moynihan and Glazer, pp. xli, 299-303, 315. The concepts of objective and subjective interest derived from the Marxist tradition and critically applied to the sort of pluralist framework used by Moynihan and Glazer are presented in Isaac D. Balbus, "The Concept of Interest in Pluralist and Marxian Analysis," Politics and Society, 1:2 (February 1972), pp. 151-177.

107. The ethnic group=interest group equation and the dichotomous model of U.S. race relations are presented respectively in Moynihan and Glazer, pp. lxxxiii, 17; and pp. xxiii-xxiv, lxxiv.

108. These data are found in U.S. Bureau of the Census, Current Population Reports, Special Studies, Series P-23, No. 54, "The Social and Economic Status of the Black Population in the United States, 1974" (Washington, D.C.: U.S. Government Printing Office, 1975), pp. 24, 41, 42 (Table 23), 55, 57, 58, 122, 134, 137 (Table 90).

109. See U.S. Commission on Civil Rights, "Social Indicators of Equality for Minorities and Women" (Washington, D.C.: August 1978).

110. Figures for top 25 Black firms' number of employees and concurrent unemployment aggregate are given, respectively, in Introduction to Afro-American Studies, 4th ed. (Chicago: Peoples College Press, 1977), p. 356; and Black Enterprise, 8:6 (January 1978), p. 7. The number of black firms in existence as of 1972 is found in U.S. Census Bureau, op. cit., p. 83.

111. Moynihan and Glazer, pp. lxvii, 15, 69, 113, 315.

112. Moynihan and Glazer, pp. xxx, lxvi, 31-36, 77, 129, 137, 239, 245-246.

The difference between North and South in the matter of segregation is largely a difference of degree; of wide degree, certainly, but still of degree.

W. E. B. DuBois,
"Segregation in the North," The Crisis,
41 (April 1934), p. 116.

Chapter 2
The Caste Model

Introduction

The problem of social inequality in societies has often called the attention of social theorists and researchers. When this inequality is associated with increasingly rigid and stable patterns apparently based on phenotypic group membership, theorists and researchers are often led to propose a paradigm relevant to this specific form of social inequality. In the case of race relations in the United States, one such paradigm proposed was the caste model.

However, the definitional ambiguities which tend to plague the caste model of race relations make coherent statement of the central hypothesis of this school difficult. In such a situation the application of the term "caste" to describe and explain U.S. race relations is problematic, and its descriptive claims often are not supported with comparative ethnographic evidence. However, perhaps three basic propositions of the model can be discerned. First, society is composed of endogamous, largely closed, culturally homogeneous units known as castes. Second, these units are held to exhibit a great deal of persistence through time and a preservation of the cultural, social, and psychological traits peculiar to them. And third, it is assumed that social interaction based on caste distinctions may be equated to social interactions based on racial distinctions. We shall take particular care to examine this last assumption, since it is central to our contention that caste and race are not cognate orders of social phenomena, though possessing superficial commonalities.

When specific instances of the use of the term "caste" by students of U.S. race relations are examined, it becomes clear that the principles sketched above do not provide the basis for policy recommendations by caste analysts. In fact, such recommendations almost invariably derive from some aspect of liberal social theory. What emerges, then, in the work of caste adherents is a literary descriptive term, "caste," whose accuracy is open to serious question.

A brief review of some prominent works which employ "caste" will illustrate this point. Generally speaking, this usage is found in the work of historians whose research interests lead them to the field of race relations.

One of the earliest references to caste is made by W. E. B. DuBois in 1903. Writing in The Souls of Black Folk, a collection of essays designed to probe the essence of Black culture, and to outline a program for its enhancement, DuBois makes repeated use of the term in portraying the social circumstances of the Black masses in the South at that time.(1) Later, C. Vann Woodward uses the term to describe the same circumstances, in the period 1877-1915, as he defends his thesis that exclusionary social barriers, far from being the direct legacy of slavery, were imposed on the South only after the defeat of Southern populism.(2) And, in an intellectual history of the same period, August Meier employs the term to characterize the state of race relations upon which various social philosophies for the advancement of Black people were projected.(3) Studies of earlier periods of Black history also reveal a proclivity for the term, as when Eugene Genovese constructs a typology of New World slavery in which the U.S. South and the Anglo-French Caribbean are held to have possessed, respectively, a "two-caste" and a "three-caste" system.(4)

And, in his analytic review of Reconstruction, Kenneth Stampp makes reference to the term to convey the racial tenor of an epoch.(5)

The term caste, and cognate terms such as "caste line," "caste system," and the like continue to be used in historical treatments of more recent periods. For example, Raymond Wolters' study of the effect of New Deal legislation and programs on Black unemployment and poverty puts race relations at that time in the mold of caste.(6) And, similarly, in a highly regarded liberal reformist statement on race relations, social commentator Charles Silberman offers expressions like "caste structure," "caste of color," and "caste system" as being reflective of basic racial realities.(7)

In none of the works cited above is a definition of caste presented which justifies its applicability to the subject matter. No theoretical statements or postulates, no matter how brief, are advanced. Rather, the term caste seems to have been chosen for its particular evocative quality and descriptive puissance, leaving the matter of theory entirely aside.

As suggested at the conclusion of Chapter 1, we shall argue here that, despite its uncharacteristic ethnographic formulation of U.S. race relations, the caste model draws upon modern liberal theory for its orientation especially as regards policy questions. Like the ethnic group model, this model's adherence to liberal assumptions is most clearly revealed in its treatment of the six fundamental concepts of race relations theory which we have advanced.

Historians seldom have advanced specific notions about the relevance of caste to American race relations. Rather, for an understanding of the theoretical assumptions which buttress the use of this term, it is necessary to turn to the work of sociologists. We shall first present a general discussion of the definition of caste, followed by an inquiry into caste and race in India, and conclude with a critique of the work of proponents of the caste model of American race relations.

The Sociological Approach

An early discussion of caste by Gait indicates the difficulties associated with defining the term. After noting that endogamy, or marrying within one's own group, however that group is defined, was itself not a suitable criterion, he settled on this definition:

> Caste may perhaps be defined as 'an endogamous group, or collection of such groups, bearing a common name, having the same traditional occupation, claiming descent from the same source, and commonly regarded as forming a single homogeneous community.'(8)

From Gait's definition, the principal definitional elements would appear to be endogamy, common nomenclature, common descent, traditional occupation, and communal setting.

In addition, Gait observes that there are different types of caste, often formed in different ways. There are "functional castes" (which he tends to equate with occupational groupings), "race castes," and "sectarian castes." Castes may be formed by migration, conversion, by change of occupation, and by amalgamation. The status of a caste depends on its position in the system of social exchanges involving food and ritual observances though "[t]he precise circumstances which determine the status of a caste vary in different parts of the country." Social mobility is variously described as occurring because of migration caused by adoption of a new, relatively in-demand occupation, or because of individual or group economic advancement which becomes incompatible with ascribed social rank and is reconciled either through fictional invention of superior ancestors, hypergamous marriage, or appeal to a mediating higher social authority.(9)

The question of how and under what conditions individual and group statuses change within a caste society is important because it leads to a detailed consideration of the rates and types of change which are characteristic of such a society. It then becomes possible to ask what kind of rigidity of social structure is most typical of a caste society. However, Gait's analysis of caste does not adequately explain how change occurs within the system nor the relation between caste society and the forms of economic production prevalent in South Asia. Though he begins his essay with a reference to the rigidity of the Hindu caste system in distinction to the relative fluidity of European social classes, this point is not taken up.(10)

A more recent discussion of caste by Inden and Marriott holds that caste is not unique in South Asia. Simpler caste systems have evolved elsewhere (e.g., Peru, Brazil, imperial Rome). They support this contention by defining caste systems as, "...moral systems that differentiate and rank the whole population of a society in corporate units (castes) generally defined by descent, marriage, and occupation."(11)

The basic elements in the authors' definition of caste are its moral system, corporateness, descent rules, endogamy, and traditional occupation. But, as seen in the definition quoted above, the primary feature which is considered to be determinative of caste is its peculiar moral philosophy. Since this philosophy is based on divinely-ordained inequality and ritualized unequal, but mutually beneficial, exchanges, Inden and Marriott maintain that any social system which has a similar moral philosophy may be described as a caste system. They dichotomize caste systems into complex and detailed, on the one hand, and rudimentary and simple on the other. Among the representatives of this latter type they include "...the black and white caste systems in the United States" and those of South Africa and Rhodesia.(12)

However, the suitability of the caste label becomes questionable when it is applied to <u>any</u> social structure in which the existence of stable patterns of social stratification can be demonstrated. Even the appearance of a moral sanction as legitimation for these patterns of stratification is not a sufficient test for caste since social inequality in most human societies tends to be rationalized by appeal to moral, ideological precepts.(13) Moreover, the attempt by Inden and Marriott to offer a generalizable definition of caste is hampered by their failure to specify the conditions of operation of social mobility under a caste regime and then to identify those conditions in other alleged caste situations; as in Gait, social mobility under caste here receives spotty, noncomprehensive treatment, the single example intended to serve for the entire differentiated system.(14)

A more suitable treatment of caste is possible if the universal aspects of the concept are separated from its unique aspects. E. R. Leach distinguishes two major uses, often ambiguously interwoven, of the term "caste" in the literature: as an _ethnographic category_ denoting specific features of Hindu society, and as a _sociological category_ having the connotative function of referring to any class structure of especial rigidity. While agreeing that caste is a structural phenomenon, Leach locates its definitional essence in the particularity of Pan-Indian civilization. Thus, he argues that the presence of more or less rigid social stratification is not alone, as a structural criterion, sufficient reason for the application of the caste label. Caste must be understood as "a _particular_ species of structural organization indissolubly linked with ... Pan-Indian civilization... (emphasis added)." Its essential quality lies in the fact that:

> ...caste _as distinct from either social class or caste grade_ manifests itself in the external relations between caste groupings. These relations stem from the fact that _every_ caste, not merely the upper elite, has its special 'privileges.' Furthermore, these external relations have a very special quality since, ideally, they exclude kinship links of all kinds (emphasis in the original).(15)

Leach also maintains that the system of social exchanges and restrictions on commensality must take place within the social context of a political economy whose division of labor mitigates economic competition, fostering instead economic interdependence if the analytic construct of caste is to be deemed appropriate. In addition, it must be recognized in caste societies that the unique feature of kinship is an exclusively internal status determinant which does not, ideally, influence social (i.e., political, economic, and ritual) relations external to caste.(16)

Leach's discussion of caste is useful in that it tends to discourage the ubiquitous application of the term. But, he does not offer any general account of how change occurs in the system, apart from certain comments about the possibilities for individual social mobility inherent in the gap between the theory and practice of the system. His observation that in the modern period castes have tended to band together as political factions seeking the redress of economic grievance in defiance of all caste traditions is a revealing glimpse at this subject.(17) However, Leach's views on caste suggest the inappropriateness of using this concept to analyze race relations, a position which puts him in opposition to Gait, Inden and Marriott, and those American sociologists of race relations who have adopted the caste approach.

Caste and Race

Before turning to a consideration of some of the views of caste model proponents, one timely issue should be addressed. We may put this issue in the form of a question: "What is the relationship between physically distinct human groups and a caste system?" India, as the foremost representative of caste in the world, has received numerous students of its society who have attempted to answer this question. Moreover, such inquiries reveal two aspects of the question: as it applies to the origins of Hindu society, and as it applies to the functioning (ancient and modern) of that society.

As to the origins of the Hindu caste system, Cox has pointed out that two sorts of explanations are most in contention: racial and cultural.(18) Risley and Ghurye have presented racial explanations for the rise of the caste system, but modern students of caste do not endorse their views. Explanations which emphasize occupation, or moral principle, or some other cultural aspect of Hindu society are more persuasive.(19) But since no hierarchy of causes has been established, one can appreciate the vagueness of Barnabas and Mehta's assertion that:

> It is likely that several factors working jointly led in [the] course of time to the emergence of the Indian caste system, its social, economic and ideological facets being specifically influenced by ... [these] factors.(20)

However, as to the necessary congruence and simultaneity of race feelings and the emergence of Hindu caste we may conclude with Hutton that:

> [c]olour prejudice and racial exclusiveness have been common enough in the history of the world, but they have nowhere else led to such an institution as caste, and it would be rash to suppose that they could have done so in India of themselves.(21)

Finally, recent studies of the functioning of caste as it remains in modern Hindu society do not give credence to the view that racial antipathies and alliances are central to the maintenance of the society.(22) From this, we should conclude that caste relations and race relations are not necessarily analogous social situations, despite superficial resemblances. Nevertheless, as we shall see, proponents of the caste model of American race relations assume that racial interaction and caste interaction are cognate social phenomena.

Caste in America (1)

W. Lloyd Warner offered a view of caste in its application to American race relations which was to become very influential.(23) Warner maintained that race relations in the South reflected the interaction of two kinds of social stratification, caste and class. The class structure was subsumed by the caste structure so that a tripartite (upper, middle, lower) division of social classes, between which movement was possible, comprised each caste. But between the castes themselves no movement or marriage was possible. The central premise on which Warner's propositions are advanced is his definition of caste whereby endogamy and social mobility restriction are deemed its quintessential features.(24)

As noted above, the correctness of Warner's definition of caste is disputable. Moreover, he raises a key issue which may really be the crucial question as regards the theoretical usefulness of the caste model. Warner gives a diagrammatic representation of the two castes, white and black, intending to show the "social skewness" of their "vertical opposition."(25) This skewness is said to reflect the fact that the caste line between the two groups has been forced upward lately by the action of the subordinate caste. The question becomes whether this type of change is characteristic of a caste society.

But, it is not a question that Warner answers. He makes no reference to traditional notions about social mobility in caste society, and thus does not compare them to his hypothesis of the rotating caste line which moves from a vertical position to a horizontal one.(26) This line rotates presumably because the social skewness which Warner notes actually represents the degree of conflict between the white caste and the black caste, conflict which hypothetically it is admitted could destroy all social barriers between the two groups <u>except</u> skin color.(27) No evidence is presented to support the inference that traditional Pan-Indian caste society produces change in this manner, or that conflict between castes is capable of generating such far-reaching, ultimately anti-caste, effects. And, the notion that skin color as an expression of racial identification, preserved by endogamy, is the essential determinative mark of caste membership and status does not find general acceptance among students of caste.(28)

Despite these definitional and theoretical difficulties, the caste model became a widely recognized paradigm for the sociological analysis of U.S. race relations. It may be possible to explain the initial adherence which the model elicited by citing, in combination with other factors, the influence of the work of Robert Park.(29) Park, it will be recalled, offered an evolutionary, natural history theory of race relations according to which they pass inevitably through four stages: competition → conflict → accommodation → assimilation. Thus, the caste model, in conjunction with Park's cyclic theory of racial contact, could be used to illuminate the causes responsible for the failure of one of America's oldest ethnic groups to progress beyond the accommodative stage and attain assimilation. Further, the preference of the model is for explanation grounded in the moral postulates of dominant American political and social ideology. This aspect, combined with its relative theoretical diminution of political and economic aspects of the race problem, may have been congenial with a time in American history in which labor struggles, Black nationalism, unpopular radical political doctrines, and general social unrest made "resolvable" social dilemmas preferable to unresolvable ones.(30)

Caste in America (2)

A good illustration of the connection between the caste model and Park's cyclic theory of racial contact is John Dollard's <u>Caste and Class in a Southern Town</u>.(31) Written in 1937, the book partakes of the historical milieu alluded to above.

Dollard sets out "to grasp and describe the emotional structure which runs parallel to the formal social structure of the community." Given the assumptions that "the social situation" patterns the affects of people and that common situations will produce common affects, he surmises that, with the passing of slavery, the imposition of a caste system has produced "a chronic frustration situation" for Black people in which aggression on their part should be expected. Since open revolt against subordination is rare, individualistic, and ineffectual, the common psychology of caste among Black folk produces other forms of aggression which aim at adjustment to the frustrating situation, i.e., at accommodation.(32)

A pattern of gains and aggressions is detailed. In education, politics, and religion, "caste patterning" produces increased assimilation of Black people and cultural conflict between regional and national mores in the schools; maintenance of white domination through the poll tax and the white primary in government and politics; and, a biracial arrangement of white institutions and black institutions (further divided into Black middle and lower class churches) in the field of religion. The white middle class enjoys an economic gain, being able to avoid farm labor, to monopolize business and professional activities, and to draw upon a steady pool of domestic servants; a sexual gain, accruing to white men, whose access to women of the lower caste is based on a projected sluttish image of them and on the derivation of "caste memory"; and, a prestige gain, exacted as deferential forms of treatment and ultimately enforceable through coercion. The Black lower class, unburdened by "sublimated expressive patterns," enjoys greater sexual impulse gratification, freer expression of aggression against fellow caste members, and relief from competition, frugality, and individual responsibility through dependence on various forms of tenantry.(33)

Moreover, Dollard explains the accommodative psychology of the Black caste as a result of the divergent moral conceptions, national versus regional (i.e., Southern), of the role of Black people in American democracy. These divergent conceptions express a moral conflict that is the basis of a culture conflict which underlies race relations in Southerntown (Dollard's fictitious name for the site of his research).(34) Racial prejudice is ultimately described as "an emotional fact" which is an "irrational affect." It tends to be drained off in the form of hostility expressed by an in-group against some out-group where free-floating aggression, a permissive social pattern, and a uniformly identifiable stigmatized group exist. The inference one can reasonably make from Dollard's analysis is that this prejudice will subside as social changes are promoted which induce a moral re-alignment of social practice with American ideals.(35)

This inference is especially justified by the 1957 preface to the book in which the author emphasizes the international difficulties which the race problem poses for the United States in its struggle with Communism, offers that evolutionary, orderly change is the preferred route to the amelioration of the caste system, and maintains that such change will accelerate the inevitable assimilation of Black people, who have no culture of their own, into American society as was the fate of all other ethnic groups. The way out of the race dilemma, then, is through moralism, i.e., re-dedication to American ideals, and it is within these ideals that the ultimate reality of the race problem is expressed.(36)

Characteristically, Dollard's moralism is predicated on a geographically dichotomous view of race relations wherein the North and South are detached and treated as separate cases, presumably with the South being the proper subject for the study of racial dilemmas. The two regions are said to have inherited from Europe different traditions, with the slave-feudal social principles of the South giving way to the "free, competitive, individualistic tradition" of the North as the latter became the mores of the nation. Hence, the conflict over race is pictured as a Southern moral one in which race prejudice as the source of that conflict stems from the imposition of an "outmoded institution" (i.e., slavery) whose demise served to reveal more plainly the irrationality of such prejudice.(37)

This dichotomous view of race relations tends to overlook much evidence against it and in so doing fails to posit a national framework as the indispensable referrent for a theoretical approach to race relations. The dichotomous approach is fundamentally misleading since it obscures similarities of practice and philosophy that have operated as regards matters of race in all regions of the United States more or less consistently. Thus, in Dollard's review of Northern history (Ch. 4), the quaint, paternalistic racial prejudice of many white abolitionists is overlooked, as well as the racial exclusiveness of many of the white settlers in the West. Instead of a view of institutional racism, Dollard offers us "regional racism" (my term). Completely unobserved, yet occurring in the epoch of his study, are the processes at work in the North and West that would culminate in the formation of racially-segregated urban ghettoes.(38)

Accommodation, and the moralism upon which it is based, constitute part of Dollard's sociological view of society. Society is a "social machine." Within the operation of this machine cultural patterns are established which leave their imprint of the mores on every individual. Every individual is, thus, a true representation of the culture; succeeding generations do not invent culture, they merely pass it on.(39) Writ-large analysis is essential and productive.

Caste, defined as a barrier to legitimate descent (i.e., as an obstacle to kinship rights) based on biological, not cultural, features, is introduced in Dollard's sociological analysis in order to explain the existence of conflict within the inertia-ridden social machine.(40) As noted, this conflict is treated as basically moral in nature and is expressed through the psychological concept of aggression which occurs on either side of the caste line. Other forms of conflict, especially economic and political, receive little attention. Moreover, no support for the preferred definition of caste is presented, except the suggestion that racial exclusion in the South is similar to the pollution concept of caste as it is known in Hindu societies.(41)

As a theoretical paradigm, the caste model outlined

by Dollard suffers from a number of debilitating limitations. Its reliance on psychological data as the ultimate form of social reality tends to neglect and diminish the connection between these sense data and other forms of social reality; these other forms, especially the political and the economic, are not very well integrated into the model. This tendency is especially apparent in the treatment of conflict whereby, in addition to its supposedly moral basis, the primary locus of tension centers on the relationship of the white middle class and the Black group.(42) The white upper class is ignored, even though its role as landlord puts it at the center of Southerntown's economy. Exploitation does not appear in the analysis, but the related phenomenon of power, in the form of coercion, is treated as the ultimate guarantor of accommodative behavior such as deference.(43) Our own conceptual framework suggests that, in race relations situations, the ability to exploit economically also may be translated into the power to penalize socially, as in the maintenance of exclusionary social barriers. However, in Dollard's analysis, exploitation and power have no relation to one another.

Similarly, exclusion is not regarded in its cultural function with reference to the subordinate group. Instead, it is presented as a social distance barrier which, though effective in politics and economics, is essentially designed to prevent sexual contact and marriage.(44) Exclusion, then, functions as a conduit for the subordinating power of the superordinate group to conveniently arrange the social life of caste subordinates.

Clearly, Dollard's view of exclusion produces a pathological view or denial of Black culture. Black social life does not constitute a "separate" or "independent" culture; the socio-cultural life of the Black lower class is described as "parasitic."(45) Middle class Black people reveal in their psychoanalytic life histories no substantial deviation from Western European norms and, for all intents and purposes, may be considered "white."(46) A matriarchal, disorganized, weak family structure, inherited from slavery, permits greater expression of physical and psychological aggression by women, since cultural bonds for instinctual repression and management are absent; as Black people leave lower class status some lower class traits survive but, in the main, their family life comes more closely to resemble the father-dominated white middle class family.(47) And, with only weak, imitative, and pathological social institutions as a basis for group life, Black social solidarity is largely passive and defensive.(48) Finally, the psychological maladjustment of the Black middle class, stemming from its disproportionately unrewarded adoption of white middle class norms under the duress of "caste barriers," is intimated.(49)

This denial of Black culture serves to make the inevitability of assimilation, theoretically and socially, all the more self-evident. Dollard's use of the term "caste," for which no ethnographic evidence whatsoever is presented, is intended to explain the disruption of the assimilative process and to accord a degree of legitimacy to a regional variation of racial inequality.(50) The domain assumptions of linear social evolution, increased historical movement from tradition (irrationality) to reason (rationality), cultural (usually predicated upon and subsuming, racial) superiority, and an equilibrium based consensually bound social order, all present in Dollard's work, make it unlikely that Black culture will be seen as anything but pathological or that its relation to a general, exclusionary system of institutional racism will be grasped.

The subject of Black culture presents similar difficulties for another classic study of race relations done from the perspective of the caste model. In Gunnar Myrdal's An American Dilemma, a related picture of Black social life is drawn.(51)

For Myrdal, the separate institutions of the Black community represent a form of social pathology because they are deviations from the American standard of assimilation.(52) Moreover, in all cultural activities, Myrdal believes that Black people are copiers, but poor copiers; they are "exaggerated Americans." Thus, they borrow European cultural traits and modify them under duress but unsuccessfully, as reflected in their tradition of individual leadership and mass passivity, their development of pressure groups as a response to the low degree of participation in the American political system, in their religious practices which are taken over from those of the white Protestant lower class, in their newspapers and schools and in their lax attitude toward crime derived from the white Southern tradition of illegality.(53)

Primarily responsible for the social pathology visible among Black people is exclusion. Though exclusion is recognized to produce economic and political effects, it is its cultural function which is given central importance. However, as in Dollard's treatment, this cultural function only expresses pathology within the subordinate group.

Exclusion produces pathology because it operates within the framework of a caste society. Caste is defined as a "type of social differentiation" in which marriage relations and movement between groups are "closed and rigid."(54) In America, the caste system emerged as the result of the demise of slavery. Caste for the superordinate white group centers on protecting its racial purity through strict endogamy, while other interests, such as enforcing deferential patterns of social etiquette and maintaining discrimination in political and economic activities, occupy a descending order of importance; hence, the famous "rank order of discrimination" is produced.(55)

Following Warner, Myrdal posits the interaction of caste with a system of social distinctions based on class. Class is chiefly determined by income and occupation, though a host of other factors is adduced as also being determinative. (In fact, caste is presented as simply an extreme case of class rigidity.)(56) The interaction of these two types of social differentiation within the same social order produces a pattern of "caste relations" which varies according to the class within each caste, region of the country, and time period.

For Myrdal, variations within the pattern of caste relations are principally attributed to regional differences between the North and the South. This dichotomous view, a characteristic of the caste school already noted, is explained by Myrdal as expressing the fundamental incongruity between two societies, one static, quasi-feudal and slave-based, the other mobile, open, and technology-based. With the demise of slavery, the static society, the Southern one, has become "a stubbornly lagging American frontier society." This being so, its disrespect for law is comprehensible since the American Creed has not fully penetrated the region.(57) The South's "tradition of illegality" combined with its rationalizations for the caste system and greater number of Black folk explain the closing off of job opportunities for them in the region's growing non-agricultural economy (especially the textile industry), their almost total disfranchisement as a result of the region's political conservatism, their inability to command any of the rewards of politics, and their sufferance of Jim Crow inspired social segregation as typified in the substandard course content of their segregated schools.(58)

In the North, on the other hand, because the American Creed operates on a formal level and because there are fewer caste subordinates, no rigid exclusionary devices exist in the labor market, the franchise is not restricted by race, no elaborate etiquette of race relations has been instituted, the Black vote secures "legal justice" and, hence, greater opportunity for protest leadership, and social segregation in public institutions is absent as evidenced by quality schools open to all.(59) The segregation that exists is attributed to three causes: one, the influence of personal prejudice at the informal level, as in the case of "_informal_ social pressure from ... whites" (emphasis in the original) being the alleged chief cause of residential segregation; two, to the poverty of the Black masses; and, three, if the Black persons are Southern migrants, to their incongruous cultural practices which may lead to increasing observed social deviance, as in the case of criminal behavior.(60)

The pivotal role played by the American Creed in

Myrdal's version of the dichotomous approach to race relations reveals his predilection to assign ultimate causal weight to consensual moralism as concerns all aspects of the problem studied. Thus, the creedal social philosophy of America, which is "gradually realizing itself," is held responsible for the homogeneity and stability of moral values in the face of the contradictory counter-acting general cultural traits of low degree of respect for law and intolerance for deviation from legal behavior norms inherited from the frontier and American puritanism.(61) These contradictory traits help establish the basis for conflict in the American conscience and the subordinate position of Black people is the most salient example of this conflict. Hence, the position of Black people in American society is "nothing less than a century-long lag of public morals," having been settled in principle long ago.(62)

Conflict for Myrdal, as can be seen, is <u>moral</u> conflict, based on consensus and occurring at the level of the individual. It is the dilemma of the average "ordinary white American" that Myrdal narrates. Other forms of conflict recede in importance and do not appear to be decisive. Conflict, in effect, becomes an equilibrium maintaining mechanism through which the social order preserves itself.(63) As Myrdal states in his conclusion:

> ...<u>[t]he important changes in the Negro problem do not consist of</u> ... <u>'social trends'</u> ... <u>but are made up of changes in people's beliefs and valuations</u>. We started by stating the hypothesis that the Negro problem has its existence in the American's mind. There the decisive struggle goes on (emphasis in the original).(64)

Myrdal's presentation of conflict, in which its social, economic, and political forms are all subsumed by the moral, has certain consequences for two other related concepts. Since "[t]he white group has the power, and, hence, the responsibility," its moral quandary must be based on a monopoly of power.(65) Power is a zero-sum game, i.e., gains for one group must represent losses for another, and caste subordinates are powerless.(66) But this conception of power completely obscures the development by racial subordinates of power bases among themselves, from which the racial status quo could be challenged (e.g., the Southern Tenant Farmers Union, c. 1934-39).

Thus, any consideration of the latent aspect of actual power relations and the unintended social consequences which may derive from them is entirely lacking, even though Myrdal's discussion of black migration and the readiness of Southern Black people to fight discrimination (c. 1943) suggest these features of the concept.(67) Moreover, because power remains at a low level of theoretical treatment and is expressed primarily through the phenomenon of moral conflict, the concept of exploitation and its related social phenomena (e.g., hierarchical social relations) virtually disappear from Myrdal's treatise. It is mentioned briefly as a past cause, developed under slavery in the South, for the "rigid institutional structure of ... economic life" which hampers the industrial modernization of the region. Apparently, in contradistinction, labor exploitation is not a problem or has been satisfactorily managed in the North.(68)

Thus, having rendered exploitation a prior determinant (implying its vitiation or absence in the present) and having limited conflict to the struggle of moral valuations based on a similarly restricted understanding of power, Myrdal is able to depict the racial beliefs of the dominant group as powerful determinants in themselves of the status of race (for Myrdal, caste) relations. These beliefs, centered on the defense of racial purity and white womanhood and the denial of amalgamation, are "active forces" in maintaining Black subordination.(69) However, since the connections between beliefs as nonmaterial social entities and the social, political, and economic agencies (i.e., institutions, secondary or primary groups) which accomplish social action presumably guided by these beliefs, are inadequately assessed, Myrdal's judgment about the power of racial beliefs is not convincing. This is especially so if one considers the author's failure to evaluate the different degrees and types of power among the various segments of the dominant racial group, and his insistent focus on causal analysis at the level of the individual; both features of the work tend to obscure the task of estimating the influence of the various segments of the dominant group in erecting and maintaining exclusionary, subordinating racial policies and the effects of those policies, transmitted and enacted at the collective level through institutions, on the national polity as a whole.(70)

The narrow formulation which Myrdal gives to some key concepts (e.g., the moral definition of conflict and power) and his minimization of exploitation are congenial with his stated aim of promoting "social engineering" within the confines of "the process of orderly growth."(71) Similarly, the controlling explanatory principles used, the principle of cumulation or "the vicious circle" and the notion of equilibrium, are presented primarily to argue that, since "everything is cause <u>to</u> everything else," single factor theories of causation centering on economics should be rejected.(72) Thus, provided that "<u>changes should, if possible, not be made by sudden upheavals but in gradual steps</u>" (emphasis in the original) and that proposals for change respect "the conservative reformist limits of average American economic discussion," purposive social action in matters of race relations can have reasonable chances of success.(73) The practical consequence of Myrdal's approach is gradualism through means of limited reform.

It should be noted that Myrdal nowhere attempts to provide supporting comparative ethnographic data for his views on caste. Instead, the use of the term is justified because it is "relative" and "quantitative"; apparently, it is a universal category of human societies.(74) By making the term a sociological category, Myrdal generalizes it beyond practical usefulness; in particular, his implicit equation of caste with race belies this error.(75)

Finally, Myrdal's concept definition (as noted above) and ultimate causal argument, being centered on a moral perspective, can be considered as support for his assertion of the supremacy of assimilation in American life. With regard to Black people, since they have no legitimate cultural tradition to preserve, create only deformed replicas of those dominant institutions from which they are barred, and themselves overwhelmingly desire assimilation, the realization of this "central element" in the American Creed will be decisively accomplished once the struggle for America's conscience is won.(76)

Recent Discussion

Subsequent to Myrdal, some later treatments of caste have attempted to use the term in the context of broadly conceived cross-cultural comparisons.(77) However, since the term is conceived as a sociological category, there are two basic problems associated with these attempts.

First, the term caste is often conceived as an ideal type, and thus potentially a universal feature of all human societies. But when a term of sociocultural analysis is stretched to such mammoth proportions, its ability to accurately assess differing social realities is called into question. Indeed, as an ideal type, the term caste simply may not be theoretically falsifiable, thus reducing its usefulness even further.(78) Hence, while van den Berghe's "competitive" versus "paternalistic" ideal type dichotomy of racial prejudice, with caste relations obtaining in the latter type, may represent an attempt at theoretical innovation, its significance may be hampered by the reservations noted.(79) A similar assessment must be made of Harris' classification of social subgroups, by the "three taxonomic polarities" of affiliation (descent or behavior), marriage regulation (endogamy or exogamy) and attitude toward social status (acceptance or rejection) in which castes are pictured as endogamous descent groups which passively accept their status, and Berreman's ideal type analysis of caste which defines it chiefly by endogamy and descent.(80)

The second problem concerns the specific content differences between caste relations and race relations which the comparative method may overlook and minimize. Van den Berghe cites the origins of the caste system in racial prejudice, and Berreman suggests that its contemporary functioning is identical to a system of race relations, neither assertion, as pointed out earlier, being supported by the literature.(81)

Harris offers perhaps the most novel interpretation of content, finding that, by his criteria, medieval Europe possessed a "restricted but bona fide caste system."(82) Berreman remarks that the routes toward melioration are different in Hindu society and the southern United States, with caste subordinates in India usually seeking improved status within the caste hierarchy while Black people in the South most often express the desire to do away with subordination altogether, but draws no conclusion from this fact.(83) However, even if the fact of a greater degree of conflict, tension, and resentment among caste subordinates in India than traditional Indian ethnography usually depicts is granted (a point which Berreman emphasizes), if the fundamental organizing principles or ethos of the two societies is different, then the different routes to melioration may have a great deal of significance and the assumption of structural similarity may not be warranted.(84)

Berreman does raise a crucial issue which may determine the essential question of the applicability of the term caste in cross-cultural research: the nature of the comparability of the economic and social relations in the base (here, Hindu India) and target (here, the U.S. South) societies.(85) If it can be demonstrated that the manner of economic organization and type of social relations which obtained in India and the U.S. South were the same during the period in which the caste model of race relations was postulated, then the validity of the model may be asserted. One such crucial question might concern the extent to which agriculture in the U.S. South and in India was characterized by capitalist relations of production during the period of the formulation of the caste school of U.S. race relations, c. 1930-49. While I do not mean to settle this issue here, it is perhaps instructive that Tindall notes that during this period (to 1937) American cotton (overwhelmingly Southern in origin) constituted between 23-45% of the world market, though Omvedt states that "towards the end of British rule) only about 35% of India's total agricultural product was consumed in market, this being itself a local village market. If, in addition to production for a world market, comparisons were made of land-owning classes, tenant classes, consumption of economic surplus, and other related variables, a sound basis for comparative treatment of caste might be established. But, in the absence of such comparability of conditions, use of the model for this or subsequent periods will only perpetuate the failure to resolve crucial theoretical questions.(86)

Conclusion

The application of the term caste to U.S. race relations has tended to produce a number of characteristic features of social analysis as reviewed herein. Taken together, these features vitiate the usefulness of this model.

As noted, the term caste is ambiguously defined: some combination of endogamy, hierarchy, and social mobility restrictions, are usually advanced in the definitions, which also make the equation (implicit or explicit) of caste with race. This last assumption is particularly questionable, and the other definitions of caste, being based on an ideal type social category, offer problems of comparability which are seldom resolved. In early formulations of the caste model, in particular, the failure to provide comparative ethnographic data and the preference for metaphoric assertion dominated the use of the concept.

A dichotomous view of race relations in the North and South, though somewhat justified by the demographic distribution of the Black population (c. 1930-40), tends to obscure the national framework within which American black-white race relations are embedded.(87) The occurrence of subordination, exclusion, and exploitative relations outside the South do not admit of explanation by the terms that the proponents of the caste model propose.

Moreover, this inability to explain race relations outside the South is also related to the peculiar formulation of certain key concepts. Exploitation is considered only as a past cause, and apparently has no discernible impact in industrial society (i.e., the North). Power is principally rendered moral in nature, and its economic and political aspects are minimized; it is expressed through conflict, which in turn centers on differing moral valuations held by caste superiors. But moral conflict, and the spiritual power it reflects, are treated at the level of the individual so that, together with the dichotomous view, problems of racial subordination which occur at the collective (i.e., structural or institutional) level (e.g., housing segregation, job discrimination) cannot be adequately conceptualized. Finally, since the principal function of exclusion is to maintain social distance barriers and to produce social pathology among the dominated, the denial of viable cultural traditions among caste subordinates is held to support the paramount goal of assimilation, though this state has never been achieved and contrary sociocultural evidence among subordinates themselves may exist as to its plausibility.

Thus, without a theory of their own that would explain U.S. race relations as a genuine caste society, caste analysts fall back on liberal assumptions about American society, especially in their approach to social change. The best example of this is Myrdal's statement, whose tone is set by its reliance on the American Creed and gradualism. This work also illustrates the similar political outlooks which unite the ethnic group and caste models.

As we argued in our critique of the ethnic group model, the subordination process which characterizes American race relations cannot be comprehended from the vantage point of liberal social theory. This same judgment applies to the caste model. A rupture with liberal social theory is very apparent in the remaining two models to be discussed, the colonial and Marxist. In the next chapter, we shall examine the colonial model.

Notes

1. W. E. B. DuBois, *The Souls of Black Folk* (New York: Johnson Reprint Corp., 1968), pp. 40, 51, 59, 69, 179, 186, 226. (Originally published by A. C. McClurg and Co., Chicago, 1903.)

2. C. Vann Woodward, *The Strange Career of Jim Crow*, 3rd ed. rev. (New York: Oxford University Press, 1974), pp. xii, 15, 46, 101-103, 118.

3. August Meier, *Negro Thought in America, 1800-1915* (Ann Arbor, Michigan: University of Michigan Press, 1963), pp. 43, 56, 79.

4. Eugene D. Genovese, "Class and Race," in Genovese, *The World the Slaveholders Made* (New York: Random House, 1969), pp. 103-113, esp. p. 107.

5. Kenneth D. Stampp, *The Era of Reconstruction: 1865-1877* (New York: Random House, 1965), pp. 14, 15, 196, 214.

6. Raymond Wolters, *Negroes and the Great Depression: The Problem of Economic Recovery* (Westport, Connecticut: Greenwood Press, 1970), pp. 15, 49, 56.

7. Charles E. Silberman, *Crisis in Black and White* (New York: Random House, 1964), pp. 96, 120, 126, 128.

8. Edward A. Gait, "Caste," in the *Encyclopedia of Religion and Ethics*, vol. 3 (New York: Charles Scribner's Sons, 1925), pp. 230-239. (Article originally published 1911.) The quote is from p. 234.

9. Gait, "Caste," pp. 231-232, 236-237.

10. Gait, "Caste," p. 230 and passim.

11. Ronald B. Inden and McKim Marriott, "Caste Systems," *Encyclopedia Britannica: Macropedia*, vol. 3, 1974 ed., pp. 982-991. The quote appears on p. 982.

12. Inden and Marriott, "Caste Systems," p. 991.

13. See E. K. Hunt, Property and Prophets: The Evolution of Economic Institutions and Ideologies (New York: Harper and Row, 1972), passim.

14. Inden and Marriott, "Caste Systems," pp. 983, 985.

15. E. R. Leach, "Introduction: What Should We Mean by Caste?" in E. R. Leach, ed., Cambridge Papers in Social Anthropology, No. 3: Aspects of Caste in South India, Ceylon and Northwest Pakistan (Cambridge, England: Cambridge University Press, 1969), pp. 1-10, esp. pp. 1-2, 5. The quotes are from pp. 5 and 7, respectively.

16. Leach, "Introduction: What Should We Mean by Caste?," pp. 5, 7-8.

17. Leach, "Introduction: What Should We Mean by Caste?," pp. 6-7, 8.

18. Oliver C. Cox, Caste, Class, and Race (New York: Monthly Review Press, 1948), p. 86.

19. Sir Herbert H. Risley, The People of India (Calcutta: n.p., 1908) and Govind S. Ghurye, Caste and Race in India, 5th ed. (Bombay: Popular Prakashan, 1969; orig. 1932) offer racial theories as to the genesis of caste. John C. Nesfield, Brief Note on the Caste System of the North-Western Provinces and Oudh (Allahabad: n.p., 1885) gives a cultural explanation rooted in occupational considerations.

20. A. P. Barnabas and Subhash C. Mehta, Caste in Changing India (New Delhi: The Indian Institute of Public Administration, 1965), p. 10.

21. John H. Hutton, Caste in India, 4th ed. (New York: Oxford University Press, 1963), p. 175.

22. See Barnabas and Mehta, Caste in Changing India; Vijai P. Singh, Caste, Class and Democracy

(Cambridge, Massachusetts: Schenkman Publishing Company, Inc., 1976); and Sidney Verba, Bashi Ahmad, and Anil Bhatt, Caste, Race and Politics (Beverly Hills, California: Sage Publications, Inc., 1971). Interestingly, this last work, a comparative study of Indian Harijans (outcasts) and African-Americans, skirts the issue of identity of caste and race while assuming it for purposes of comparison between the two social groups, a curious method indeed.

23. W. Lloyd Warner, "American Caste and Class," American Journal of Sociology, 42 (September 1936), pp. 234-237.

24. Warner, p. 234.

25. Warner, p. 235, fig. 1.

26. Social mobility in India under the caste system would seem to involve generally migration and the taking up of a new occupation, individual rise through acquisition of wealth and hypergamous marriage, fictional descent claims to higher caste status, and in the days of the Hindu kings, appeal to royal power for reclassification. See Kathleen Gough, "Caste in Tanjore Village," in E. R. Leach, ed., Cambridge Papers, pp. 26, 56; Gait, "Caste," p. 237; Inden and Marriott, "Caste Systems," p. 985.

27. Warner, p. 236.

28. A critique of race theories of the origin of the Pan-Indian caste system is found in Cox, Caste, Class, and Race, pp. 82-96.

29. Stanford M. Lyman, "The Race Relations Cycle of Robert E. Park," Pacific Sociological Review, 11 (Spring 1968), pp. 16-22; and R. E. Park, Race and Culture (New York: The Free Press, 1950), p. 104.

30. The turbulent history of the United States in the period 1930-45 is probably most visibly reflected in the history of the labor movement at that time. Brecher estimates that more strikes occurred in 1944 than in any

other previous year of American history; Rayback notes that in 1934, one-seventh of the total industrial labor force was involved in work disputes and in 1936-37, almost one-half million workers engaged in sitdown strikes. Preis documents the occurrence, in the 2-year period 1945-46, of 9,735 strikes involving 8,070,000 strikers, and resulting in a total of 154,000,000 man-days lost in production (computed from author's annual figures, page cited below). Finally, in the South, among agricultural workers, Foner records that by 1936 the Southern Tenant Farmers Union, begun in Arkansas in July 1934, had more than 25,000 members, 80% of whom were Black, in Texas, Mississippi, Tennessee, Oklahoma, and Missouri, before becoming defunct in 1939. See Jeremy Brecher, _Strike!_ (Greenwich, Connecticut: Fawcett Publications, 1974), p. 271; Joseph G. Rayback, _A History of American Labor_, expanded and updated (New York: The Free Press, and London: Collier-Macmillan Limited, 1966), pp. 330, 354; Art Preis, _Labor's Giant Step: Twenty Years of the CIO_ (New York: Pathfinder Press, 1972), p. 283; and Philip S. Foner, _American Socialism and Black Americans: From the Age of Jackson to World War II_ (Westport, Connecticut: Greenwood Press, 1977), pp. 349-356.

31. John Dollard, _Caste and Class in a Southern Town_, 3rd ed. (Garden City, New York: Doubleday and Co., 1957) (originally published by Yale University Press, 1937).

32. Dollard, pp. 2, 16, 17, 63, 252-253, 289-313. The quotes are from pp. 8, 16, and 252.

33. On education, politics, and religion, see Dollard, Chs. 9-11; on the economic, sexual, and prestige gains of whites, see Chs. 6-8; and on the gains of the Black lower class, see Ch. 12.

34. Dollard, pp. 60, 197, 366-367.

35. Dollard, pp. 442-446.

36. Dollard, pp. viii-xii.

37. Dollard, pp. 51-52, 53.

38. See C. Vann Woodward, American Counterpoint: Slavery and Racism in the North-South Dialogue (Boston: Little, Brown and Co., 1971), pp. 140-183, 212-233; and W. E. B. DuBois, John Brown (New York: International Publishers, 1972) (originally, 1909), pp. 123-144. See also, Leon F. Litwack, North of Slavery: The Negro in the Free States, 1790-1860 (Chicago: University of Chicago Press, 1961), pp. 214-246. As for the processes at work in the North and West, for example, on Chicago, see Drake and Cayton, Black Metropolis, 2 vols., rev. and enl. ed. (New York: Harper and Row, 1962); and, on Harlem, Gilbert Osofsky, Harlem: The Making of a Ghetto, Negro New York, 1890-1930 (New York: Harper and Row, 1968).

39. Dollard, pp. 26, 416.

40. Dollard, pp. 62-63.

41. Dollard, p. 353.

42. Dollard, pp. 89, 128.

43. Dollard, pp. 175, 179, 250-251, 253, 333.

44. Dollard, pp. 127, 171, 211, 350.

45. Dollard, pp. 268, 432-433.

46. Dollard, p. 454.

47. Dollard, pp. 57, 153, 270, 413-414, 451, 454. Aside from the ideological function of the pathological model, recent evidence based on empirical research contradicts Dollard's version of the Black family; see Herbert G. Gutman, The Black Family in Slavery and Freedom, 1750-1925 (New York: Random House, 1976), esp. pp. 257-326.

48. Dollard, pp. 71, 331.

49. Dollard, pp. 427-428, 449.

50. The appearance of legitimacy for Southern race

relations is conveyed by the author (ibid., pp. 49, 56, 207, 212) in a number of ways. Most pertinent is his adoption of what Gutman (op. cit., pp. 541-544) calls the "retrogressionist" view of Reconstruction: freedom for the slaves meant cultural chaos and rule by savages for the genteel South. Modern historical scholarship, beginning with the revisionist work of DuBois, tends to judge such sentiments as more conservative racial propaganda than historical fact: "Negro domination" was nowhere a fact, most Reconstruction governments were interracial coalitions led by native white Southerners or other whites, and most were of short, unstable duration, though significant social welfare legislation (e.g., public schools) did emerge, often with the strong support of the freedmen. See W. E. B. DuBois, Black Reconstruction (New York: Atheneum, 1935); Kenneth D. Stampp, op. cit.; and Robert Cruden, The Negro in Reconstruction (Englewood Cliffs, New Jersey: Prentice-Hall, 1969).

51. Gunnar Myrdal, An American Dilemma: The Negro Problem and Modern Democracy, 2 vols. (New York: Random House, 1972) (originally published, 1944).

52. Myrdal, pp. 927-929.

53. Myrdal, pp. 712, 822, 863-868, 882, 915-920, 952, 976.

54. Myrdal, pp. 667-668.

55. Myrdal, pp. 57-61, 207-208, 221-222.

56. Myrdal, pp. 673-675.

57. Myrdal, pp. 221-222, 459, 532-533.

58. Myrdal, pp. 88, 281-289, 395, 440, 497, 628, 880, 946, 949-950.

59. Myrdal, pp. 45-46, 88, 291, 383-384, 439, 723, 879-880, 945-946.

60. Myrdal, pp. 622, 628, 969-970.

61. Myrdal, pp. 3, 14, 15-17, 23, 1021.

62. Myrdal, pp. lxix, lxx, 21, 24.

63. Myrdal, pp. lxix, 384-385, 573, 585.

64. Myrdal, p. 998.

65. Myrdal, p. 422. This statement will be recognized as essentially an expression of classical liberalism's equation for moral responsibility, i.e., knowledge + potent actor = moral responsibility or decision-making entitlement.

66. Myrdal, pp. lxxiii-lxxiv, 110, 507, 725, 853-854, 923, 1004, 1010.

67. Myrdal, pp. 200-201, 1013-1014.

68. Myrdal, pp. 220-221.

69. Myrdal, pp. 58, 60, 101, 109.

70. To illustrate: though Myrdal repeatedly points to the psychic involvement of the ordinary white American in allegiance to the anti-amalgamation doctrine of caste relations, no similar picture of the white employer is given. The latter's involvement in caste dogma is deemed to be merely the result of opportunitistic rational calculation, i.e., use Black labor where labor is scarce or unions are strong. However, Myrdal does not consider the difference in effective social power between these two individuals and the possibility that this difference, when transposed to the collective level for employers, may offer the employers an interest in Black labor as degraded labor remunerated below prevailing standards, and as such, a source of extra profits. See Myrdal, op. cit., pp. 389, 393-394.

71. Myrdal, pp. 512, 1059; Myrdal offers a definition of "social engineering" as "...deriving scientific plans for policies aimed at inducing alterations of the anticipated social trends...." on the last cited page.

72. Myrdal, pp. 75-78, 1033-1034, 1047-1057, 1065-1070. It is well known that one of the central axes along which social theorists have divided concerns the use of a conflict or consensual model to explain social order. Consensualists often employ some notion of equilibrium, while conflictualists develop ideas related to hegemony, domination, and differential access to social resources and rewards. It is possible to locate Myrdal's use of the concept equilibrium within the consensualist organismic school of functionalist sociology associated with Herbert Spencer, later represented in the United States by William Graham Sumner and Robert Ezra Park. However, unlike Spencer or Sumner, Myrdal adds the notion of purposive social action to his schema, in accordance with his desire to promote reforms. Here, he is closer to Park and John Dewey, both liberal reformers. See, on Spencer's influence on American sociology, Richard Hofstadter, Social Darwinism in American Thought, rev. ed. (Boston: Beacon Press, 1967), pp. 31-50; and Robert L. Carneiro, "Herbert Spencer," in the International Encyclopedia of the Social Sciences, 1968 ed., vol. 15, pp. 121-128; on Park's use of the term equilibrium and his reformer's stance see, respectively, R. E. Park, "The Nature of Race Relations," in Edgar T. Thompson, ed., Race Relations and the Race Problem: A Definition and an Analysis (Durham, North Carolina: Duke University Press, 1939), pp. 4-5; and Park, "Social Planning and Human Nature," Publications of the American Sociological Society, 29 (August 1935), pp. 19-28; on Dewey's liberal reformism, see J. Dewey, Liberalism and Social Action (New York: G. P. Putnam and Son, 1935); and on the divergent assumptions underlying conflict and consensus models as competing paradigms, see Jonathan H. Turner, The Structure of Sociological Theory (Homewood, Illinois: The Dorsey Press, 1974), pp. 25-27, 38-39, 73-74, 78-91; Lewis Coser, The Functions of Social Conflict (New York: The Free Press and Macmillan, 1956), pp. 15-31.

73. Myrdal, pp. 214, 518, 1023-1024.

74. At one point, as justification for the use of the term caste, a mysterious "Hindu acquaintance" is cited; Myrdal, p. 668, note c.

75. For a similar attempt at the universal application of the term by writers who greatly influenced Myrdal in his formulation, see W. Lloyd Warner and Allison Davis, "A Comparative Study of American Caste," in Edgar T. Thompson, ed., Race Relations and the Race Problem, pp. 219-245; a version of Warner's earlier diagrammatic treatment of caste and class (cited above in n 23) is presented by Myrdal in op. cit., p. 691.

76. Myrdal, pp. 505, 927, 928-929, 998, 1018.

77. See Pierre L. van den Berghe, "The Dynamics of Racial Prejudice: An Ideal-Type Dichotomy," Social Forces, 37 (December 1958), pp. 138-141; Marvin Harris, "Caste, Class, and Minority," Social Forces, 37 (March 1959), pp. 248-254; and Gerald D. Berreman, "Caste in India and the United States," American Journal of Sociology, 66 (1960/61), pp. 120-127.

78. Karl Popper's formulation of the principle of falsifiability with regard to scientific hypotheses is found in his The Logic of Scientific Discovery (New York: Harper and Row, 1968), pp. 27-48, 78-92. While Popper's epistemology may not be entirely appropriate to social science, in the absence of conceptual clarity among advocates of the caste model of race relations as a specific case, his principle for the testability of theories may be useful. This lack of clarity is especially apparent in Berreman's article, where it is argued that mere differences in "cultural details" are not important to comparisons of social systems, yet no theoretical principle is adduced for this assertion. See Berreman, op. cit., pp. 121, 122.

79. Van den Berghe, pp. 139, 141.

80. Harris, pp. 252, 253, 254; Berreman, p. 120.

81. Van den Berghe, p. 140; Berreman, pp. 121-124.

82. Harris, p. 253.

83. Berreman, p. 125.

84. Berreman, pp. 124-127. In this context, Leach holds that as low castes, under socio-economic pressure, come to protest their caste position by partaking of such modern techniques of melioration as unionization, they cease to operate as a caste but rather operate in "defiance of caste principles." See Leach, "Introduction: What Should We Mean by Caste?," pp. 6-7.

85. Berreman, pp. 121-122.

86. George B. Tindall, The Emergence of the New South, 1913-1945 (Baton Rouge: Louisiana State University Press, 1967), pp. 401-402; and Gail Omvedt, "Women and Rural Revolt in India," Occasional Papers, No. 6, Program in Comparative Culture (University of California, Irvine, January 1978), p. 27.

87. Demographic research, especially more recent work, shows a greater degree of rural-to-urban migration within the South during this period than the proponents of the caste model generally conclude. Since caste is fundamentally a rural agricultural phenomenon, the distribution of the Black population at that time is an important consideration. See Henderson H. Donald, "The Urbanization of the American Negro," in G. P. Murdock, ed., Studies in the Science of Society (New Haven, Connecticut: Yale University Press, 1937), pp. 181-199; T. L. Smith, "The Redistribution of the Negro Population of the United States, 1910-1960," Journal of Negro History, 51:3 (July 1966), pp. 155-173; and, Reynolds Farley, "The Urbanization of Negroes in the United States," Journal of Social History, 1 (Spring 1968), pp. 241-258.

> Cultural domination, because it is total and tends to oversimplify, very soon manages to disrupt in spectacular fashion the cultural life of a conquered people. This cultural obliteration is made possible by the negation of national reality, by new legal relations introduced by the occupying power, by the banishment of the natives and their customs to outlying districts by colonial society, by expropriation, and by the systematic enslaving of men and women.
>
> Frantz Fanon,
> The Wretched of the Earth, 1961, p. 236.

Chapter 3
The Colonial Model

Introduction

Recent interest in a colonial analysis of U.S. race relations may be traced to the work of Frantz Fanon.(1) When the most advanced revolutionary Third World group of the time, the Black Panther Party, adopted his views on colonialism as applicable to the situation of Black folk in the United States, the currency of the colonial paradigm was assured.(2,3)

Earlier usage of this paradigm was most noticeable in some of the pronouncements of the Communist Party (CPUSA) in the Depression of the 1930s.(4) But our concern centers around the 1960s and '70s and those writers who surveyed the turbulence of the racial scene, convinced that the turmoil and the basic nature of U.S. race relations could only be comprehended and explained by the phenomenon of colonialism.

Unlike either the ethnic group or caste models, the

colonial model of U.S. race relations takes the subordination process of American ethnic and racial relations as the central datum in its analysis. It is this perspective which makes it a superior vantage point to the ethnic group and caste models, and in certain aspects, the Marxist model, also.

The colonial model considers it axiomatic that oppression breeds resistance. But, typically, it understands this resistance to involve the clash of two weltanschauungen: that of the colonized versus that of the colonizer. In this struggle, the colonizer seeks to erect and maintain an elaborate system of exclusion designed to debase, control, and exploit the colonized; racial and cultural prerequisites are institutionalized into all points of contact between the two groups. But in response to this oppression, the colonized find that their culture and its integrity (historical and emergent) become sources of the strength to survive and the will to resist. Once started on the road to the defeat of colonialism, the colonized fashion their culture into a weapon of struggle, and reinvigorate it with new forms and new content.

As Fanon describes the colonial experience, it is a social world, made up of compartments for the colonized and the colonizer, respectively, in which the oppressed are pictured as biologically inferior, culturally degraded and evil.(5) But the very process of colonization compels the colonized to assert their humanity; in other words, built into colonialism is the dialectic between oppression and resistance. Since decolonization, for the colonized, is literally the process of turning upside down an entire social order, of "...the replacing of a certain 'species' of men...," it necessitates struggle. Violence will play a large role in this struggle because colonialism itself was imposed and maintained through violence. And through this violent struggle, the colonized actually create themselves as a new people, complete with demands and programs for the recognition of a cultural tradition and identity that is the logical antithesis of colonizer mockery and derogation.(6)

We shall argue in this chapter that the colonial model possesses a certain resonance, not often found in the other perspectives, with the reality of the American racial subordination process. It is unmatched in its ability to convey the social-psychological consequences of oppression, which it correctly understands as a product of exclusion. But paradoxically, this strength falters when proponents of the model consider two subjects directly related to its portrayal of colonial reality within the United States: the subject of the culture of the oppressed is not always addressed unambiguously; and, the subject of the relations between the capitalist political economy, this culture, and that of the racially-dominant segment of the population does not find generally agreed upon importance. This last mentioned difficulty recalls a similar difficulty -- perhaps, more appropriately, a reticence -- on the part of ethnic analysts to undertake this task. But, as regards colonial analysts, their general ringing denunciation of assimilation makes it risky to attribute to them similar motives in their uncertain confrontation with political economy.

The colonial model generally revolves around four key propositions:

First, when viewing a colonized society, the social cleavage in that society which is held to subsume all other cleavages -- ascribed, economic, political, and social -- is that between the colonizers and the colonized.

Second, the central focus of the model is the total structure of domination in the colonized society. This structure is considered to be the primary source of the enforcement of colonizer privilege and the deprivation of the colonized.

Third, the single most important topic of theoretical interest, when viewed in relation to the total structure of domination, is that of culture, most often the culture of the colonial (often indigenous) subjects. This culture is usually regarded as both the manacle with which the oppressor has shackled the colonized and as the key to the potential for survival, revitalization, and struggle of the colonized people.

Finally, the struggle between the colonizer and the colonized which the total structure of domination engenders is held to be amenable to solution only by the achievement of self-determination by the colonized people. Often, it is argued that self-determination is possible only through a war of national liberation.

Before turning to an inspection of the literature, it should be remarked that the use of the terms of analysis of a particular model does not always indicate congruence with that model or its conclusion. For example, Carmichael and Hamilton make numerous references to the "colonial situation" of Black people in America, variously using such expressions as "colonialism," "indirect rule," "colonial politics," "political colonialism," "colonies," "colony," "economic colonization," and "American colonialism."(7) But, the substance of the analysis provided by Carmichael and Hamilton is not in line with the fundamental tenor of the model whose terminology they so profusely adopt.(8) Similarly, James Boggs pointedly refers to Black people as "a semi-colonial people" who have suffered exploitation and underdevelopment.(9) However, Boggs' general analysis makes it clear that he understands the problematic situation of Black folk to flow from the class contradictions of an advanced capitalist state.(10) He, too, should not be considered a practitioner of the model though certain of its terms appear in his work.

A general orientation to the colonial model is provided at both the practical and theoretical level by two analysts, one a renowned Black nationalist leader and the other a Black social scientist. Perhaps the greatest oratorical exponent of a colonial view of U.S. race relations was Malcolm X. His fiery speeches were often filled with invective directed at the nightmarish reality of "second class citizenship" for Black folk in the midst of "the American Dream." This status, he argued, amounted to nothing more than "twentieth-century colonization" and revealed America's true nature as a "colonial power."(11)

As regards theory, Robert Staples provides an overview of the colonial model of race relations as it applies to the United States.(12) Noting that a shift in the theoretical perspective of theories of race relations, from assimilationist and biological determinist to Pan-Africanist, Marxist, and internal colonial, has taken place, Staples holds that the object of "internal colonialism" theory is the "structural inequality between racial groups" and the "social processes" which create and sustain "racial differentials."(13)

Under this model, according to Staples, culture exhibits a dual nature. It is both an instrument of oppression by reason of the deformation and replacement of traditional values by the oppressor; and, it is an asset in the struggle to survive, since some useful indigenous cultural forms do persist and are created even under colonization.(14) Because colonialism is not static, the model also must comprehend changes through time which have been wrought on the system of internal colonialism, whereby each change in the system correspondent to a change in the historical situation represents a link in the chain of racial oppression. The common base of each link is white dominance and Black submission. The model, as Staples delineates it, is also concerned with "status ordering systems." The rigid inferiorization of the native and his culture leads to differences in prestige, occupation, and income which always result in an invidious comparison with the colonizer.(15)

Staples argues that certain basic concepts underlie the colonial model. Generally, these concepts specify the nature of the unequal relations between the colonized and the colonizer: e.g., "dependency," "privilege," and "racism."(16)

Sub-groups of the Model

In the application of the four basic propositions noted above, the proponents of this model tend to split into two camps: those who consider the racial and ethnic identifications of colonialism as transcendent of, and yet somewhat responsive to, the capitalist political economy form one sub-group, while those who reckon the colonial situation a direct outcome of the functioning of American capitalist democracy form another. This distinction is not always hard and fast, and there are many points of agreement between the two sub-groups. Foremost of these is the concentration on exclusion as the curious form of social inclusion which consistently relegates the colonized to subordinate status and which is always accompanied by a justificatory ideology of racial privilege. But the first sub-group tends to center its attention on the fact of exclusion itself, seeing in it the essence of colonialism. The second sub-group determines colonialism to be not only the product of socio-economic processes, but also to be directly influenced by them; hence, its insistence on pursuing the significance of class differences within the colonized population and the colonizing population, too.

The Internal Colony: Race Only

With this orientation, we are ready to turn to a consideration of the first sub-group within the model. The statements examined in this sub-group share two basic characteristics: first, each tends to define the colonial situation according to its highly visible racial features and, second, the ideology of racial privilege (racism) which invariably accompanies the colonial situation is held to be not directly responsive to the capitalist political economy, instead independently interacting with it. Thus, for analysts so persuaded, differences internal to the colonizer and colonized populations are leveled and not treated as significant. Moreover, these proponents tend to overlook those structural tendencies within American capitalism which may form a real material base for the sustenance and nurturing of racist dogma. Finally, these analysts tend to present the culture of the oppressed as an apolitical assemblage of static ethical traits.

Our critique of this sub-group, in this section and in the conclusion of the chapter, will address the points raised above. Class differences within the Black community exist -- as between the petty bourgeois farmer, artisan, shopkeeper, or professional, and the working class household, service, operative, or unskilled laborers -- and these differences must be taken into account.(17) Similarly, class differences within the racially dominant group must not be overlooked since control and power are hierarchical and asymmetrical in the colonizer population, and not evenly distributed. The question of the relevance of this datum for the colonial model is either denied or unaddressed by adherents in this sub-group. As for racism as an ideology, the above class considerations taken together with the documentation of consistent inequalities in the wage contract with capital as between white labor and Black labor, may provide a significant check on the interactive notion of racial ideology that this sub-group advances.(18) That is, racism, despite its interactive appearance, may have bases within the political economy which are deeper than those acknowledged. And, as regards culture, no total picture emerges which gives both its normative aspects for the colonized and the circumstances within the social context which develop or retard these aspects.

In the first statement under review, racism is presented as an "interactive" ideology with the American capitalist political economy. Jeffrey Prager, writing in the Berkeley Journal of Sociology, follows Sartre in maintaining that white racial privilege is at the heart of the colonial relationship between whites and Third World people in the United States. "The colonial theory" which he elaborates denies that racism is an epiphenomenon used wittingly by the capitalist ruling class for its own ends.(19)

According to Prager, the system of privilege, with racism as its negative corollary, emerged in the eighteenth and nineteenth centuries and was "ensconced" in the twentieth. Both the white capitalist and the white worker benefited from this system and both participated in its construction. White workers, with their concern for job security in a limited job market, are especially culpable.(20)

Prager's development of the model contains the denial of false consciousness among white workers, asserting that they do, indeed, know what they are protecting and from whom.(21) For Marx and Engels, false consciousness represents the ideological veil in a society which prevents true social relationships from being seen and comprehended; typically, it arises on the twin bases of the separation of mental from physical labor, and the mastery of the means of ideological production by a ruling class, who uses this control to further ideologies that accord with and defend its own interests.(22) So, here, Prager is asserting that no such ruling class deception is involved as regards the defense of racial privilege by white workers. Further, he contends that racial stratification and class stratification are "contiguous" processes which have "separate and distinct" purposes, the demands of racism perhaps even being contrary to those of capitalism, though the two processes are at once "independent" and "interactive."(23) This presentation leads one to believe that the author has set up a sort of causal parallelism between race and class.

Prager goes on to insist that any adequate theoretical account of U.S. race relations must consider the accumulated gains over time that have accrued to whites. Such an account also would have to understand the "racial dimension" of this society, like the economic one, to have its own base (privilege), its own separate reality, and its own organizational demands on society; in a word, it would have to understand racism as an independent social force "...with a life and dimension all its own."(24)

It follows, in Prager's outline of the colonial model, that the abolition of capitalism will not summarily eliminate racism; only a project of decolonization can hope to accomplish this.(25) But, paradoxically, when the author presents evidence to support the colonial model, this evidence is much more in line with the domain assumptions of another model of race relations, the Marxist political class model, than with Prager's chosen theoretical vehicle. Low occupational status, lack of entry to management level jobs, the cyclical nature of employment progress with successively fewer low-skill low-pay jobs available, and the failure of education to equalize social mobility rates are all indicia which could be read as testifying to the super-exploitation of Third World peoples in the United States, as much as the colonial status for which Prager argues.(26) In fact, an essential difference between these two theoretical modes, Marxist political class and colonial, which Prager mentions -- the concept of "decolonization," a primarily cultural, social, political, and non-economic construct -- remains here relatively unelaborated.(27)

Moreover, since Prager is so concerned to emphasize the conscious replication of the structure of privilege based on the decisions of whites, and the economic gains that they reap thereby, he falls into one of the major errors of this model: <u>the failure to adequately distinguish among whites</u>.(28) Though he appears conscious of the need to make such distinctions, his work here leaves the impression that white workers and white capitalists share amicably in the spoils of racial privilege.(29) This is a major weakness of his presentation of the colonial model, one which seems to divide the proponents of this theoretical model into two camps as sketched above: those who explicitly incorporate an analysis of capitalist political economy and the white ruling class into their writings, and those who do not, preferring instead to see economic forces in general as not primary, or at least not ultimately determinative, in the comprehension and description of colonial or neo-colonial race relations.

In the preceding statement, the subjects of the structure of domination and the racial ideology which reinforces it were addressed. In the next statement, not only are racial ideology and colonial structure analyzed, but the subject of culture receives attention and elaboration in the version of the colonial model given by Robert Blauner in <u>Racial Oppression in America</u>.(30)

Black culture, as outlined by Blauner, stems from six basic sources: the African past, the "neo-African"

South (where African cultural ways and language were adapted to a new context), slavery, emancipation and migration, "the lower-class component," and response to racist subjugation. This last-named source, paradoxically, has led to the creation of a "political history" in the course of which Black folk have established much of their culture.(31)

Black people, and other Third World people to varying degrees, Blauner maintains, form "internal colonies" which are subjected to "internal colonialism." The geographical-spatial relationship which obtains under traditional colonialism does not, by its absence, invalidate the application of the concept of colonialism to the domestic American situation since a common process characterized both types. This process, which he calls "the colonization complex," consists of the mode of entry, cultural impact, bureaucratic domination, and racism.(32) Noting that immigration and colonization historically are the two principal means by which nations incorporate new major population groups, the author denies that the experience of European immigrants is directly comparable to that of Third World people because of the dissimilar processes at work.(33)

Blauner asserts that under internal colonialism, cultural conflict assumes primary importance. Culture itself becomes a method of control as the colonizer penetrates the culture of the colonized people, distorting or destroying it, and transforming it according to "the cultural imperatives" of the dominant group.(34) Historically, the cultural conflict which ensued between Europeans and Africans and Asians produced a "unifying thread" of racist belief which helped to cement the settlers' fragmented society while conversely devaluing all aliens.(35) In the United States, the most important consequence of this racial control, expressed through cultural hegemony, has been the creation of a system of racial privilege, ultimately founded on exclusion, that allows white groups to assimilate and enjoy greater material rewards and to suffer less pervasive labor discipline.(36) Blauner posits a causal sequence in which racial privilege is generated by exploitation which, in turn, is based on control, which often assumes manifold guises.(37)

However, Blauner's depiction of the causal relationship between racism, as an inherent feature of colonialism, and capitalist labor exploitation unties the two. Though according to Blauner, modern race relations originated in the economic expansion of medieval Europe, under colonialism, labor discipline was transcended by the issue of control itself, centering especially on the assignment of place and the penetration and manipulation of the natives' culture. Exploitation, as first cause, was displaced by the need for racial control as an end in itself. In the United States, it is this basic phenomenon which has allowed European immigrants a measure of cultural autonomy while assimilating toward Anglo-conformity at the same time that they escape and benefit from the cultural oppression and dehumanization which has been the lot of peoples of color; as Blauner sums up, "white ethnics [are] exploited, but not colonized."(38) Thus, the "immigrant analogy" stands rejected by reason of the colonization complex, the element of choice, the "colonial labor principle" which made the key equation of unfree labor with people of color, differences in initial urban concentration, access to employment in centers of industry, and geographical dispersion, and the lack of subjection to cultural oppression.(39) Furthermore, Blauner, like Prager, denies that whites in general, and white workers in particular, experience false consciousness in the defense of their racial privilege.(40)

Racism itself is variously defined by Blauner as "...a propensity to categorize people who are culturally different in terms of noncultural traits, for example, skin color, hair, structure of face and eye...," and as "a system of domination" whose objective side is determinative, though it does also contain "a complex of beliefs and attitudes...."(41) Institutional racism, specifically, is defined as a mechanism of exclusion built on the interplay of the various aspects of social life so as to maintain a pattern of subordination; this pattern is characterized by its unintentional and indirect manner and by the importance which it ascribes to institutional or structural role over individual attitude or personality.(42)

Blauner subsumes racism under the category of race consciousness which he appears to assign a separate independent causal sphere. Criticizing contemporary sociology for its tendency to reduce race problems to either economic or psychological causes, and mindful of the assumption of seminal European thinkers, including Marx, that ethnic consciousness would decline as the modern industrial period progressed, the author counters that race consciousness is "a rational project" undertaken by man as part of the quest for identity and community.(43) But, race consciousness, whose fundamental core is rational, displays both rational and irrational elements: as a project for self and group discovery, it is rational; as racism, it is irrational. The principle of racial control in colonial labor systems reflects this irrational element. Using a Weberian analysis, Blauner concludes that, historically, race consciousness was submerged in irrational elements as it became institutionalized (in Weber's parlance, "routinized") in the form of racial oppression with the advent of conquest, slavery, and colonialism.(44)

But, the introduction of the concept of irrationality is contradicted by Blauner's separation of racism from ethnocentrism and by his denial of the false consciousness of whites, two observations which suggest the rationality of racism.(45) But the most important error that the introduction of the concept of irrationality causes is the author's inability to adequately distinguish among whites as benefactors and perpetrators of racism. His colonial labor principle describes the differential proletarianization experienced by the multicultural, multi-racial U.S. labor force, and this principle is connected to institutional racism as the basic colonial mechanism used to ensure racial privilege.(46) However, since racism is defined in social-psychological terms grounded in irrationality, the social-psychological rewards of racism are not separated from its economic rewards. Blauner can then argue that the marginal increment in life chances attributable to racial privilege is greater for the white working class, though the middle and upper classes enjoy greater class privilege.(47) Completely missing is an account of the white ruling class and its pre-eminent access to all rewards of racism, be they social-psychological, political, or economic and a qualitative distinction between the pathology of the individual racist and the structural, pathological rationality of institutional racism. Blauner himself is aware that these distinctions must be made when he comments that not all whites have "effective power" in race relations; but, it is not an insight which is extended and broadened.(48)

However, Blauner finds further justification for his view that race constitutes a separate causal sphere by borrowing Weber's concept of status and proceeding to label racial groups as "status groups." But since race and class interpenetrate, creating labor patterns which reflect the ability of racism to modify social mobility and stratification, this designation is quickly replaced in favor of the formula that racial groups are "interest groups." At any rate, because the reality of racial groups in American life is unquestionable, the "status concerns of race" are themselves real and have a base in social life.(49)

A critical assessment of Blauner's version of the colonial model might begin by pointing out the unsuitability of his theoretical view of culture. Blauner seems to prefer the cultural-essence, or elementarist, method of cultural analysis whereby a number of traits or elements are held to comprise the existence of culture; if some element is missing, it is argued that a culture does not exist or is pathologically deficient. Though he is critical of this holistic view of functionalist social science, his own move to redefine the South as "neo-African" -- so as to better align Black culture with the holistic definition of culture as "distinctive language," "unique religion," and a "national homeland" -- belies such criticism.(50) While this call to redefinition is valuable in itself for the fresh viewpoint on Afro-American culture which it stimulates, it should not be tied to a view of culture which one-sidedly assigns primacy to the spiritual, immaterial aspect of culture: "the mystique of Soul" and "the underlying ethos" of far-removed West African seventeenth-century societies do not constitute the single most important theme of Black culture as Blauner implies.(51) His own statements that culture must be seen as an open-minded, dynamic process, and that, for Black people, the "single most important source" of their culture has been the political history, "the unique socio-political experience," that has been created out of their struggle against racism reveal a more promising line of analysis.(52)

We will return to examine at length, in the concluding segment of this chapter, some of the issues raised here in connection with Blauner's work. Nonetheless, one more critical observation at this point is in order.

That is, the fundamental contradiction in Blauner's formulation of the colonial model, which sums up the problems so far noted, would seem to be dissociation of racial control from its end, exploitation. The author does this by arguing that racial control has become an end in itself, and that racial oppression transcends class oppression because of the cultural hegemony present in the former.(53) Both declarations are predicated on his assertion that the phenomena of race constitute a causal sphere all their own in human affairs.

The Internal Colony: Race and Class

Turning to the second sub-group in the colonial model, we note that there is much more emphasis placed on the role of the relatively privileged strata of the colonized population, the buffer group. Undoubtedly, the greater role assigned to a class analysis of the colonial predicament is responsible for this focus.

On the other hand, both sub-groups of the model display a noteworthy ability to capture the psychological feeling-tone of the subordination and oppression of the colonized. This basic strength of the model stems from its ability to portray exclusion in both its negative (i.e., social barriers) and positive (i.e., coalescing of communal resources) aspects. Hence, the prominence of the themes of racial privilege, institutional racism, and culture. But although the two subgroups share these themes, they do not analyze them in the same way.

Because the second sub-group is more concerned, generally, to locate its analysis of the colonial situation within the American capitalist social order, it seeks to portray the effects of the colonial relation between the races as direct consequences of capitalism. In the literature reviewed below, these effects concern the interpretation of the spontaneous violence of the colonized, the consideration of appropriate and inappropriate economic strategies, the analysis of political strategies, and the expression of a class-influenced outlook on domestic colonial oppression from the viewpoint of the colonized.

In summary, we may say that the statements included in the second sub-group share two essential features. First, the colonized group is analyzed according to its racial characteristics <u>and</u> its class position. And, second, class position itself is regarded as important (especially as regards two entities -- the buffer group, and the ruling class) because capitalism is held to be the direct determinant of colonial relations. These two points represent a tendency, not always explicit, of this sub-group. But, it is this tendency which accounts for the assertion by most of these writers of a direct causal link (past and continuing) between racial ideology and capitalist political economy. And, the program of culture offered here is typically focused on political culture (i.e., ideology) precisely because it is in the ideological sphere that the racist policies pursued by capitalist society generate the most resistance (i.e., the movement for self-determination) on the part of the colonized.

Our critique of this sub-group will center on its definition of the domestic colony. Although a crucial term in its analysis, it is often not presented in systematic or detailed fashion. Additionally, we shall want to address the question of the link between capitalism and racism as it is treated by both sub-groups. But let us first examine the statements of the second sub-group, beginning with one in which the general views of these analysts on the sociopolitical consciousness of the colonized is given skillful, authentic presentation.

H. Rap Brown, in the autobiographical Die Nigger Die!, begins by stating that Black people are "a colonized people" in the United States, and that the most important aspect of colonization is "the sub-cultural phase."(54) For Brown, this importance derives from the control function which certain colonial subjects perform in the interests of the ruling class; these individuals constitute a buffer group used to disseminate favorable ideology and cultural norms.(55)

The Black community, according to Brown, is controlled by whites for the benefit of whites. He does not extensively distinguish among whites, and the types and amount of rewards they receive from institutional racism, but he does declare that capitalism is the chief beneficiary of racism and that poor whites, though exploited, are not colonized and, thus, make unlikely allies because of their inability to overcome racism.

Brown states that racism, though structural in nature, is based on an attitude, the concept of racial superiority, which cannot be destroyed under capitalism; however, he posits no formal causal relationship between racism and capitalism other than colinearity. Moreover, Brown declares that the problem of exclusion, which racism generates, is solved by desegregation, not integration.(56)

Brown's own conviction is that "racism, capitalism, colonialism and imperialism" rule the lives of "people of color" in the world and all "colonized minorities" -- e.g., the Mexican-American, the Puerto Rican, the Native American, Japanese-American, etc. -- in the United States.(57) He believes that only the taking of state power by the dispossessed (which includes poor whites) can accomplish the destruction of inhuman societies built on the profit motive, and thus ensure the elimination of poverty and racism.(58)

According to Brown, a liberation movement must be created, guided by "a people's ideology" founded upon political principles. Orthodoxy and dogmatism must be resisted in the construction of this ideology since, following Fanon, Brown argues that Marxist analysis must be "extend[ed]" to comprehend colonialism. The enemy is the system, capitalism.(59)

Further, Brown asserts that the liberation ideology of Black people cannot be based on blackness alone since blackness is co-optable, especially by the neo-colonial buffer group. Political nationalism must be separated from cultural nationalism since the latter tendency, detached from politics, exhibits narcissism and enervation of the will to struggle, and because successful cultural revolutions occur only after decisive armed confrontation. Culture, then, can only have meaning if it is political.(60)

Finally, Brown maintains that the political expression of capitalism has always been oppression and exploitation. This being so, only violence is likely to dislodge this system. The central term which underlies the struggle against the social order is power.(61)

In the next two pieces of analysis examined, the authors' primary intent is to interpret the spontaneous violence of the Black ghettoes and their potential for revolutionary action. The first statement considers the outbursts in Black communities during the 1960s from a class-influenced colonial perspective.

In a series of articles appearing in Freedomways, J. H. O'Dell applies the colonial model to U.S. race relations.(62) O'Dell holds that racism is "the chief ideology of colonialism" and alienation is "inherent" in the relationship between colonizer and colonized. The basic mechanisms which ensure colonialism are land ownership monopoly, forced labor, the poll tax, or similar fiscal measures designed to void the franchise of the colonized, and the establishment of a system of racial segregation (exclusion).(63)

Since slavery, and particularly the defeat of Reconstruction, O'Dell contends that the foregoing mechanisms have created the following condition:

> Segregated by law, disfranchised, robbed of its share of wages by discriminatory employment patterns, confronted by a police power and illegal mobs acting in the role of an occupation force, the Negro American community was imprisoned in a colonial relationship....(64)

In O'Dell's argument, it is most important to understand that colonial relations in America are based on the quality of the institutional mechanisms of colonial rule and do not necessarily require a specific land relationship (e.g., indigenous people to explorer/settlers) for the validity of their application.(65)

He argues, moreover, that the effects of the racism and exploitation which are inherent in U.S. capitalist society are expressed in the colonial relationship, and that this relationship is fundamentally anchored in economic deprivation, i.e., capitalist exploitation.(66) In the wake of the urban rebellions which have rocked America, "the decision-makers at the top" are reluctantly willing to sacrifice certain racist practices in return for the loyalty of Black people in defense of America's interests; this is the essence of "neo-colonialism," viz., minor concessions in return for protection of the status quo.(67) He sees the rebellions themselves as protests against the "special exploitation" of Black people which the ghettoes serve to facilitate. The revolts must not be attributed to the lawlessness of the Black lumpenproletariat, but must be understood as being rooted in the resentment of all segments of the Black community at police brutality, joblessness and a poor quality of life.(68)

Finally, according to O'Dell, the nature of the "Black Revolution" is being transformed, as much by the deepening awareness of the people as by the failure of the governmental policy of containment, from a radical attack on racism to a revolutionary assault on capitalism itself.(69) He argues that, eventually, "internal domestic colonialism," with its tripartite historical base of the expropriation of Indian and Mexican land, African slave labor, and European immigrant labor, and its fascist "Military State," will be defeated by a broad-based progressive democratic coalition of the organized Black urban poor, students, and a revitalized labor movement.(70)

It is just this question of organization that the next statement investigates. Though the colonial situation engenders resistance, it is the conscious, long-range organization of that resistance which the next analyst considers the only meaningful response to the degradation of colonial life imposed by capitalism. In a sparse, coiled prose, Soledad Brother George Jackson's writings leave a stark impression of the reality of Black suffering and oppression.(71)

Jackson explicitly maintains that Black people lead a "colonial existence" and that the "black colonies" have been locked in an economic depression since the end of the Civil War.(72) The "Black Colony" has now become the principal repository of revolutionary potential in the United States. But in order for this energy to be released, a political vanguard -- the author proposed the "Vanguard Black Panther Communist Party" -- must be created. This vanguard will lead a united front made up of ideologically diverse progressive elements, and it must be multi-national in character; racism is the most serious obstacle which stands in the way of its realization.(73)

Once in place, Jackson asserts that the vanguard must deploy secret military units to unleash "People's War" against the American power structure on its ultimate battlefield -- the cities. Following "foco theory," Jackson argues that in the early stages of the urban guerrilla warfare, the political and military arms of the vanguard should function separately, the better for the latter branch to be able to employ "limited selective violence tied to an exact political purpose."(74) In the battle which will engulf the populace, the vanguard party must concern itself with the creation of a "revolutionary culture" which flows from the creation of an "autonomous infrastructure," the fifth of the five major principles which guide the people's prosecution of urban guerrilla warfare. "Dual power" must be created.(75)

Jackson understands "culture" to center on "institutions." The culture of the ruling class, enemy culture, is based on the principle of "hierarchical control." Thus culture is divided into two types of institutions: inhibitors, such as the prisons, the courts, the army, the police, the law, which are designed to discourage and curtail certain kinds of activity, and actuators, such as "the flea market" (consumer society), the mass media, the foundation, the corporation, the universities and the primary schools, the state-controlled unions, which are designed to encourage and promote certain other kinds of activity.(76)

The institutions of ruling class culture under monopoly capitalism generate "pathogenic character types" which are expressed by means of two central institutional modes: repression (especially via the prisons) and institutional racism. When the "cultural traits" of capitalist society (e.g., individualism) are not adequate to prevent behavior which threatens the ability of bourgeois law to carry out its main task of protecting property relations, then imprisonment and retaliatory violence result.(77) Such imprisonment is clearly "an aspect of the class struggle," and the people must be made to realize that all such crime has its roots in the unjust socio-economic conditions imposed and perpetuated by the ruling class.(78) So much for all this talk of "Black social disorganization."

As for racism, Jackson maintains that it is "a fundamental characteristic of monopoly capital," and is a complex psycho-social by-product of private enterprise. It is a matter of "ingrained ... attitudes conditioned through institutions."(79) Its function historically in the U.S. capitalist economy has been to divert the resentment and insecurity of the white population (and of white workers in particular), caught in "status competition" that is inexorable under the system, on to the backs of domestic colonial subjects (e.g., Native Americans, Afro-Americans, Chicanos, Asians, etc.) and away from experiencing any "status deprivation" in regard to the class above which exploits all non-property-owning wage-earners.(80) At bottom, psychologically, the "authoritarian personality structure" of racism, grounded in the "vulnerability" to capitalist exploitation of the white working class, is recognizable in its "dual nature" usefulness as social release for a people "processed" to conformity and to hate that which is different, and yet longing for the freedom to decide.(81) The exclusion which racism crystallizes is consciously understood and used by the exploiter (here, the racially superordinate group) as a way of defending and maintaining his position against the exploited.(82) Thus, Jackson denies false consciousness.

For Jackson, the task of revolutionary culture is to break the "life cycle" of reactionary, enemy culture. A community infrastructure, based on the day-to-day survival needs (e.g., for food, clothing, shelter, employment, etc.) of the oppressed, must be developed under the leadership of a political vanguard.(83)

And, in a reformulation of Marx's classic edict, Jackson asserts that this political vanguard will itself be led, not by the working class, but by "the outlaw" and "the lumpen."(84) The violence of the establishment will call into being the counter-violence of the oppressed, and the Black revolutionary, "the doomed man," will guide its force. Self-determination can only be realized through a revolution triggered by a clandestine, highly skilled army well-trained in counter-terrorism. "The outlaw and the lumpen will make the revolution. The people, the workers will adopt it."(85)

Having reviewed the subjects of the general outlook of the colonized and spontaneous violence, we take up another aspect of the colonial model as expressed in the second sub-group: the question of economic strategies. For the colonized, the distinction between appropriate and inappropriate economic strategies is crucial. As the next statement makes clear, the essence of these economic issues revolves around developing a correct analysis of American capitalism.

In The Myth of Black Capitalism, Earl Ofari takes a colonial perspective on U.S. race relations. The Black "neo-colony" is not "underdeveloped," it is "over-exploited." Its economic super-exploitation is compounded by another oppressive burden, that of white racial discrimination: a "dual oppression" of race and class afflicts Black America.(86)

Ofari understands white racism to be a "peripheral manifestation" and "offspring" of capitalism. Racism has been "institutionalized" into the body politic by the system of "capitalist exploitation and oppression."(87)

Self-determination for Black people, however, can only be achieved through the prior destruction of U.S. imperialism and the victory of socialism, according to Ofari. Thus, he asserts that revolutionary Black nationalism, which takes a class analysis as basic to its program and principles, will be the ideological vehicle of the struggle for self-determination and the abolition of the "colonial structure" of oppression.(88)

Ofari notes the ineffective history of American Marxism in dealing with the race question, and the generally complicitous relationship of white labor to the economic pillage of the Black ghettoes. He ascribes both failings to the ability of racism to disrupt and divide the working class and its allies.(89) His treatment implicitly eschews the notion of false consciousness as regards white racism.

Finally, in discussing economic strategies, Ofari concludes, after devoting much of the book to a critique of Black business ventures that have been capitalistically inspired, that the Black businessman is being groomed by the corporate power structure for one of the essential roles of neo-colonialism, viz., membership in a buffer elite. This group, the "neo-black elite," will perform a control function in the Black ghettoes as it transforms the potentially revolutionary demand of the

Black masses for community control into system-maintaining Black capitalist control of these communities, thereby also seeking to limit the possibilities of future outbreaks of disruptive violence.(90)

On the question of the definition of the "neo-colony," Ofari offers no formal statement. Those statements which can be culled from the text provide only inferential and general definition.(91) However, Ofari would seem to base his definition of the Black neo-colony on race and class, but he leaves the matter of culture unaddressed. We return to these issues in the concluding segment of this chapter.

In the last piece of literature under consideration, the discussion of political strategies for the oppressed is central but the two essential features of this sub-group also shape the argument. That is, the internal colony is defined by its racial and class features, and these class features express the determinative negative influence of capitalism. Therefore, as in Ofari's view, the buffer group receives a great deal of attention.

Robert L. Allen, in Black Awakening in Capitalist America, begins by asserting that Black America is "an oppressed nation, a semicolony" which is undergoing the transformation from "colonial nation into a neo-colonial nation," much like the experience of many former colonial areas.(92) Colonialism itself is not to be understood simply as a fixed historical context involving the colonizing nation and its overseas possessions. Rather, following O'Dell, Allen argues that the real essence of colonialism is to be found in the quality of the institutional relationship between the colonizer and the colonized.(93)

Allen asserts that in the process of the change from "domestic colonialism" to "domestic neo-colonialism," the role of the native bourgeoisie becomes crucial.(94) Though colonialism itself induces class divisions in the indigenous population, the better to maintain its direct rule, these divisions become vital in the strategy of indirect rule which neo-colonialism must pursue. Since neo-colonialism is the granting of formal independence while seeking to retain economic-political and military domination by other means, a "certain strata" of the colonized population is recruited to assist in this project.(95) In the United States, Allen believes that a segment of the Black bourgeoisie is being prepared for this role by "America's corporate elite" in the wake of the urban rebellions, which are directly comparable to "colonial insurrections"; the key to this neo-colonial strategy of corporate America is the Black student, especially at the high school and college levels.(96)

Thus, according to Allen, the response of the corporate capitalist to the decay and turmoil of American urban centers has been to seek to create:

> ...a <u>ghetto</u> <u>buffer</u> <u>class</u> clearly committed to the dominant American institutions and values on the one hand, and on the other, in rejuvenating the black working class and integrating it into the American economy (emphasis added).(97)

For Allen, the policy of containment of urban rebellions by combining a massive show of force with little expenditure of ammunition, initiated after 1967, and programs aimed at Black capitalism, community development corporations, and job training are all illustrations of this two-sided strategy; containment is especially designed to buy time so that the buffer group may be formed and take its place.(98)

However, the author notes that two economic forces threaten to dispose of the corporate elite's neo-colonial strategy. One is automation, whose impact is severely felt among unskilled Black laborers, and the other is recession, which causes the curtailment of corporate expenditures, social welfare, and hiring programs being among the first cuts to be made. In addition, the paucity of the job training programs and of the suitable new jobs created annually, the flight of businesses to the suburbs from the central cities, and the role of labor unions in defeating special programs aimed at "unemployables," all militate against the long-term success of the corporate strategy.(99)

In Allen's explication of the colonial model, a direct causal relationship between capitalism and racism is asserted. Colonial slavery with its capitalistic economic framework is responsible for racism and its subsequent institutionalization.(100)

Another key element in his schema is power. Specifically, Allen denies that political power is based on popular suffrage, arguing instead that the real base of such power in American society is the control of "valued resources and critical institutions." Such control and its correspondent power do not depend on the popular electorate for their exercise.(101) This amounts to an implicit rebuttal to the dispersed-power thesis generally preferred by those who adopt the point of view of the ethnic group model. Further, Allen contends that power in a social order is based ultimately on the existence and propagation of "social mythologies," chief among which in the United States is the sanctity of private property, and on the disposition of force.(102) As to the colonial situation in particular, he quotes Fanon's conclusion that decolonization is fundamentally a question of "relative strength," i.e., of power.(103)

Allen's view of colonialism derives much of its substance from Fanon's writings. Hence, Allen's arguments about the dichotomous division of the colonial world into natives and colonizers, the role of the police in maintaining that division, the outlets of inner-directed violence and religious mysticism for the aggression that the colonial subject accumulates, the creation of native elites by the colonial power and the ambivalence of these groups toward the national liberation struggle, the granting of formal independence (the analog in the United States, Allen notes, is the rash of civil rights legislation post-1954, guaranteeing the political equality of Black people) to the colony as the crisis brought on by the liberation struggle deepens, and the attempt to subvert that independence through neo-colonialism, all find resonance in Fanon. In fact, Allen maintains that Fanon's description of colonialism is directly applicable to the situation of the Black semi-colony, c. 1969.(104)

When Allen moves to consider the particulars of the U.S. situation for Black people, he begins by postulating that Black nationalism must be understood as a constant, permament and recurring substratum in the psychological orientation of the Black community. Moreover, Black nationalism exists in a dialectical relationship with assimilationism in the "collective black psyche."(105)

Elaborating a crisis theory of this dialectical relationship between Black nationalism and its assimilationist counterpart, he holds that in times of stress in race relations the nationalistic and separatist psychological tendencies of the Black masses find overt expression. This overt expression, which Allen terms "intellectual advocacy," generally is made by members of the Black middle class while the ongoing nationalistic sentiments, the "latent nationalism," of the Black masses is often overlooked until this stressful period. Nationalism among Black people in the United States ultimately results from the denial of sufficient "productive space" for them by a capitalist social order predicated on racism and exploitation.(106)

Culture as a weapon of struggle against oppression and exploitation assumes a central role in the nationalism associated with the pre-revolutionary phase of the liberation effort. Movements and sects dedicated to the reclamation or redefinition of Black cultural forms spring up. What in other countries has been described as messianism and millenarianism Allen equates with the "traditional black nationalism" espoused by such groups as the Black Muslims. Such movements display a tendency to either dissolve eventually into social desuetude or to become the germinal, prototypic influence in the development of revolutionary nationalistic politics. Allen finds evidence that nationalistic feeling among Black folks is taking the latter course.(107)

Allen declares that a chief factor capable of greatly influencing the direction that protonationalist movements will take is the Black middle class. This class is characterized by ambivalence which stems from its privileged position in society. In politics, this ambivalence manifests itself in "bourgeous nationalism," centered on reforms, Black capitalism, and cultural mysticism, and "revolutionary nationalism," which poses the question of the complete and necessary restructuring of society as the only possible route to Black liberation. It is the ambivalence of this class, coupled with the co-optable political manifestation of this instability in bourgeois nationalism, on which the white, corporate power elite bases its plans to penetrate the ghettoes, in the wake of the rebellions, and install leadership favorable to the status quo. And for Allen, this process is in essence no different from the process of neocolonialism in underdeveloped countries.(108)

The concept of self-determination completes the theoretical inventory of Allen's presentation of the colonial model. Arguing that the problem of programmatically and analytically synthesizing racial oppression and class-based exploitation must be addressed, he proposes that efforts to institute community control, nationwide, in Black communities, led by a national, coordinated, independent Black political party, offer the most practical, meaningful resolution of this problem. Leadership of this political vehicle must be in the hands of members of the Black lower classes, and the party must not aim for Black economic self-sufficiency, such a project being both unattainable because of the nature of corporate capitalism and undesirable because of the likelihood that it would simply foster the rise of a new class of exploiters, i.e., the Black business elite and its followers.(109) Such community development as is undertaken must substitute "capitalist property relations" with "communal (property) relations," and it must be controlled democratically by the community itself.(110)

As Allen sees it, self-determination, however, cannot be won through the exertions of the Black community alone. Without the reorganization of the total structure of white society, the burdensome relations of racist oppression and economic exploitation which sustain that society would sooner or later re-impose themselves on Black people. This means, above all, that a simultaneous struggle at the national, governmental level must be waged, and this necessity, in turn, raises the question of allies.(111)

Finally, the author observes that the international context of poverty, underdevelopment, imperialism, and racism makes it likely that the solution to America's race problems will have international repercussions. Such a solution presages the strategy which corporate white America will pursue in the world.(112)

In offering a preliminary critical assessment of Allen's formulation, it should first be pointed out that, like other authors (e.g., Prager, Ofari) already considered, Allen also rejects the notion of false consciousness as applicable to the white worker and his defense of racial privilege. This rejection is implicit in his treatment of the negative reaction of labor unions to job training and preferential programs.(113)

This positive similarity is matched, however, by one that is negative: Allen's use of the word "nation" is left at a rhetorical and journalistic level; and no formal definition of this key term is provided. Here, this matter is crucial since the author attributes rights and prerogatives to Black people, primarily the right to self-determination, which have generally been derived from specific definitions of "nation."(114) Perhaps, like Ofari, Allen understands "the Black nation" to be a cultural amalgam based on race and class, but this orientation is left unstated.

Culture itself is another critical flaw in the author's work. Only reference to the destructiveness of slavery as concerns the African past and the subjection to cultural imperialism mark his treatment of this topic.(115) Though Allen intends his work to be an "analytic history," the analysis appears to encompass primarily the political and economic aspects of Black history in the twentieth century. The political and economic bases of culture are not tied to a consideration of its immaterial, psycho-social and institutional forms as an integrated whole.(116) Black culture, then, is not adequately presented as a processual, interactive, dynamic entity in this work.

Conclusion

The works inspected here present a view of U.S. race relations which parts company with the assumptions and theories of mainstream political science and sociology on this issue, and this view is also critical of American society in general. Many of the ideas and concepts expressed find no counterpart in traditional approaches.

Perhaps the most important concept of this nature is institutional racism. Postulated as a structural mechanism based on exclusion and subordination, it is held to be one of the central phenomena which defines the colonial nature of race relations. Usually, it is denied, either explicitly or implicitly, that the superordinate group experiences false consciousness in defending and maintaining its racial privilege (Prager, Ofari, Jackson, Allen, and Blauner). However, this assertion regarding false consciousness must be understood as a general expression of disdain for older Marxist analyses which tended to ignore racial privilege, and not as a definitive statement on the false consciousness notion itself. Since favorable objective and subjective conditions for revolution must simultaneously exist, it is possible to comprehend the ideology of racial privilege *at the level of the subjective* as not being false consciousness at the same time that *at the level of the objective* it is. The point that certain colonial model proponents seem to be making is that Marxist analysis cannot have relevance to U.S. race relations so long as it continues to deny the significance of racism as a material force in American society.

Another striking concept developed by colonial model adherents is the idea of the internal or domestic colony. Often referred to as a "nation," the internal colony primarily is identified as the product of exclusion and subordination; it is the "place" of the colonized.

But, use of the concept reveals an unresolved problem in the model: lack of a clear definition of "colony" or "nation." The problem of definition of the group which is being oppressed and exploited is basic to the colonial school of analysis. Ofari apparently equates Black people with "an oppressed national minority group" who possess the right to self-determination.(117) Prager, in the work cited above, is interested primarily in describing the impact of racism on the class structure and the relation between the two. However, his statements about this relationship would seem to indicate that, for him, Black and other Third World colonies are defined primarily by their race.(118) Like Ofari, Jackson, Brown, and Allen also present views of the internal colony which revolve around its racial characteristics and its class position. Thus, the works reviewed suggest the dichotomy already noted: one group seeming to prefer definitions that are based on race and ethnicity (Prager, Blauner), and another those which associate race and class (Ofari, Jackson, Brown, Allen). Again, a clear definitional statement of this important term must be formalized if the model is to be extended and developed.

Another concept which is centrally employed in this model is that of culture. Though few lengthy definitions of culture are provided (Jackson, Blauner), it becomes the principal ground of the struggle which colonialism engenders. The buffer group, composed of usually pliant members of the colonized populace who rise to prominence under neo-colonialism, is seen as a result of the cultural conflict between colonizer and colonized. Within the internal colony itself, the prominence of the buffer group stems in part from the class differences introduced in the colonized population.

Of the two lengthy discussions of culture referred to above, Blauner's attempts a more comprehensive treatment. He offers six sources of Afro-American culture, the last and most important being the political history of struggle of Black people against racism. But this source is not satisfactorily explicated, nor is his elementarist definition of Afro-American culture acceptable. We shall offer our own position on culture.

At the heart of the political history of struggle against racism as the key process in the elaboration of Afro-American culture stands the replacement of African production and social relations of production by Euro-American production and social relations of production. This crucial abrupt transformation was to have a profound effect on all aspects of Afro-American life.

To production, and social relations of production, must be added a third processual sphere of human activity essential to all cultures, that of a special category of social relations which are stable, crystallized around certain roles, symbols, or rituals, and of long duration. These social relations may be called cultural institutions. The processual interaction method of culture study seeks to understand culture as the interaction of these three delimited, permeable, spheres of human activity. Blauner's discussion of culture, particularly of Afro-American culture, fails because the cultural-essences method which he employs focuses only on the cultural institutions sphere of culture in a mystical, idealist way. The two other processes are neglected except for mention of the concept of "political history," which is not sufficiently developed.(119) Thus, if the colonial model is to progress at all on this point, we hold that it must abandon all static conceptions of culture in order to recognize the changing character of the culture of the colonized.

Finally, the most challenging question which the colonial model raises concerns the investigation of the nature of the link between the ideology of racial privilege and American capitalism. Since empirical evidence exists which demonstrates a connection between racism against Black people and income inequality among whites, and loss of income to Black workers, there is reason to believe that this area of research must be pursued.(120)

But, no clear picture emerges of the causal relationship between racism and capitalism. The concept of exploitation, which is central to any linking of these phenomena, is sometimes presented as being in sort of a revolving door relationship with racism, each component in the relationship being separate and independent, yet interacting with the other (Prager, Blauner). Another perspective holds racism to be in a direct causal relationship with capitalist exploitation (O'Dell, Ofari, Jackson, Allen) while simultaneously recognizing the ability of the effect, racism, to influence the cause, capitalism (Ofari, Jackson). Still another view posits no formal causal relationship between the two but is essentially in agreement with the direct cause argument (Brown). From this it can be gathered that the subject of capitalism, its political economy and its particular form of exploitation are treated as fundamental and determinative by some writers in this school (O'Dell, Ofari, Jackson, Brown, Allen) and as secondary or co-determinative by others (Prager, Blauner); generally, however, the first group does not dispute the ability of racism to guide social interaction much in the manner stressed by the second group. What this internal division amounts to are the two camps in the model spoken of earlier.

The most important consequence of this division is the limitation it places on the discussion of the colonizing superordinate group. The segments within this group, and the differing qualitative and quantitative nature of the rewards each segment reaps from racial privilege, are often obscured or neglected when no specific conception of the link of this racial privilege to capitalist political economy is given. Likewise, unfortunately, even those writers who attempt this connection often do not specify the nature of the segments and of their respective rewards. This whole area seems to be the one most in need of further efforts if a colonial model of race relations integrated into a capitalist political economy is to be realized.

However, it is clear that the resolution of this question of the link will not be forthcoming as long as key terms remain ambiguous. "Racism" is the most pressing example. Historical practice in other societies compared with the American experience, together with suitable conceptions of human nature, must be explicated. While this task awaits completion, we should like to offer our own view on the question of the link. We shall do this in conjunction with our criticism of Robert Blauner's finding that racism and capitalism now have a tenuous relation at best. Since, as in our critique of the ethnic group model, we maintain that the facts of hierarchy and socioeconomic inequality inherent in American capitalism bear very directly on Black/white relations, we shall propose a plausible manner in which to argue the connection.

In his presentation on racism, Blauner carefully separates rational race consciousness from the irrational. But in doing so, he loses sight of the historical situation (i.e., modern American capitalist society) whose ideological contours shape the concept under examination. This happens because he introduces the concept of irrationality by means of a social-psychological view of racism, represented as the ideas of "the white ... and black ... collective unconscious" and "the white racial mind," so that racism becomes defined through writ-large analysis of the *individual*, insecure, personality-fragmented racist.(121) A part/whole fallacy is committed which results in the diminution in importance of exploitation and its concomitant, hierarchical power relations.

We may expand our criticism by providing an alternative formulation to Blauner's equation of racial groups with status and interest groups. If the terms of this equation are extended so that its racial and political economic aspects interact, it is possible to offer a plausible explanation of their connection.

Blauner contends that racial groups are both status groups and interest groups whose concerns are real since race is a real phenomenon in American society. While this contention is acceptable at the level of generalization, it does not reveal the particular links to the political economy of capitalism that racial groups may have in their status and interest aspects. In order to do this, it would be necessary to understand that the system-threatening nature of the status relations between racial groups, as embodied in cultural conflict, does not stem solely from the status relations themselves, but also from the fact that these status relations are correlatives of and adjuncts to the actual and potential irreconcilable objective interests of the racial groups.(122) For the dominators, those objective interests include maintenance and replication of the exclusion, subordination, oppression, cultural privilege and advantage over, and <u>exploitation</u> and <u>exploitability</u> of the target groups; but, within the dominant racial group, disparities in power and status cause variable subjective allegiance to these interests. For the dominated, the diametrically opposed objective interests include mitigation and ultimate destruction of the exclusion, subordination, oppression, cultural privilege and advantage, <u>exploitation</u> and <u>exploitability</u> imposed by the dominant group; again, variable subjective attachment to these interests is noted in the dominated group; but power and status disparities tend to be less pronounced though clearly present (e.g., the buffer stratum). The explosiveness (potential or actual) of race relations stems precisely from the fact that the differing objective interests of racial groups tie into the fundamental class antagonisms of capitalist society.(123) That is why the destruction of institutional racism, which conceptually encompasses exclusion, subordination, and cultural (or racial) privilege and advantage, would drastically alter capitalist social relations and capitalist property relations.

Moreover, the status aspect of race relations draws its profundity from its relation to the divergent objective interests of the racial groups involved. These objective interests, for the dominators, express the social ideas and context which represent <u>the concatenating force</u>, capable of organizing social relations along the desired lines, released by the central phenomenon of capitalist society, exploitation, and its concomitant, exploitability, i.e., the creation of those conditions necessary to perpetuate and extend capitalist exploitation into the future. Inclusion of the concept of "exploitability" negates the argument of the displacement of exploitation since it points to the <u>continuing</u> process which facilitates exploitation.

This concatenating force is the plausible link between the status and interest aspects of race relations and the political economy of capitalism. When combined with Blauner's own findings, this view suggests that for white groups in the United States, the link has been structured as localized labor discipline, Anglo-Conformity assimilation, and generally unrestricted legal access to productive space.(124) For Third World groups, in degrees of applicability, the link has appeared as more extensive labor discipline, colonialism (or neocolonialism) which includes institutional racism and token (numerical and symbolic) representation in certain (usually political or occupational) endeavors, and limited access to productive space at all levels.

Thus, in sum, when Blauner defines racism primarily as an irrational manifestation of the otherwise rational, independent phenomenon of race consciousness, capable of sustaining its own status and interest orientations, and especially when he argues that racial control has become an end in itself, he is distancing himself from the very theoretical ground which would enable him to integrate his model with some conception of its relation to capitalism. But, because his presentation has the general effect of obscuring and making secondary the concept of exploitation, no such integration is possible.

The problem of the explanation of racism, together with other aspects of Black/white race relations, in a capitalist political economy also has compelled the attention of another group of writers who draw upon the tradition of social inquiry bequeathed by Karl Marx. As we shall observe in the next chapter, proponents of the Marxist (we use this adjective only to denote the socio-political reference of these writers, not to equate their views with those of Marx himself) model entertain serious disagreement as to the proper interpretation of the ideology of racial privilege. It is significant that of the two salient Marxist positions on this issue, one -- the notion of racism as a semi-autonomous, or "independent," social force -- bears a superficial resemblance to the approach of the first sub-group of this model delineated at the outset of this chapter.

The crucial difference, however, is that the concept advanced by the Marxist writers is visibly anchored in the class analysis of Marxist theory. We turn now to the Marxist model, the last perspective to be examined.

Notes

1. Most important in this regard is his Wretched of the Earth (New York: Grove Press, 1968). Also of note is A Dying Colonialism (New York: Grove Press, 1965).

2. The Panthers' identification with Fanon's work is seen in Gene Marine, The Black Panthers (New York: The New American Library, 1969), pp. 44-45; and, in Huey P. Newton, Revolutionary Suicide (New York: Random House, 1973), pp. 122-126.

3. For the purposes of this chapter, I have chosen to regard as basically similar the terms "colonial" and "neo-colonial" when applied to U.S. race relations by theorists and writers. Though a distinction does obtain between the two, viz., neo-colonial relationships are a post-independence phenomenon, I hope to demonstrate below that the terms and the conclusions drawn from them do admit of a qualitative similarity.

Other terms which will be regarded as cognates of the above are "internal colony," "internal colonialism," and "domestic colonialism." And, though traditional Marxism's reliance on the categories "national minority" and "nation" is often pictured as being at odds with the terms so far listed, these Marxist terms will be examined here when the predominant sentiment of the writer is judged to be congruous with the sentiments usually expressed by the proponents of this model.

4. See Wilson Record, The Negro and the Communist Party (New York: Atheneum, 1951), pp. 55-60. From 1928 to 1935, Record states that the CPUSA's position on Black people in the United States' South was that they constituted "an oppressed nation" suffering "intense exploitation and heavy oppression" and were thus capable of pursuing a program of "national liberation" and "self-determination."

5. Frantz Fanon, The Wretched of the Earth, trans. Constance Farrington (New York: Grove Press, 1968; orig.

Maspero editeur S.A.R.L., Paris, France, 1961), pp. 37-38, 41.

6. Fanon, pp. 35, 36-37, 38, 43, 86, 94, 212; the quoted phrase is found on p. 35.

7. Stokely Carmichael and Charles V. Hamilton, Black Power: The Politics of Liberation in America (New York: Random House, 1967), pp. 5, 10, 14, 15, 18, 22, 23, 25, 30-31, 182.

8. Carmichael and Hamilton confound the theoretical clarity of their work even further by making an allusive reference to the "subordinate caste" position of Black people in American society; *op. cit.*, pp. 27-28.

9. James Boggs, Racism and the Class Struggle: Further Pages from a Black Worker's Notebook (New York: Monthly Review Press, 1970), pp. 37, 42.

10. Boggs' earlier work, The American Revolution: Pages from a Negro Worker's Notebook (New York: Monthly Review Press, 1963), makes this point, especially in the essay "Rebels with a Cause," pp. 75-87.

11. These quoted phrases are taken from the phonographically recorded text of a speech, "Ballots or Bullets," delivered April 3, 1964, First Amendment Records, Philadelphia, Pennsylvania, 1 vol. side A; from "The Black Revolution," delivered April 8, 1964, reprinted in G. Brietman, ed., Malcolm X Speaks (New York: Grove Press, 1965), pp. 45-57; and from a recording of "Message to the Grass Roots," delivered November 9, 1963, Grass Roots L.P. Co., Detroit, Michigan, 1 vol. side B.

12. Robert Staples, "Race and Colonialism: The Domestic Case in Theory and Practice," The Black Scholar, 7 (1976), pp. 37-48.

13. Staples, pp. 37, 39-40.

14. Staples, p. 39.

15. Staples, p. 40.

16. Staples, pp. 40-42.

17. The classes named in the text are described for Black people in Introduction to Afro-American Studies, 4th ed. (Chicago: Peoples College Press, 1977), pp. 267-272, 347-351.

18. Indirect evidence for the existence of the greater inequality of the wage contract with capital for Black labor is given by Landry in the form of the analysis of twentieth century income ratios and occupational indices of dissimilarity; Bart Landry, "The Economic Position of Black Americans," in H. Roy Kaplan, ed., American Minorities and Economic Opportunity (Itasca, Illinois: F. E. Peacock Publishers, 1977), pp. 50-108, esp. pp. 55-63, 68, Table 2.5, 69, Table 2.6.

19. Jeffrey Prager, "White Racial Privilege and Social Change: An Examination of Theories of Racism," Berkeley Journal of Sociology, 18 (1972/73), pp. 129, 130.

20. Prager, pp. 137-139.

21. Prager, p. 144.

22. The conception of false consciousness held by Marx and Engels is discussed in two letters by Engels: see Frederick Engels, "Engels to C. Schmit in Berlin, London, Oct. 27, 1890," and "Engels to F. Mehring in Berlin, London, July 14, 1893," in Karl Marx and Frederick Engels: Selected Works in One Volume (New York: International Publishers, 1968), pp. 694-699, 699-703.

23. Prager, pp. 131-132, 133, 136.

24. Prager, pp. 126, 127, 133, 145, 146.

25. Prager, pp. 128, 134, 144, 146.

26. Prager presents this evidence on pp. 140-142 of his article.

27. Prager, pp. 134, 146.

28. Prager, pp. 137, 139, 140, 142, 144.

29. Prager takes Lester Thurow, Poverty and Discrimination (Brookings Institute Press, 1969) to task

for not making these distinctions as regards the "racial differentiation by class" of the gains that white people receive (Prager, p. 144).

But Victor Perlo in Economics of Racism, USA: Roots of Black Inequality (New York: International Publishers, 1975), pp. 131-132, 147-149, 158, 225-226, counters Prager by contending that since capitalists control over 90% of all employment in this country, the patterns of discrimination in employment which exist are largely their work. Furthermore, he generalizes the case of "Ma Bell" (The American Telephone and Telegraph Co.), which in 1973 had a fifteen million dollar consent decree brought against it by reason of its past racist, exclusionary job entry and promotion policies, to argue that American capitalism reaps forty-six billion dollars annually in super profits based on racist distinctions in employment which hold down the wages of both Black and white workers.

30. Robert Blauner, Racial Oppression in America (New York: Harper and Row, 1971).

31. Blauner, pp. 133-146; in a sense, Blauner and Allen may be read as complementary views on the subject of Black culture. The concept of "political history" corresponds directly to the substance of Allen's "analytic history," while the other concepts are not articulated in Allen's work. See Robert L. Allen, Black Awakening in Capitalist America (Garden City, New York: Doubleday and Company, 1969), to be discussed below.

32. Blauner, pp. vii, 54, 84-85.

33. Blauner, pp. 52-53, 67-68.

34. Blauner, pp. 30-31; Blauner cites Harold Cruse, The Crisis of the Negro Intellectual (New York: William Morrow, 1967), and borrows the quoted phrase from him.

35. Blauner, p. 119.

36. Blauner, pp. 29-31, 35.

37. Blauner, p. 22.

38. Blauner, pp. 29-31, 36-42, 65-67, 68-70; note here, that the author employs the notion of displacement in his causal analysis of racism with much the same effect as that achieved by liberal writers like Moynihan and Glazer or conservatives like Banfield, *viz*., the role of capitalism is minimized or obscured. For Moynihan and Glazer, slavery and segregation have been displaced by the internal weaknesses of the Black group as cause for the continuing existence of Black social degradation and racism; see Moynihan and Glazer, *Beyond the Melting Pot*, 2nd ed. (Cambridge, Massachusetts: M.I.T. Press, 1970), pp. xxxix-xl, 31-36, 39, 45, 50-53, 59, 69, 84. For Banfield, racial discrimination, now moribund, has been displaced by social class prejudice as the reason for the hostility that Black people often encounter; see E. C. Banfield, *The Unheavenly City Revisited* (Boston: Little, Brown, 1974), pp. 79-80, 87-91. While Blauner does directly cite capitalist exploitation as the *initial* factor instigating racism, something which none of the other authors mentioned above would even consider, nonetheless, his argument for the continued existence of racism as an autonomous force predicated on internal colonialism and the need for racial control tends to overlook the *continuing* role played by capitalism.

39. Blauner, pp. 10-11, 56-70; Allen, too, vigorously rejects the ethnic group model (Blauner's "immigrant analogy"), though for its more contemporary failings, e.g., its failure to account for the uniqueness of Black people as manifested by their subjection to racism, the decline of city hall as an avenue to power as metropolitanism increases, the non-viability of small business as a power base in the age of monopoly, the inability of Black capitalism to do more than create a small, nouveau-riche, privileged class in the Black community, and, the general obsolescence of the mass of unskilled Black laborers in a highly technological, automated economy; see Allen, *op*. *cit*., pp. 50-54.

40. Blauner, pp. 28, 116.

41. Blauner, pp. 112, 380-381.

42. Blauner, pp. 185, 187-188.

43. Blauner, pp. 2-4, 19-20.

44. Blauner, pp. 20-21, 31n; Blauner's treatment of race consciousness suggests an analogy to Weber's analysis of the irrationality of bureaucracy due to the routinization of charisma; see H. H. Gerth and C. Wright Mills, eds., From Max Weber: Essays in Sociology (New York: Oxford University Press, 1946), Ch. XI, "The Social Psychology of the World Religions," esp. pp. 281-282, 282, 295, 298-299.

45. Blauner, p. 279; I am intrigued by the confluence between Blauner and Cox on this point and on others -- e.g., exclusion serves to block avenues to cultural parity, capitalist labor exploitation as the first cause of modern race relations, the ranking of domestic ethnic groups as being roughly correlated to the international standing of their respective homelands, and that the attitudes alone of white people are not determinants in race relations since power is the fundamental issue -- while no mention is made of Cox's work either in the text, chapter footnotes, or the index; see Blauner, pp. 22, 29, 279, 280. The work by Cox referred to is Oliver C. Cox, Caste, Class, and Race (New York: Monthly Review Press, 1948).

46. The concept of differential proletarianization is sketched in Robert L. Allen, "Racism and the Black Nation Thesis," Socialist Revolution, 6 (January-March 1976), p. 149. The concept is used to describe the different levels of access to productive space and its valued attributes (e.g., income, occupational prestige, mobility, education) that have characterized the process of the formation of the American labor force from racially and ethnically diverse population groups.

47. Blauner, p. 26.

48. Blauner, p. 32.

49. Blauner, pp. 28-29, 39, 61.

50. Blauner, pp. 128-129, 136.

51. Blauner, pp. 129n, 143-144; Blauner's mystical conception of Black culture is reminiscent of DuBois' treatment of the subject in a similar manner; see W. E. B. DuBois, The Souls of Black Folk (New York: Washington Square Press, 1970).

52. Blauner, pp. 140-141, 144, 153.

53. Blauner, pp. 67, 146.

54. H. Rap Brown, Die Nigger Die! (New York: The Dial Press, 1969), p. 8.

55. Brown, pp. 1-2, 8, 10, 40-41, 47.

56. Brown, pp. 3-4, 124-125.

57. Brown, pp. 124-125, 143.

58. Brown, p. 128.

59. Brown, pp. 128-129.

60. Brown, pp. 14, 130-131.

61. Brown, pp. 128, 129, 144.

62. J. H. O'Dell, "Colonialism and the Negro American Experience," Freedomways, 6 (1966), pp. 296-308; "A Special Variety of Colonialism," Freedomways, 7 (1967), pp. 7-15; "The July Rebellions and the 'Military State,'" Freedomways, 7 (1967), pp. 288-301; and "The Contours of the 'Black Revolution' in the 1970's," Freedomways, 10 (1970), pp. 104-114. The articles will be respectively referred to hereafter by the following abbreviated titles: "Colonialism," "A Special Variety," "The July Rebellions," and "Contours."

63. J. H. O'Dell, "Colonialism," pp. 296-297, 300, 303-305.

64. O'Dell, "Colonialism," p. 305.

65. J. H. O'Dell, "A Special Variety," p. 8.

66. O'Dell, "A Special Variety," pp. 9-10.

67. O'Dell, "A Special Variety," pp. 12-14.

68. J. H. O'Dell, "The July Rebellions," pp. 290-292, 294.

69. J. H. O'Dell, "Contours," pp. 108-111.

70. O'Dell, "Contours," pp. 111-115.

71. George Jackson, Soledad Brother: The Prison Letters of George Jackson (New York: Bantam Books, 1970); and, Blood In My Eye (New York: Random House, 1972). The two works will be referred to respectively by the following titles: Soledad Brother, and Blood In My Eye.

72. Jackson, Soledad Brother, pp. 37, 183.

73. Jackson, Blood In My Eye, pp. 9, 37, 93-94, 114.

74. Jackson, Blood In My Eye, pp. 26-29, 48-49, 161-162.

75. Jackson, Blood In My Eye, pp. 38, 56-59; the four other principles are mobility, infiltration, ambush, and camouflage.

76. Jackson, Blood In My Eye, pp. 77-79; the terms "inhibitor" and "actuator" are mine.

77. Jackson, Blood In My Eye, pp. 85, 86, 89.

78. Jackson, Blood In My Eye, pp. 90, 91.

79. Jackson, Blood In My Eye, pp. 94, 157.

80. Jackson, Blood In My Eye, pp. 105-106.

81. Jackson, Blood In My Eye, pp. 106, 144, 146. Jackson is here relying on the work of Wilhelm Reich, principally The Mass Psychology of Fascism (New York: Farrar, Straus, and Giroux, 1970). Jackson further typologizes white racists as overt, unconscious, or self-interdicting. This last type is the object of his special ire and condemnation since the ability for truly non-racist conduct is not deemed possible. These comments are made as the conditions necessary for "unitarian conduct" on the part of the white Left and the Black vanguard in creating the united front are reviewed. He ultimately concludes that a verification test of the principle of "unitarian conduct" and its necessary conditions will be provided by the practice of the multiracial political prisoners' defense movement, centering around his own and other such cases (Jackson, Blood In My Eye, pp. 93-96).

82. Jackson, Blood In My Eye, p. 157; on this point, he is basically in agreement with Cox; see Caste, Class, and Race (New York: Monthly Review Press, 1948), pp. 475-476.

83. Jackson, Blood In My Eye, pp. 36-37, 50, 159.

84. Jackson, Blood In My Eye, p. 105. Jackson points out that although the proletariat is still a revolutionary class, its power and numbers have been diminished by automation, government-controlled unions, the military-industrial complex, National Guard strikebreakers, right-to-work laws, and so on. In fact, the working class can be separated into two "mutually exclusive and conflicting sections," the ultra-right conservative, and the left or neutral. The right-wing section constitutes a "new pig class" and is the backbone of governmental repression. It helps to create an "inverted stratification of revolutionary potential" with petit-bourgeois and upper class students and professionals displaying revolutionary consciousness while a sizeable section of the working class defends the status quo. Historically, the "short-term economic interests" of labor were satisfied, thus providing the key to compromising and vitiating the labor movement as its leaders developed ties with the ruling class (Jackson, Blood In

My Eye, pp. 38, 53-54, 148).

On the contention of the inadequacy of classical Marxism's view of the proletariat in light of some of the factors Jackson discusses, see the similar opinion of Stanley Aronowitz, who argues that a new working class consciousness must be built around the campus radical and the rebellious, alienated, anti-union young worker. Aronowitz, however, labeling Black demands such as those portrayed by Jackson "particularistic," does not see the possibility of Black leadership of the cultural revolution which he advocates as essential to the revitalization of proletarian struggles. See Stanley Aronowitz, False Promises: The Shaping of American Working Class Consciousness (New York: McGraw-Hill, 1973), Ch. 8, "The New Workers," esp. pp. 404, 407, 413-414, 423, 426-430, and 434-442.

85. Jackson, Blood In My Eye, pp. 48, 67, 105, 106.

86. Earl Ofari, The Myth of Black Capitalism (New York: Monthly Review Press, 1970), pp. 96-98, 123n.

87. Ofari, pp. 9, 25, 79.

88. Ofari, pp. 98-99, 122-123.

89. Ofari, pp. 55-56, 95.

90. Ofari, pp. 68, 85.

91. See, for example, the long footnote on p. 123 (ibid.) in which Ofari offers the following statement: "The notion that blacks in America are a colonized nation is gaining a more widespread acceptance. Like many neo-colonies abroad, black America is in many ways treated by the white ruling class as a separate and distinct politically and socially oppressed national grouping. Although upwards of 90 percent of black America belongs in one form or another to the working class, the oppression is not strictly class in origin."

92. Robert L. Allen, Black Awakening in Capitalist

America: An Analytic History (Garden City, New York: Doubleday, 1969), pp. 1, 13-14.

93. Allen, Black Awakening, p. 8; the piece by O'Dell which Allen uses is "A Special Variety of Colonialism" referred to above in n 62. Staples also defends the applicability of a colonialist framework to U.S. race relations by referring to O'Dell's position; see Staples, "Race and Colonialism," p. 46.

94. Allen, Black Awakening, pp. 2, 11, 17.

95. Allen, Black Awakening, pp. 11, 14, 16-17.

96. Allen, Black Awakening, pp. 2, 17, 262.

97. Allen, Black Awakening, p. 194.

98. Allen, Black Awakening, pp. 207-209, 213, 217-221.

99. Allen, Black Awakening, pp. 226-227, 237-238.

100. Allen, Black Awakening, p. 185.

101. Allen, Black Awakening, p. 187.

102. Allen, Black Awakening, pp. 55-57.

103. Allen, Black Awakening, p. 63; he cites Fanon, The Wretched of the Earth, p. 48.

104. Allen, Black Awakening, pp. 60-65.

105. Allen, Black Awakening, p. 89.

106. Allen, Black Awakening, pp. 89, 115-118.

107. Allen, Black Awakening, pp. 121-126; interestingly, Harold Cruse makes just the opposite argument, contending that formal, orthodox revolutionary ideologies (which he equates with "Marxist-Communism") only make headway among Black people in periods characterized by assimilationist integrationism. See Harold Cruse,

The Crisis of the Negro Intellectual, p. 226.

108. Allen, Black Awakening, pp. 47-48, 99, 125-126, 223, 252-253.

109. Allen, Black Awakening, pp. 265, 274-279.

110. Allen, Black Awakening, p. 278; Allen's arguments here draw heavily from W. E. B. DuBois, The Dusk of Dawn (New York: Schocken Publishers, 1968), in which DuBois' idea of the Black economic "co-operative commonwealth" was outlined.

111. Allen, Black Awakening, pp. 281-283.

112. Allen, Black Awakening, pp. 283-284.

113. Allen, Black Awakening, pp. 115, 237-238.

114. I have in mind the two seminal works which leftists in this country usually cite when arguing about Black folk and what constitutes a "nation": J. Stalin, "Marxism and the National Question," in Bruce Franklin, ed., The Essential Stalin (Garden City, New York: Doubleday and Co., 1972), pp. 54-84; and V. I. Lenin, "The Socialist Revolution and the Right of Nations to Self-Determination," in Lenin on the National and Colonial Questions (Peking, China: Foreign Language Press, 1970), pp. 1-19. A good summary of this debate is M. Frank Wright, "The National Question: A Marxist Critique," The Black Scholar (February 1974), pp. 43-53.

115. Allen, Black Awakening, p. 13.

116. Allen's weakness here is more one of not thoroughly assessing the suggested interaction, offering instead limited vignettes of particular events and leaders, rather than ignoring it altogether. See, for example, the discussion of the Garvey and Black Muslim movements (ibid., pp. 100-102, 106-110).

117. Ofari, p. 98.

118. Prager, p. 146; it is here that he argues for

the transcendent nature of racism over and above the class structure and its purposes. Since colonialism is based ultimately on racism, and since racism does not exert the same social alignment that capitalism does and will not be stilled by the demise of the latter, it follows that the neo-colony must be defined principally by its racial identification.

119. A general orientation to the subject of culture study may be found in A. L. Kroeber and Clyde Kluckhohn, Culture: A Critical Review of Concepts and Definitions (New York: Random House, 1952). Criticism of the cultural-essences, or elementarist, view of culture is offered in C. J. J. Vermeulen and A. de Ruijter, "Dominant Epistemological Presuppositions in the Use of the Cross-Cultural Survey Method," Current Anthropology, 16 (March 1975), pp. 29-52.

The term "processual interaction," which I have coined, relates most closely to the view of culture and its study expounded in an appendix to the Kroeber and Kluckhohn book; see A. G. Meyer, "The Use of the Term Culture in the Soviet Union," in Kroeber and Kluckhohn, op. cit., Appendix B, pp. 414-423.

120. Reich establishes the Black/white income ratio as a "measure of racism" which directly affects income inequality among whites: where greater racism, there also greater income inequality among whites. This finding stems from the application of specific statistical tests derived by Reich to 1960 census data. See Michael Reich, "The Economics of Racism," in David M. Gordon, ed., Problems in Political Economy: An Urban Perspective (Lexington, Massachusetts: D. C. Heath, 1971), pp. 107-113. Moreover, Perlo has found, also using census data (c. 1970-72), that although 96% of all employed Black workers are wage or salary earners, their aggregate income amounts to only 60% that of white workers. Racism is a plausible explanation for a large part of this differential. See Victor Perlo, Economics of Racism, U.S.A., pp. 18, 156 (Table 24).

121. Blauner, pp. 118-119, 165, 292; Blauner's use of Hartz' theory of the cultural fragmentation of

settler societies is most important here; see Louis Hartz, The Founding of New Societies (New York: Harcourt, Brace, Jovanovich, 1964), referred to by Blauner on the first pages mentioned in this footnote.

122. The concept of interest, in both its subjective and objective aspects, is delineated in Isaac D. Balbus, "The Concept of Interest in Pluralist and Marxist Analysis," Politics and Society, 1 (February 1971), pp. 151-177. My use of the term "objective interest" follows Balbus.

123. While the classically Marxist distinctions of bourgeoisie and proletariat still obtain, the more recent development of American capitalism in its monopoly stage has led some class analysts to offer detailed critiques on the changing composition of the classic categories and the increasingly important intermediate categories. See, for example, Erik Olin Wright, "On Class Boundaries in Advanced Capitalist Countries," Studies on the Left (1976), pp. 3-42.

124. This concept is taken from Allen, Black Awakening, p. 115. It comprises group access to production, and those material and social resources which allow the elaboration of a pattern of group life, in culture, politics, and social relations.

At best, Marxian hypotheses are "servants, not masters."

Oliver Cox,
Caste, Class, and Race,
1948, p. xi.

Chapter 4
The Marxist Model

Introduction

The application of Marxist thought to the problematic nature of Black/white race relations in the United States can be traced back to Marx himself. In the era of the U.S. Civil War and Reconstruction, Marx, from a limited base of first-hand knowledge, generally expressed himself as favorable to abolition and the cause of democratic rights for Black folk.(1) But an astute student of and participant in the race problem observed, at the height of the Depression, that Marxism would get nowhere in the United States until it was "modified" to meet the specific conditions of America, and not Europe.(2)

Chief among these specific conditions are the relations between those parts of the American populace which are of European ancestry and those which are of African ancestry. However, early policies inaugurated by the adherents of Marxist socialism in the United States did not seem to take into account this specific condition.

For instance, there is Eugene V. Debs' famous declaration, uttered in 1912 as the presidential candidate of the Socialist Party, that socialism in America had "nothing special to offer" Black people: they were oppressed as all workers are oppressed under capitalism, and the basic nature of their oppression was economic, not racial.(3) The Socialist Party itself, splintered into reformist, centrist, and radical factions, failed to move beyond Debs' colorless formulation of the class struggle and did not effectively confront racism, at times surrendering to it, for example, as in the practice of maintaining segregated local chapters in the Deep South.(4)

From 1919, when the Socialist Party ruptured into several new organizations, to 1924, the main expression of the Party's concern with race centered around its affiliation with The Messenger, a Black radical magazine in Harlem edited by A. Philip Randolph and Chandler Owen.(5) Randolph and Owen enjoyed some success, the former polling over 200,000 votes as a Socialist Party candidate for state comptroller in 1920, but this effort did not initiate party work in the South where the bulk of Black people, despite increasing migration, still resided.(6) Nor did it change the Party's view of the race problem, perhaps best expressed by the 1912 resolution of the Tennessee Socialist Party's platform which declared that "'the question of race superiority' had been 'injected into the mind of the white wage-worker' only as a 'tactical method' of the 'capitalist class to keep workers divided on the economic field.'"(7)

This platform declaration and other statements like it are the source for the early pronouncements of American Marxism that racism is an epiphenomenal appendage of capitalism. It is a manipulable ruse created and used by the ruling class to divide workers. And since the existence of racism is not essential to the capitalist order, the white worker experiences and acts with a "false consciousness" when he defends racial privilege, and unwittingly, the very system which exploits him. This mechanical view of racism assumes great importance in the history of American Marxism's early perspective on race relations.

Out of the splintering of the Socialist Party in 1919 emerged the Communist Party (CP). In 1920, the Communist Party expressed this view of the race problem: "The racial expression of the Negro is simply the expression of his economic bondage and oppression, each intensifying the other. This complicates the problem, but does not alter its fundamental proletarian character."(8) And in 1925, William F. Dunne, speaking for the Party, attributed racial prejudice to the history of slavery and to the conscious policy of the capitalists of igniting and inflaming racial antagonism.(9) Though the Party's introduction, after 1928, of the colonial theme into its analysis of Black/white race relations represented a new slogan, much of the Party's subsequent history reveals an inability to critically engage the subject of racism with any long-range practical or theoretical success.(10)

Other radical voices in the Depression years of the 1930s continued the theoretical imaginative drought inherited from European social democracy and worsened by racist paternalism within the ranks of the radicals themselves.(11) Norman Thomas offered the Black man salvation if he would cast his lot with the Socialist Party, though he lamented that white workers were often won over by the "appeals to race prejudice" of the exploiting class.(12) And, Ernest Rice McKinney argued that, although capitalism will make concessions, the ultimate hope for Black workers was to become part of a racially-unified labor movement under the leadership of a revolutionary party, presumably his Workers Party. Only then could the "special problems" of Black folk stemming from their "double ... exploitation" (i.e., race and class) be seriously addressed.(13) McKinney's recognition of the "special problems" of Black people was an uncharacteristic observation for the period, but neither he nor Thomas confronted the material stake of the white working class in racism. Moreover, both writers rejected both the CP's colonial Black Belt position, according to which Black people in the South constituted a nation, and the nationalism of the Black petit bourgeoisie. In sum, however, their views were compatible with a mechanical interpretation of racism and its attendant effects.

This brief historical sketch of some of the earlier Marxist analyses of U.S. race relations serves to underscore the discussion of Marxist interpretations which have been presented since. In this latter group, some of which will be discussed below, major points of interpretation are discernible. (As mentioned, the term

"Marxist" is used to denote the tradition stemming from Marx.)

First, the division of society into classes which are socially contiguous and politically antipathetic is held to embody the fundamental reality of modern industrial society. The bourgeoisie, or owning and ruling class, and the proletariat, or working class, are the main classes, and the latter is exploited by the former. As adversaries in the quest for state power, their incessant conflict is the basis for the class struggle.

Second, the quest for state power as the basis of class struggle has as its goal the attainment of control over the means of production. The disposition of the control of production greatly affects social relations of production and superstructural phenomena such as ideology.

Finally, racism, as a superstructural phenomenon, is considered to be a product of capitalism. But, beyond this point, it is sometimes argued that racism has become "an independent force" with a life of its own, or, as with the older view already mentioned, that it is essentially a mechanical ideological quantum manipulated, created, and perpetuated by the ruling class itself.

Sub-groups of the Model

The last domain assumption outlined above will serve as the organizing principle for the separation of this model into two sub-groups. The first sub-group portrays the ideology of racial privilege as an inevitable product of capitalism; that is, racism becomes a specific ideological tool fashioned by the ruling class in order to achieve one of its main ends, the weakening of the working class as one group of workers is set against another. In the history of American Marxism, this view has a long tradition; we shall designate it the mechanical view.

Of more recent lineage is the view which holds that, despite its origins in the economic relations of American slavery, the racial ideology of privilege now demonstrates the capacity to influence significantly all social relations between racial groups, economic and non-economic. We shall designate the second sub-group by this view; for it, racism has become "an independent force." As we shall state in the conclusion of this chapter, we prefer the phrase "semi-autonomous force" since it better conveys the conviction of this second sub-group that, though it is directly exacerbated by the capitalist socioeconomic context, racism also calls upon its own injurious devices. This view must be carefully distinguished from the first sub-group (racial characteristics only) of the colonial model's view of racism, discussed in Chapter 3, which does not treat seriously the American capitalist order as the inescapable backdrop for the machinations of racism. We turn now to an examination of the first sub-group.

The Mechanical View

Perhaps the clearest expression of the mechanical view of racism is given by Oliver C. Cox in Caste, Class, and Race.(14) For Cox, racial prejudice is "the socio-attitudinal matrix supporting a calculated and determined effort of a white ruling class to keep some people or peoples of color and their resources exploitable."(15)

To this basic kernel of interpretation are added several other propositions. Exclusion serves the purpose of maintaining exploitability since "[t]o grant cultural parity is to eliminate the basis of intermarriage restrictions; and to permit intermarriage is to make cultural discrimination on the basis of race impossible."(16) Skin color, of itself, has no intrinsic meaning, and is rather a "symbol of relatively unlimited cultural opportunity" and this symbol retains its desirability only so long as the white racial group enjoys a dominant position; hence, "[t]he value of a white skin tends to depreciate directly with cultural advantage."(17) Racial conflict is a system-threatening phenomenon aimed at subverting the entire racial order and it is based on the fact that "...Negroes and whites in the United States stand toward each other in the relationship of subordination and superordination, a relationship implying suspended conflict."(18) The destructive force of this conflict is derived from the "economic content of racial prejudice."(19)

In the end, Cox finds that the race problem is a class problem or in his terminology, a "political-class" problem.(20) The rationalizations used by exploiters of labor have changed through various historical periods, with racial differences being heavily employed in the modern period.(21) The specific nature of the racial rationalization used and the social arrangements which attend it will depend on the "exploitative situation" of the white dominant group.(22) As for the problems which beset Black people, the author makes it clear that their only solution lies in Black people joining the white democratic proletarian movement to achieve socialist democracy.(23)

In this movement, Black people will be "auxiliary" and not leaders, since they tend to be "conservative" though they are "indeed more decidedly potentially communists than whites."(24) They will produce no hoped-for "great leader" because maintenance of friendly ties with the white dominant racial group tends to blunt criticism and aggressiveness; their great leader "will almost certainly" have to be a white man, especially since Black people are often mistrustful and impatient with their own leadership.(25)

These outlandish and patronizing views are a direct result of one of the author's central themes, _viz_., that assimilation is the principal social force active among the Black masses. This force acts in a "centrifugal" manner on the Black racial group, impelling its members outward into the larger society.(26) This insistence on the overwhelming importance of assimilation is tied to two other themes: a pathological view of Black culture, and a denial of the substance and possibilities of Black nationalism. Black folk have not been allowed to participate in the "civic pride" of the nation, by conscious design of the white ruling class, so that, as "a people without a culture peculiar to itself," they have constructed only a "truncated pattern" of the dominant culture.(27) Only those institutions are initiated and survive in the Black community to which Black people are denied access; such institutions and endeavors are reactions to racism. What remains of Black social life reflects "the planned cultural retardation" and "social degeneracy" of the Black masses, again a direct consequence of white ruling class policy. The resultant "spiritual and physical instability" and "dependence" of Black people make them "more easily exploitable."(28)

Being without a true culture, and possessed of a racial solidarity which is defensive, temporary, and evaporates as white reproach declines, Black people are not likely to generate or support nationalistic doctrines or leaders.(29) Any Black leader who espouses nationalism will not encourage a large, active following because the all-consuming assimilative urge of the Black masses makes an infertile ground on which to sustain such movements. The "destiny" of Black folk is "cultural and biological fusion with the larger American society" and in this they are "old Americans" responding like "most other American immigrants" to the "American cultural trait" of assimilation.(30)

The conclusions which Cox reaches about the nature of culture, the possibility of nationalism, and the prevalence of assimilation among Black people all hinge on his dichotomous approach to the United States. The North and the South represent "two nationalities" with the South occupying a subordinate position as a result of the Civil War.(31) Since that time, the proletariat of the North has advanced toward democracy by exercising the franchise while the proletariat of the South remains weak and divided by racial antagonism. The Southern ruling class, "aristocratic and fascist," knows very well that its power rests on its ability to sow and perpetuate race hatred.(32) The ruling class of the North is no less manipulative in regard to this matter, but the constraints of its international position and the unwelcome strength of organized labor make it more amenable to propagandistic use of religion and other social values in an attempt to picture its interests as if they were those of all citizens.(33) When Cox discusses race relations, he is almost exclusively concerned with the South, while the North recedes in importance as a place where Black folk have already been carried closer toward "social equality" by "the stronger white proletariat."(34) In fact, Cox's entire presentation of a class anslysis of American society is tilted by this one-sided regional approach: labor unions and their policies on racial matters are rarely reviewed while whole sections and chapters are devoted to an exegetical critique of the function of race etiquette, the role of poor whites in racial conflict, the emphasis on sex in race relations, and so on as these matters involve race relations, especially in their manifestation in the South.(35)

Of course, the author's concentration on the South is understandable as the natural consequence of his attempt to criticize the caste school of race relations theory. Many of the works by authors in this mode employed research done in the South in the construction of their arguments.(36) Cox insists that these social scientists have confused the nature of caste relations with that of race relations by making "incommensurate arrays" between caste and such social phenomena as racial etiquette, hypergamy, endogamy, passing, socially accepted division of occupations, and negative intermarriage sanctions. He maintains that caste relations are not racial in origin nor based on color, but rather are based on the desire of the caste to protect its divinely-ordained cultural heritage, or dharma. Amalgamation does not affect the relations between castes since they are based on culture not race, but it does significantly alter the relations between races.(37)

The principal weakness of Cox's analysis of the caste system appears to be the static, unchanging quality which he imputes to it.(38) This is quite ironic since one of the major points that he raises in criticizing the caste school of race relations analysis is their own imputation of moral sanction, stasis, and social equilibrium to a situation fraught with the perils of conflict, pathological psychological maladjustment, and impending crises.(39) One author whose work Cox dismisses retorts that the book's premise rests on a specious definition of caste which incorrectly narrows its application to the pre-British colonial Hindu society of India.(40) Notwithstanding this charge, later treatments of the caste system of India do portray it in somewhat livelier terms than those chosen by Cox.(41)

However, Cox steadfastly maintained that the caste school of race relations analysis never demonstrated that caste and race are cognate social systems which produce commensurate experiences.(42) But, granted this point, the author's own conception of race relations remains marred by problematic issues.

Critics often contend that Cox leaves no room for the functioning of social psychology, here in the form of racism, in any autonomous way. A "real Marxist" approach "must see the whole configuration of the Negro problem in the United States -- the socio-economic basis and the superstructural rationalizations -- psychological and ideological."(43) Liberal critics are usually content to point to the ironic parallel between a Marxist who belittles race and conservative or liberal ethnic analysts of race relations who do the same.(44)

The basis of such criticism is found in the excessively mechanical view of racism which Cox presents. In an obverse corollary of some colonial analysts' view which dismisses or minimizes the differential access of the colonizing population to the rewards of racism, Cox addresses only those rewards, principally economic, which are commanded by the ruling class and fails to consider any others. The result is that he is unable to account for the material stake in racism held by white workers, and the general white populace.(45) To this principal error must be added another of equal severity: a distorted view of Black culture and the denial of Black nationalism. Nowhere is Cox more inaccurate or inexplicably unattentive to historical data than in his summary dismissal of nationalism among Black people. The historical significance of such figures as Henry MacNeil Turner, Martin R. Delaney, Benjamin 'Pap'

Singleton, Henry Highland Garnet, and Marcus Garvey is apparently completely lost to him.(46) And, by taking a position which is in essential agreement with the "Frazierian tradition," Cox supports this denial of nationalism on the contention that no distinctive group life survived slavery which could become the basis for nationalist movements.(47) The possibilities of Black culture, and the meaning of racism for the development of that culture, are negated and this prevents the author from seeing the potential for popularly-demanded social change which inheres in the relationship between capitalist exploitation and cultural oppression.(48)

Both the failure to account for the material interest of the majority of the superordinate racial group, and the denial of Black culture and Black nationalism constitute serious errors which may be traced to the mechanical view of racism which is at the heart of Cox's formulation of a theory of race relations. But, though these flaws impair the utility of his model, Cox still makes an essential contribution. The social phenomena of modern race relations are located squarely in the political economy of capitalism, linked to two fundamental concepts: exploitation and power. Racial groups are "power groups" which "stand culturally or racially as potential or actual antagonists." As power groups, "races are defined by intergroup conflict" and relations between these groups harbor "latent conflict attitudes" which on the part of the dominant group are always at bottom, defensive rationalizations. The differences in power between the superordinate and subordinate groups, expressed as the antagonism of a "latent power-group relationship," tend to divide the society vertically in two.(49) What remains to be accomplished is the combination of Cox's understanding of the centrality of capitalist exploitation in the initiation and maintenance of modern racial prejudice with a more general theoretical account of the ways in which this phenomenon actuates and has penetrated the social psychological and ideological realm of modern society.

A more recent expression of the mechanical view of U.S. racism is represented by the next statement. Though Victor Perlo's Economics of Racism U.S.A. raises issues which augment economic considerations, his discussion of American race relations ultimately does not sustain this broader approach.(50)

As regards this broader context, Perlo develops a notion of the "special needs" of Black people based on the greater degree of exploitation from which they suffer. The concept of "super-exploitation," defined as the substandard wage rate paid Black labor, is introduced as support for this contribution.(51) But, no reference to the possible colonial nature of Black oppression is made, and the subject of culture is only fleetingly presented.(52)

Instead, Perlo concentrates on discussing the economic base for racism. Noting that the Black/white median family income ratio exhibits a cyclical tendency and does not generally exceed the 50-55% range (1945-73), he attributes this low primary index of standard of living among Black people to economic differentials which operate in the labor market. Four exploitative mechanisms, the first two being most important, express this differentiation: differential employment and promotion, differential pay rates, differential access to work and consequent rates of unemployment, and differential property ownership and receipt of property income.(53) The net effect of this differentiation is to concentrate Black workers in lower paying jobs and industries. When this effect is coupled with "super unemployment," i.e., the persistently higher rates of unemployment which Black people suffer based on the "hidden unemployment" of officially uncounted employable teenagers, part-time workers, and the contingent labor force of those seeking work but unable to find it, the result is the relegation of the Black masses to "the semi-permanent reserve army of the unemployed."(54) Thus, although Black people are overwhelmingly members of the working class, they receive less per capita income for their labor and are therefore more dependent on transfer payments, i.e., socially provided income, which, in effect, subsidizes their exploitation.(55)

Perlo asserts capitalist responsibility for racial oppression and subordination because white capitalists can make greater profits from the lower wage rates paid to Black workers, and can also use these wage rates as a depressant on the cost of white labor. Capitalism itself is held to have produced racism, and the economic advantage which capitalists command through racial discrimination is adjudged the prime social force in the maintenance and perpetuation of racism.(56) Perlo's justification for the asserted causal link confines itself to economic data.

Moreover, the role of white workers, and of the white population in general, in the maintenance and perpetuation of racism is consistently minimized. Perlo concedes that white workers are infected with racist attitudes and behavior, and that they enjoy material advantage from such predispositions, but, in his assessment, they appear as a smaller ancillary social force in a society dominated by the power of capitalism.(57)

Thus, Perlo's analysis of racism inclines toward a mechanical view, especially since exclusion is treated solely as a function of the capitalist class, while the role of the white proletariat is largely ignored. And although the author's notion of the "special needs" of the Black community promises to mitigate this mechanical approach, precisely because it recognizes that racism has indeed wrought a special oppression on Afro-Americans, it fails to do so as a consequence of the one-sided economic representation of those needs. Had Perlo considered the substance of those needs more extensively, especially as regards culture, the need of the Black community to confront and defeat the racism of the white proletariat and professional strata, in addition to that of the ruling class, would have become apparent.

Moreover, Perlo's failure to broaden the notion of "special needs" to include culture appears paradoxical in the light of his discussion of monopoly capital's decision "to create a layer of Black capitalists under its control and loyal to it."(58) The cultural distortion which results from this colonial strategy is not analyzed, and this deficiency, in turn, results from the absence of any conception of institutional racism in Perlo's work. Such a conception certainly would analyze, in addition to the economic sphere, the social and cultural institutions in which this "layer" (or buffer group) would operate.(59)

In sum, though Perlo's model of race relations is a notable improvement in certain particulars over earlier Marxist versions, the problem of explaining racism beyond immediate economic advantage remains unaddressed. Though Perlo recognizes the fact of Black leadership in recent social and proletarian struggles, this acknowledgment is reduced in significance by his uneven portrayal of the sources of racism which that leadership must overcome.(60) It is as if the material stake in racist economic patterns which Perlo himself uncovers, together with the cultural norms and roles of racist subordination and oppression which he does not discuss, do not constitute the social basis in reality for the real acts of racism committed by white workers; instead, Perlo attempts, for the most part, to absolve them.(61) This solution is very unlikely to produce an analysis of racism, at the personal and structural level, which is able to encompass its totality, comprehend its workings, and envision the circumstances for its demise.

A Transition

The problems in the analysis of racism which the work of Cox and Perlo manifests were often accompanied, in other Marxist interpretations, by newer ideas on this subject. This mix of old and new views tends to give these other statements a transitional character, since they do not entirely adopt a mechanical view of racism, yet only implicitly offer another formulation. Paul M. Sweezy's The Theory of Capitalist Development, written in 1942, may be taken as an example of such a transitional statement.(62)

Writing in the shadow of fascism in Europe, Sweezy raises the subject of racism as part of his discussion of modern imperialist societies. Curiously, however, although Sweezy is willing to concede an "expansionist dynamic" all its own to militarism, and even concedes that the nationalist sentiments of the masses are not "artificial," a similar concession is not made in regards to racism.(63) Sweezy asserts that all three of these social ideologies -- i.e., militarism, nationalism, and racism -- become important under the imperialist stage of capitalism, but only racism is discussed in somewhat mechanical terms. Sweezy's treatment of racism is further extended, but in a manner which contradicts a mechanical approach, by his statements that racism is "not novel" under imperialism and that racial discrimination offers "substantial material rewards" to portions of the dominant racial group: the first statement would seem to cast doubt on the causal nexus between capitalism and racism, while the second attests to the basis for widespread popular support and exclusionary racial systems and ideologies.(64)

Moreover, Sweezy's discussion raises a difficult question concerning the ideological nature of racism: Is racism "an independent social force," possessed of its own dynamic and capable of independently directing social action? Because of its ability to promote and secure preferential access to production and the attendant material values and because of the virtually limitless social-psychological reservoir of ego-gratifying invidious spiritual values which it is able to fill and to tap, racism lends itself to such a portrayal. And the testimony of perceptive members of subordinated racial groups about the effects of racist exclusion on their institutions and cultures corroborates the potency of this destructive social force.(65) However, the independent force conception of racism often tends to blur the relationship between this phenomenon and capitalist exploitation, picturing the latter as secondary or nonoperative, and it concedes a permanence to "human nature" and irrationality which ultimately may be very misleading.

The Independent Force

The difficulties in Sweezy's transitional statement point to the need for a clearer understanding of the non-material factors responsible for racism. It is particularly with regard to social psychology and the social relations between dominant and oppressed groups that these factors must be elaborated. More recent statements from the Marxist tradition have attempted this task.

Three such statements specifically comprise our representatives of the second sub-group in the Marxist model. Their common thread is a view of racism that does not confine it solely to the realm of economic calculations; it becomes a social force with disastrous consequences, and its economic and non-economic bases are sought. In the first statement, by Baran and Sweezy, a social psychological treatment of racism is extended from a Marxist analysis of the American political economy. Their aim is to demonstrate the connection between racism and its contemporary historical context. In the second and third statements, both by worker-cum-revolutionary theoretician James Boggs, the appropriate programmatic framework for a Marxist view of U.S. race relations is the central topic of discussion. We begin with the work of Baran and Sweezy.

A somewhat inferential statement of the independent force notion of racism is found in Paul A. Baran and Paul M. Sweezy, Monopoly Capital.(66) The problem of race relations for the U.S. ruling class, the authors assert, is one over which they do not "have the power to shape and control...."(67)

The authors reach this conclusion by way of an analysis of three factors which, under monopoly capitalism, are responsible for the position of "permanent immigrants" which the majority of Black people occupy: "a formidable array of private interests"; "socio-psychological pressures generated by monopoly capitalist society"; and, the declining demand for unskilled labor. These factors operate in such a way that "pariah group" status and increasingly permanent unemployment among Black folk are assured.(68)

Baran and Sweezy provide a definition of Black people as "a substantial segment of the urban working class," and the documentary evidence presented about their conditions of living tends to deal with some aspect of production, e.g., unemployment statistics, government employees by race.(69) Further, they argue that what has been often lauded as a revolutionary breakthrough toward equality for Afro-Americans is really nothing more than the step from the bottom of "the ... agricultural ladder" to the bottom of "the urban-industrial ladder" via migration, with the consequent incremental rise in standard of living. In both situations, and particularly in the last-named which has come to predominate since 1960, Black people are trapped at the bottom.(70)

What traps them are, of course, the three factors already mentioned, the first and third of which reflect the character of the exploitation of this group. The second factor, social-psychological impulses, is linked to an exacerbation of "*existing* racial prejudices" (emphasis added) and also to the basic class framework of monopoly capitalism through the notion of "an irregular and unstable 'status hierarchy.'"(71)

Baran and Sweezy state that monopoly capitalism did not create racism, though capitalism did in its earlier colonialist stage as a justificatory ideology for the exploitation of African and indigenous New World labor.(72) From this predominantly economic view of the genesis of racism, they give a much more flexible account of its current function in monopoly capitalist society since, with the augmentation of the two class framework by numerous intermediary "social strata and status groups, largely determined by occupation and income," racial prejudice now serves as the litmus test for the invidious comparisons of status which individuals and status groups are constantly making, and are conditioned to make.(73) Presumably, the ruling class does not have to tell the white populace to make such comparisons and act on them since the mythology of social mobility has already become a popular shibboleth. However, the authors do not deal with this mythology and its exact workings are left unstated. The picture which emerges, then, of modern day racism in the United States is of a social-psychological complex of attitudes designed to heighten status superiority in relation to "a special pariah group ... which acts as a kind of lightning rod for the frustrations and hostilities of all the higher groups...," attitudes which produce gratification and which respond to "a deep-rooted psychological need" to avoid status envy of those above by heaping contempt on those below.(74)

Baran and Sweezy argue that these attitudes, as racial prejudice, have assumed an autonomous ideological existence in much the same manner as the constraints generated by the inherent contradictions of monopoly capitalism prevent its rational absorption of the economic surplus which it produces. Excess capacity, the relentless pursuit of profitability, the changed nature of technological innovation from investment stimulant to profit maximizer, and the changed nature of competition itself under monopoly, all produce a normal tendency toward stagnation which are not controvertible by the conscious will of the ruling class.(75) Just as the capitalists cannot solve the problems of investment and utilization of an ever-growing surplus, neither can they solve the race problem, especially as it involves those areas (e.g., housing, private employment) which impinge on these structural difficulties.(76) Thus, an independent ideological status is implied for racism by the authors' treatment.

This imputation of the inability on the part of the ruling class to manipulate the race problem is contradicted by the authors' own discussion of just such an attempt to control: the strategy of tokenism. The apparent inconsistency is explained by referring to two spheres of social action, one "administrative" and juridical, in which the corporate rulers have power, and another, apparently more amorphous and less cohesive, in which their power is either diluted or negated entirely.(77)

The trouble with the conception of race relations put forward by Baran and Sweezy, in this particular and in general, concerns the vagueness with which the links between capitalist exploitation and racism are argued. Unlike other chapters in the book which draw on a wealth of critically supportive materials, the authors seem content here to rest their case on minimally-documented assertions: The most glaring example is their failure to specify the types and amounts of rewards which white workers (and whites in general) receive from racism.(78) By not elaborating the material stake of the white superordinate group, the case for the autonomous ideological nature of racism is weakened; this also gives the discussion of the social psychology of racism a one-sided appearance. The discussion of these subjects seems impressionistic and sketchy.

This failure to depict in detail the particular economic relationships which buttress and sustain racial subjugation is compounded by the absence of any conception of institutional racism. Certainly, a consideration of the gain in profits and savings on wage bills that accrue to capitalists because of the operation of exclusionary social and job-related practices would strengthen the verification of the existence of a set of stable, exploitative social relations, encompassing social, economic, and political phenomena, which promote racial subordination and oppression. But Baran and Sweezy do not make such calculations, leaving their conception of racism with the salience of social-psychological factors while little detailed attention is given to an accounting of material interests. Consequently, their conception of racism is partial, tending to forego the task of presenting a systematic formulation of the manner in which material and social-psychological factors are integrated in the maintenance of racism, and thereby eschewing the possibility of presenting a useful political economic model of institutional racism.

Perhaps Baran and Sweezy's conception of racism may be considered an improvement over that of Cox precisely because they are willing to raise the question of the importance of the non-material side of this phenomenon. But, as pointed out above, their development of this aspect is too sketchy and unspecific about the relation of non-material to material factors in order to provide a suitably integrated model. The conceptions of Cox, and of Baran and Sweezy, suggest theoretical statements which address separately each side of the phenomenon, material and non-material, but which collectively still leave the job of theoretical synthesis ahead.

Still, there are important departures from early Marxist perspectives on race relations contained in Baran and Sweezy's work. The automatic extirpation of racist attitudes and beliefs is no longer considered an immediate consequence of the end of capitalist exploitation. Though white racial prejudice is "a unique ... transitory historical phenomenon," its eradication, even in a socialist society, will probably take "decades rather than months or years," as part of a "difficult and protracted process."(79) And, in a refocusing of Marx, the authors find that:

> The revolutionary initiative against capitalism, which in Marx's day belonged to the proletariat in the advanced countries, has passed into the hands of the impoverished masses in the underdeveloped countries who are struggling to free themselves from imperialist domination and exploitation.(80)

This acknowledgment, in an age of Third World decolonization, formal independence, and revolution, has an historical resonance with the development of economic, political, and social processes that earlier Marxist treatments lack (such as that of Cox, written at a time when most of Africa was still formally colonial, and Latin America and Asia were European "spheres of influence"; but written also on the eve of the Chinese Revolution).

Indeed, the inadequacy of Marxist approaches to race relations, based on this lack of historical resonance, has led to sharp criticism. Critics most often cite Marx and Engels' own racism, and the failure of Marxism to develop specific postulates regarding the particularity of Black (and Third World) oppression or to recognize this particularity in the realm of culture.(81) This last criticism represents a theoretical lacuna which is increasingly being addressed in the works of those concerned with a Marxist perspective on race relations. For example, Harold M. Baron maintains that slavery necessitated the development of a whole "culture of control" replete with "political and cultural imperatives" which, as institutional racism, ensures the exclusion, subordination, and exploitation of the Black masses.(82) And Robert L. Allen finds racism to be "...an ideology ... perfectly capable of playing at least a semi-independent role in subsequent social developments."(83) A further illustration of efforts to strengthen the ability of Marxism to comprehend racial oppression is found in the work of James Boggs.

Boggs is especially critical of the failure of American Marxists to recognize the fundamental importance of racial antagonism in the light of the specific development of American capitalism and the changed nature of labor especially since World War II. In *The American Revolution*, he points out that changes in production have diminished the size of the production work force.(84)

These changes in production, stemming from automation and cybernation, are creating an ever increasing mass of unemployed workers and the impossibility of their absorption. As this process spreads, social conflict will increasingly revolve around jobholders versus the jobless, since the social costs of maintaining a large and growing dependent human mass of unemployed and unemployables will generate friction and resentment. This conflict ultimately is predicated on the realization of the end of forced socially necessary labor which technology now makes possible for the first time in human history. With this realization, American society stands poised on the verge of an "Age of Abundance."(85)

However, Boggs maintains that organized labor will not promote this realization because its very existence depends on the defense of the older mode of production. Its interests coalesce with those of the capitalist in maintaining the old system, but instead of profits organized labor is concerned to protect its jobs, its escalator clauses, and its pension plans. And, most important, organized labor (especially the craft labor unions) will not countenance any change in the peculiar form of social mobility by which it arrived at its preferred status, *viz.*, climbing over the backs of Black people first and all other newly arrived immigrants.(86)

But it is upon Black people, according to Boggs, that leadership of the coming social revolution has devolved precisely because "the strength of their cause and its power to shake up the social structure of the nation comes from the fact that in the Negro struggle all the questions of human rights and human relationships are posed." Taking the initiative since 1960, Black folk have developed a momentum which surpasses the listless labor movement and qualifies them as "the one revolutionary force dominating the American social scene."(87) Black oppression has never been solely a matter of race, involving instead race, class, and nation. It has been made to appear solely a race question by the pivotal role of exclusion, especially after the Civil War. The initial division of the working class during the American colonial period was ratified by the defeat of Reconstruction and this separation has imparted to the Black struggle its "distinctive revolutionary character." American Marxists often fail to see this because of their refusal to recognize the special status of Black workers as workers and the necessity of leadership which flows from this position.(88)

In a later work, Boggs expands his criticism of American Marxism.(89) The mechanical view of racism which it often propounds obscures the fact that white workers have always formed, as a race, a class above Black people. The specific mode of formation of the American proletariat gave white workers an economic and social stake in the defense of racial privilege, something undertaken and maintained without false consciousness.(90) The mechanical view cannot see this stake; and because it cannot, abstract slogans of labor solidarity have been promulgated, ignoring the reality of racism as a social force. Unable to see this social force, Marxists likewise have been unwilling to assess the growing counter-revolutionary character of white labor and its direct relationship with the social disquietude resulting from recent Black efforts at irreparably damaging the racial status quo. In Boggs' opinion, until Marxist theory advances to meet the particularities of the American class struggle, its analysis will continue to be incorrect and unproductive.(91)

Boggs himself begins the task of making the necessary reformulation of hypotheses so that Marxist theory derives greater explanatory power from historical perspective. The historical particularity of the class struggle in the United States derives from the role in production assigned to Black people as a solution to the problem of the changing organic composition of capital, i.e., the need of capitalists to counteract the falling rate of profit generated by existing capital through investment in cheap human labor power.(92) The human exploitation inherent in capitalism confined Afro-Americans to "capitalist semi-colonialism" under slavery and spawned a racist ideology of justification. This ideology, pervading every segment and institution of American society, went on to acquire "a dynamic of its own." Later, after slavery, colonial status continued as Black people were assigned "the scavenger role" in production, in which they continue today.(93) In this role, they form an "under-class" whose experience is directly analogous to the colonial peoples of the world who form a "world underclass," exploited and racially subjugated.(94) Black communities are underdeveloped as a direct consequence of capitalist development, though their colonial experience differs from the external phenomenon because internal underdevelopment results from an acute exhaustion of human resources in the process of industrialization, not from the absence of technology and industry as in the Third World abroad. Further, the presence of the colonized <u>within</u> the boundaries of the oppressing nation makes for a complexity not found in other more classic situations.(95)

Boggs continues by pointing out that, as a consequence of the semi-colonial nature of Black labor, a "horizontal platform" was created ensuring all members of the superordinate racial group the benefits of racial privilege. For white workers, this has meant a pattern of social mobility always dependent on "a reserve army of black labor to scavenge the dirty, unskilled jobs in the fields and sweatshops." This is the true meaning of

America's labor history.(96) For white capitalists, the super-exploitation of Black labor has been the principal means whereby surplus profits could be obtained in order to enlarge "the total social capital available for modernization" and maintain the value of existing capital.(97)

The foregoing analysis leads Boggs to conclude that the coming revolution in America must center on "putting politics in command," since historical precedents set in underdeveloped countries are untenable.(98) And, the central political question, capable of revolutionizing the entire American social system, is the struggle for Black Power. This phenomenon, being an antithetical ideological response to the development of American capitalism, manifests itself in the growing strategic concentration of Black people in the nation's cities. Once a political program is drawn up around the grievances and needs of "[t]he people at the very bottom of the Black community..." and is enacted by a leadership organization fighting for community control, Black Power will advance the struggle for power from the "liberated areas" of Black communities to the cities and finally to the national government itself.(99) Black people are now "the only revolutionary social force at this stage" in American history and their leadership of a struggle for national power stems from the fact that their survival as workers displaced by technology and their hopes for counteracting the imposed underdevelopment of their communities can only be realized with the creation of a new society which overturns the racial domination ingrained in all existing institutions.(100)

Boggs' model of race relations centers on exploitation, with the derivative concept of super-exploitation being introduced but not defined. Conflict and exclusion also are accorded central theoretical importance since the first expresses the system-threatening nature of the Black movement and the second illuminates the specific configuration of the American class struggle and its special effect on Black labor.(101) Power receives detailed attention, as formulation of the "scientific concept of Black power" and as the fundamental calibrator of race relations. The aspect of latency is recognized in the assertion of the need for "parallel hierarchies" of social control in the Black community, created through mass struggle and addressed to Black social needs.(102) All of these concepts are elaborated within the framework of the development of American capitalism.

Boggs' use of the colonial theme to describe Black oppression, especially as regards the buffer group, is somewhat consonant with the opinions of the colonial model. He even asserts that a "war of national liberation" will be necessary in order to achieve Black freedom. But the subject of culture receives far too little attention, leaving his colonial descriptions lopsidedly grounded on racial expressions of class conflict.(103)

Similarly, though the author pronounces both white capitalist and white worker guilty of racism, the incessant focus on the cupidity, short-sightedness and counter-revolutionariness of white labor tends to obscure the role of white capital; the latter's specific material interests (e.g., lowered wage bill) and levers of power (e.g., hiring practices) are not elaborated beyond the assertion already noted above.(104) Thus, although Boggs has progressed a great distance from early Marxist treatments of race relations, his analysis still wants a completeness, a detailed specification, of the relationships uncovered and their interaction. His discussion of the role of white allies is an analytic step in this direction, but the effort must be extended.(105)

Another criticism which must be raised concerns the location of the development of Black Power in the cities. This strategy is not cognizant of the many sizeable obstacles confronting the construction of this ideological force; and, Boggs' mention of federal assistance in regards to Southern cooperative land development plans strikes a curious note indeed.(106) The city may be <u>the</u> battleground, but it remains here a battleground whose topography is only dimly perceived.

What emerges from Boggs' work, especially in the later book, is a progression toward a colonial perspective on race relations without using some of its key propositions, at the same time that a class analysis in racial terms is advanced.(107) Hence, culture, as pointed out, is not extensively discussed nor is any consideration given to self-determination or the distinguishing characteristics of the Black semi-colony, other than its potential for revolutionary leadership. Other leftists, particularly Black Marxists, have been more attentive to the full implications of the colonial view.(108)

Conclusion

The concept of exploitation dominates the theoretical panoply with which Marxist theory confronts human society. Armed with this polemical lance, many additional concepts -- e.g., alienation, ruling ideas, class -- are adduced in support of Marxism's critical thrust. The interaction of the economic and non-economic aspects of a social order comprises the analytic base from which Marxism begins its study of society.

However, the most problematical feature of a Marxist interpretation of social reality, given the ultimate primacy which it assigns to materiality, becomes the correct determination of the balance between material and non-material factors in a given social or historical situation and of the directional tendencies of this dialectic. The works reviewed in this chapter suggest that when American Marxism focuses its attention on race relations, the resultant discourses too often neglect the impact of non-economic factors on materially exploitive social relationships.

The treatment of exclusion illustrates these neglected factors. It is either pictured as an overwhelmingly economic phenomenon responsive to capitalist market decisions (Cox, Perlo), or as on a many-sided phenomenon whose social and cultural aspects, though acknowledged, are not adequately elaborated or understood (Baran and Sweezy, Boggs). In the first case, the non-economic aspects of culture appear only as capitalist culture; in the second case, the oppositional nature of the subordinated group's reaction to capitalist culture's racial oppression, though granted the semblance of legitimacy, is nonetheless denied the status of a culture in its own right. Both views are congruent with the Marxist domain assumption of the assimilation of elements of bourgeois culture to the creation of proletarian culture, which assumption, in turn, reflects Marxism's historical roots in cultural evolutionism.(109) But neither view moves toward an understanding of the function of exclusion in non-economic social realms nor of its fundamental responsibility for creating the conditions for the emergence of a culture of struggle among the racially oppressed.

Since the cultural function of exclusion is not often recognized, it becomes possible to argue (as does Cox) that the superordinate racial group does not maintain an interest in racial oppression except so far as its dominant members are concerned. Or, one can argue (as does Perlo) that, even granted the material stake in the racial status quo that all members of the superordinate racial group have, nevertheless their racial prejudices do not stem from genuinely felt cultural norms which defend racial privilege but rather from the conscious machinations of a handful of this group. Though other lines of analysis are possible within this context (e.g., Baran and Sweezy's social-psychological approach), none of them promises to provide a full accounting of the function of exclusion, especially in its cultural aspects. Only the interpretation of exclusion offered by Boggs begins to approach this subject in a comprehensive manner.

Moreover, because American Marxists, as evidenced here, have only partially understood the role of exclusion in the perpetuation of racism under capitalism, they have also been unable to deal successfully with the subject of Black nationalism. The particularity of American historical experience, which is confirmed by the existence of exclusion on the basis of race in matters of governmental philosophy, social norms, political relationships, and economic pursuits from the earliest days of the republic, has been slighted in preference for the more or less mechanical application of theoretical precepts developed in European circumstances. To this preference must be added the outright racism or concessions made to racism of Marxist theorists which have further vitiated Marxist approaches to Black nationalism in particular and to race relations in general. The result has been an often disastrous combination of doctrinaire dogmatism and ill-disguised paternalism.

In order for Marxism to comprehend the nature of race relations in twentieth-century industrial societies, it must turn to the subject of culture. The study of the contradictory development of a culture of struggle among the subordinate racial group in contradistinction to the culture of oppression of the dominant racial group, both developed within the historico-social context of capitalism, is the only route toward a correct assessment of the relationship of exclusion to capitalist exploitation.

The structural critique of American capitalist society which Marxist analysts develop provides an historical context within which to place a theoretical statement on race relations. The concepts of exploitation, conflict, and power are assigned central explanatory positions with the first concept being invoked as the cause of racial subordination, and the second and third as the social mechanisms by which this subordination is maintained. But because exclusion is conceptually delimited in the sphere of economic relations, the Marxist structural critique of the American context does not provide a successfully integrated theoretical model of how the actual dynamics of capitalist race relations work based on the interaction of economic variables such as exploitation and super-exploitation with non-economic variables such as exclusion, subordination, and culture. It is the relative inattention to the special nature of these non-economic variables, as reflected in the fact that none of the works considered here offers an explicit formal conception of institutional racism, that hampers the Marxist perspective on race relations.

This perspective is only likely to promote clarity in the theoretical comprehension of race relations once the non-economic variables are fully incorporated. "The independent force" conception of racism offers some possibility of considering superordinate group defense of racial privilege beyond economic calculation, but this approach does not appear to enjoy wide acceptance in Marxist writings (only Baran and Sweezy, and Boggs, of those examined here, employ it). Indeed, this notion is much more prevalent in a competing paradigm, the colonial model.

But some proponents of the colonial model who are receptive to the independent force notion (e.g., Blauner) are often content with only a cursory examination of capitalist political economy. It is here that the Marxist model enjoys a great potential advantage, since a skillful explication of U.S. race relations from its premises ought to be able to incorporate this more comprehensive view of racism into its already powerful set of economic critiques.

Once accomplished, this synthesis would extend Marxism's transitional view of human nature so that racism would be considered an "independent," or semi-autonomous, social force only under the proviso of two negative sociological conditions, the first a necessary condition and the second, a sufficient and fulfilling one: first, that capitalist exploitation continue unabated and structurally unaltered, especially by attempts to replace it with a non-exploitative political economy; and, second, that no large-scale, prolonged, intense campaign be launched to root out all traces of racist practices and ideology in the cultural, political, social, national, and international spheres of life of the people. These two conditions correspond to the domain assumptions of Marxism which, in the first instance, asserts the indispensability of socialist revolution for true human emancipation, and in the second, promulgates the standard of genuine democratic relations between people as the most powerful antidote to the poisonous practices and ideologies of the past.

Thus, only in so far as these two negative conditions are not controverted would racism be considered an independent social force free to roam the ideological contours of its milieu which is, in turn, bounded by certain socio-historical limits. Any move toward the negation of these two conditions as far as racism and its attendant effects are concerned should demonstrate, in Ernest Kaiser's words, that:

> The personality pattern is not immutable human nature at all. It is almost completely the complex end product of all the shaping social influences -- economic and superstructural (i.e., cultural). That is why philosophic materialists and sociologists are correct when they insist upon thorough social change in the long run knowing that psychological change will follow inevitably in its wake. That is why ... [it] is basically correct [to emphasize] socialism as the eventual way out of the capitalist morass and jungle of Jim-crow, cruelty, cynicism, and exploitation of workers, Negro and white.(110)

Notes

1. See "Karl Marx and the Negro," *The Crisis*, 40 (March 1933), pp. 55-56.

2. W. E. B. DuBois, "Marxism and the Negro Problem," *The Crisis*, 40 (May 1933), pp. 103-104, 118.

3. Quoted in Sterling D. Spero and Abram L. Harris, *The Black Worker: The Negro and the Labor Movement* (New York: Atheneum, 1972) (originally published, 1931), p. 405.

4. S. M. Miller, "The Socialist Party and the Negro, 1901-20," *Journal of Negro History*, 56 (July 1971), pp. 220-229.

5. Spero and Harris, *The Black Worker*, p. 411.

6. James Weinstein, *The Decline of American Socialism: 1912-1925* (New York: Random House, 1967), pp. 75n, 73-74; Spero and Harris, *The Black Worker*, p. 407; Harold Cruse, *The Crisis of the Negro Intellectual* (New York: William Morrow, 1967), pp. 40-43.

7. Quoted in Weinstein, *The Decline of American Socialism*, p. 69.

8. Quoted in Wilson Record, *The Negro and the Communist Party* (New York: Atheneum, 1971) (originally published, 1951), pp. 21-22.

9. Record, *The Negro and the Communist Party*, pp. 27, 318n.

10. Record, *The Negro and the Communist Party*, pp. 54-119; Robert L. Allen, *Reluctant Reformers: Racism and Social Reform Movements in the United States* (Garden City, New York: Doubleday, 1975), pp. 227-238.

11. Allen, *Reluctant Reformers*, pp. 218-222; Cruse, *The Crisis of the Negro Intellectual*, pp. 144-146, 147-170.

12. Norman Thomas, "The Socialist's Way Out for the Negro," Journal of Negro Education, 5 (January 1936), pp. 100-104.

13. Ernest Rice McKinney, "The Workers Party's Way Out for the Negro," Journal of Negro Education, 5 (January 1936), pp. 96-99.

14. Oliver C. Cox, Caste, Class, and Race: A Study in Social Dynamics (New York: Monthly Review Press, 1959) (originally published, 1948).

15. Cox, p. 475.

16. Cox, p. 388.

17. Cox, p. 387.

18. Cox, p. 431.

19. Cox, p. 475.

20. Cox, pp. 333, 485-486; in Chapter 10, pp. 153-173, Cox outlines his definition of a "political class" as a conscious, organized, antagonistic social entity geared to conflict over state power in distinction to the "social class," a purely conceptual sociological convention used to describe part of a cooperative status system that is unorganized, conscious only of its status, and complementary and supportive to other parts of the status system.

21. Cox, pp. 486-487.

22. Cox, p. 351.

23. Cox, pp. 571-575.

24. Cox, pp. 571, 574, 582.

25. Cox, pp. 572-573, 581-582.

26. Cox, pp. 403, 452-454, 545, 568, 571.

27. Cox, pp. 368-369, 569; it now becomes clear why Cox never touches on the subject of Black culture in his often brilliant critique of Myrdal's An American Dilemma: In essence, Cox agrees with Myrdal's pathological view. See Myrdal's position in An American Dilemma (New York: Random House), vol. 2, Chs. 43, 44, pp. 927-994. The critique by Cox appears in Caste, Class, and Race, pp. 504-544.

28. Cox, pp. 369, 381-382.

29. Cox, pp. 403, 453, 545-546.

30. Cox, pp. 545-546, 571, 572.

31. Cox, pp. 403-404; incidentally, the author, true to his mechanical and implied epiphenomenal view of racism, dismisses the question of slavery in the causal skein of the Civil War since it was "merely" a part of other essential conditions which sparked the conflict.

32. Cox, pp. 569-570, 576, 577.

33. Cox, pp. 254-255, 256, 277-278, 279, 281.

34. Cox, p. 570.

35. A ten-page discussion of organized labor may be found in Cox, pp. 277-278, 204-212. The other subjects here mentioned are treated extensively in the critique of Myrdal already referred to (see n. 27 above) and elsewhere in the book.

36. Cox, pp. xv-xvi; of the seven works on race relations cited on p. xvi as being indispensable, six deal with the South in terms of caste analysis.

37. Cox, pp. 13, 54, 55-57, 80, 93-96, 424, 447-450.

38. The discussions provided of caste occupation and of outcasting typify this problem; see Cox, pp. 438-441, 459-461.

39. Cox, pp. 495-496, 504.

40. Everett C. Hughes, review of Caste, Class, and Race in Phylon, 9 (1948), pp. 66-68.

41. See, for example, Willian and Charlotte Wiser, Behind Mud Walls: 1930-1960 (Berkeley, California: University of California Press, 1963); and, Ronald B. Inden and McKim Marriott, "Caste Systems," Encyclopedia Britannica: Macropedia, vol. 3, 1974 ed.

42. Oliver C. Cox, comment on Hughes' review of Caste, Class, and Race, in Phylon, 9 (1948), pp. 171-172. Cox's assertion that a fully developed caste society is found nowhere outside of Brahmanic India is made in Caste, Class, and Race, p. 539.

43. See Ernest Kaiser, "Racial Dialectics: The Aptheker-Myrdal School Controversy," Phylon, 9 (1948), pp. 296-297, 302.

44. See Raymond S. Franklin and Solomon Resnik, The Political Economy of Racism (New York: Holt, Rinehart and Winston, 1973), pp. 173-174.

45. An accounting of this interest is estimated in Louis L. Knowles and Kenneth Prewitt, eds., Institutional Racism in America (Englewood Cliffs, New Jersey: Prentice-Hall, 1969).

46. Garvey is mentioned tangentially in the book twice; Cox, pp. 432, 571. The other persons mentioned are treated in Robert L. Allen, Black Awakening in Capitalist America (1969), Ch. 3, pp. 89-127; Delaney is briefly reviewed in Iva E. J. Wells Carruthers, "Black Power and Integration: A Reformulation of the Theory of Race Relations," Ph.D. dissertation, Northwestern University, 1972, pp. 15-16, 46; Bishop Turner's nationalist aspirations are reviewed in Edwin S. Redkey, Black Exodus: Black Nationalist and Back-to-Africa Movements, 1890-1910 (New Haven, Connecticut: Yale University Press, 1969), pp. 24-46; on Singleton, see Walter L. Fleming, "'Pap' Singleton, the Moses of the Colored Exodus," American Journal of Sociology, 15 (July 1909), pp.

61-82; the standard work on Garvey is E. David Cronon, Black Moses: The Story of Marcus Garvey and the Universal Negro Improvement Association (Madison, Wisconsin, 1955). Also of note is Theodore Vincent, Black Power and the Garvey Movement (San Francisco: Rampart Press, 1971).

47. Cox, p. 452; the "Frazierian tradition" of viewing Black culture as pathological and devoid of any meaningful African survivals is reviewed in Charles A. Valentine, Culture and Poverty (Chicago: University of Chicago Press, 1968), pp. 20-24; the quoted phrase is borrowed from this author.

48. This inability is all the more unexpected since Cox, basing himself on his analysis of U.S. race relations, makes two predictions which have been borne out by subsequent history. The first concerns the use of force in a hypothetical situation involving racial antagonism. In maintaining that the state would use whatever force necessary to restore the racial status quo, Cox may be read as accurately presaging the tumultuous events in 1967 in such cities as Plainfield, New Jersey, Detroit, Michigan, and tens of others. In the other instance, he disputes the assertion by members of the caste school that racial etiquette and segregation will persist even after the attainment of political equality in the franchise by contending that exclusionary social barriers of this nature could never withstand such an essential change in the power relationship between the two races. Events since 1954, and particularly in the South, tend to support Cox; see, for illustration of the profound effect on race relations produced by the fall of many overt segregationist practices, Anthony Lewis and The New York Times, Portrait of a Decade: The Second American Revolution (New York: Random House, 1964), pp. 70-103; and, Benjamin Muse, Ten Years of Prelude: The Story of Integration Since the Supreme Court's 1954 Decision (New York: The Viking Press, 1964), pp. 201-209. The predictions made by Cox appear in op. cit., pp. xxxviii; 495, 501.

49. Cox, pp. 318-319, 427, 433, 461, 488, 503.

50. Victor Perlo, Economics of Racism U.S.A.: Roots of Black Inequality (New York: International Publishers, 1975).

51. Perlo, pp. 157, 198.

52. Perlo's Ch. 2, "The Black People," contains no discussion of Black culture and subsequent references to the topic in the text are of the most ephemeral nature. Perlo, pp. 11-25, 41, 257.

53. Perlo, pp. 53-54, 56, 69-70.

54. Perlo, pp. 90-91, 96-99, 106.

55. Perlo, pp. 18, 155-157.

56. Perlo, pp. 9, 127-129, 142, 146-147, 162; the author produces calculations, based on the case of ATT's discriminatory wage pattern, designed to argue for the existence of at least forty-six billion dollars in superprofits in the 1972 total profits of $173 billion realized by employers and self-employed persons; half of this $46 billion dollar figure is attributed to the super-exploitation of Third World workers (principally Black and Spanish-surnamed) and the other half to the "indirect profits" resulting from downward pressure on the wages of white workers; Perlo, pp. 147-149.

57. Perlo, pp. 5, 86-87, 128, 155, 166.

58. Perlo, pp. 191-192.

59. A suggestive treatment of how a model of institutional racism might work is given by Harold Baron, "The Web of Urban Racism," in Louis L. Knowles and Kenneth Prewitt, eds., Institutional Racism in America, Appendix, pp. 134-176, esp. pp. 170-171. Baron, however, like Prager and Blauner, concludes here that capitalism and racism are only "interlaced" and not constituents in a direct causal relationship.

60. Perlo, pp. 9, 211.

61. Perlo, pp. 5, 155, 197-214; see Baron's essay in Knowles and Prewitt, eds., _op_. _cit_., pp. 160-164, for a discussion of the norms and roles which typify institutional racism.

62. Paul M. Sweezy, _The Theory of Capitalist Development: Principles of Marxian Political Economy_ (New York: Monthly Review Press, 1942), pp. 327-328.

63. Sweezy, pp. 308-310.

64. Sweezy, pp. 310-311.

65. Certainly one of the most perceptive and critical was William Edward Burghardt DuBois. In an activist scholarly career that spanned over sixty years, he offered evidence of the ability of racism to divide society in two in the decade preceding the works of Sweezy and Cox analyzed here; see W. E. B. DuBois, "A Negro Nation Within the Nation," _Current History_, 42 (June 1935), pp. 265-270, and, "Does the Negro Need Separate Schools?," _Journal of Negro Education_, 4 (July 1935), pp. 328-335. In these two articles, DuBois argues that the exclusionary policies of American labor combined with the rapid job-displacing technological changes occurring in industry make the further development of Black institutions such as the church, the school, and community business enterprises a necessity for the Black "nation" of 12 million (c. 1935).

66. Paul A. Baran and Paul M. Sweezy, _Monopoly Capital: An Essay on the American Economic and Social Order_ (New York: Monthly Review Press, 1966).

67. Baran and Sweezy, p. 271.

68. Baran and Sweezy, pp. 263, 266-268.

69. Baran and Sweezy, pp. 257, 261, 269.

70. Baran and Sweezy, pp. 257, 258, 263.

71. Baran and Sweezy, p. 265.

72. Baran and Sweezy, pp. 249, 251 (n. 2), 271; the authors cite as the authoritative source for these opinions Cox, <u>Caste, Class, and Race</u>, and Eric Williams, <u>Capitalism and Slavery</u> (Chapel Hill: University of North Carolina Press, 1944).

73. Baran and Sweezy, p. 265.

74. Baran and Sweezy, pp. 265-266; this social-psychological portrait of racism very closely resembles that made by George Jackson; see <u>Blood In My Eye</u> (New York: Random House, 1972), pp. 94, 105-106, 144, 146, 157.

75. Baran and Sweezy, Ch. 4.

76. Baran and Sweezy, p. 271.

77. Baran and Sweezy, pp. 271-277.

78. Baran and Sweezy, p. 264.

79. Baran and Sweezy, pp. 264-265 (n. 18), 266 (n. 20).

80. Baran and Sweezy, p. 9.

81. See Carlos More, "Were Marx and Engels Really White Racists?," <u>Berkeley Journal of Sociology</u>, 19 (1974-75), pp. 125-156; Dennis Forsythe, "Radical Sociology and Blacks," in J. Ladner, ed., <u>The Death of White Sociology</u> (New York: Random House, 1973), pp. 226-233; Earl Ofari, "Marxism, Nationalism, and Black Liberation," <u>Monthly Review</u>, 22 (March 1971), pp. 18-33; and Michael Albert, <u>What Is To Be Undone</u> (Boston: Porter Sargent Publisher, 1974), pp. 146-179.

82. Harold M. Baron, "The Demand for Black Labor: Historical Notes on the Political Economy of Racism," <u>Radical America</u>, 5 (March-April 1971), pp. 1-46, esp. pp. 3, 4, 16, 36.

83. Robert L. Allen, <u>Reluctant Reformers</u>, esp. pp. 2, 276, 284.

Allen's work here may be read as a logical extension, in certain particulars, not only of Sweezy's work already mentioned, but also that of Paul A. Baran in The Political Economy of Growth (New York: Monthly Review Press, 1957). Baran had spoken of the politics of imperialism having "a dynamic of their own ... their own momentum"; and, of "a socio-psychological 'climate'" in Japan permitting the adoption of Western technology. At the same time, he denied the long-term viability of racism as an ideological prop to the imperialist system. Baran further maintained that since "...socialism in backward and underdeveloped countries has a powerful tendency to become backward and underdeveloped socialism...," national liberation movements in the Third World, even where successful, constitute only the conditions for the worldwide elimination of imperialism, requiring for fulfillment, the leadership of the advanced countries once themselves on the road to socialist democracy. See Baran, pp. viii, ix, 118, 132, 160, 250, 295. Allen appears to have jettisoned the culturally-biased judgments on the potential of Third World revolutions and to have re-directed the application of the "independent force" conception to racism, its materially sustaining component, and its concomitant social-psychological states, e.g., white resentment; see Allen, Reluctant Reformers, Ch. 8, pp. 261-296.

84. James Boggs, The American Revolution: Pages from a Negro Worker's Notebook (New York: Monthly Review Press, 1963), p. 16.

85. Boggs, The American Revolution, pp. 37, 40-41, 47, 50.

86. Boggs, The American Revolution, pp. 21-24, 45, 54.

87. Boggs, The American Revolution, pp. 81, 83-84, 85.

88. Boggs, The American Revolution, pp. 76, 77, 78, 85-86.

89. James Boggs, Racism and the Class Struggle:

Further Pages from a Black Worker's Notebook (New York: Monthly Review Press, 1970).

90. Boggs, Racism and the Class Struggle, pp. 15, 73-74, 98-99, 151.

91. Boggs, Racism and the Class Struggle, pp. 30, 54-55, 126-127.

92. Boggs, Racism and the Class Struggle, pp. 153-155.

93. Boggs, Racism and the Class Struggle, pp. 134, 135, 155.

94. Boggs, Racism and the Class Struggle, pp. 22, 50, 54, 125.

95. Boggs, Racism and the Class Struggle, pp. 134, 137, 138, 172-173.

96. Boggs, Racism and the Class Struggle, pp. 93, 97, 152, 167.

97. Boggs, Racism and the Class Struggle, pp. 154-155, 167.

98. Boggs, Racism and the Class Struggle, pp. 165-166.

99. Boggs, Racism and the Class Struggle, pp. 39, 46, 52, 118, 138, 142, 184.

100. Boggs, Racism and the Class Struggle, pp. 56, 127-128, 131, 169, 174.

101. Boggs, Racism and the Class Struggle, pp. 126, 131; on the crucial importance of exclusion see also Boggs, The American Revolution, p. 86.

102. Boggs, Racism and the Class Struggle, pp. 44, 74, 115, 119, 139.

103. Boggs, Racism and the Class Struggle, pp. 57,

58, 63-64, 68, 73, 158-159.

104. Boggs, Racism and the Class Struggle, pp. 10, 14-15, 30, 92, 95, 125-126, 159, 170.

105. Boggs, Racism and the Class Struggle, pp. 76, 120-121, 130.

106. Boggs, Racism and the Class Struggle, p. 143. The problems which specifically face Black Power in the mayoralty are reviewed and analyzed in my paper, "Black Power in Office: The Limits of Electoral Reform."

107. Boggs argues that the class struggle has been "incorporated" within the national (i.e., nation-state) struggle of races brought about by the creation of a colored world underclass in revolt against the white race (Racism and the Class Struggle, pp. 49-50).

108. See Black Workers Congress, "The Black Liberation Struggle, The Black Workers Congress, and Proletarian Revolution," Atlanta, Georgia, 1974; Tony Thomas, "Leninism, Stalinism, and Black Nationalism," International Socialist Review (October 1970), pp. 15-19, 35-38; and M. Frank Wright, "The National Question: A Marxist Critique," The Black Scholar (February 1974), pp. 43-53.

109. Marxism's disposition toward the utility of certain features of bourgeois culture may be gauged in M. Frank Wright, "The National Question: A Marxist Critique," and, V. I. Lenin, "Proletarian Culture," in V. I. Lenin: Selected Works (New York: International Publishers, 1971), pp. 620-621. The influence of evolutionism on Marx is assessed in Marvin Harris, The Rise of Anthropological Theory (New York: Thomas Y. Crowell Co., 1968), pp. 217-249.

110. Ernest Kaiser, "Racial Dialectics: The Aptheker-Myrdal School Controversy," p. 301.

Practice without thought is blind;
thought without practice is empty.

K. Nkrumah,
Consciencism,
1970, p. 78.

Chapter 5
Review, Critique, and Conclusion

Periodization of U.S. Race Relations Theory

Before turning to the task of suggesting the most viable lines of theoretical synthesis from among the competing paradigms which have been reviewed, it may be useful to consider briefly the historical development of the field of race relations inquiry in the United States. Broadly stated, three main periods are discernible.

In the first period, coinciding with the rise of the academic disciplines of anthropology and sociology in the late nineteenth century and ending with the conclusion of World War I, the dominance of Spencerianism and the spread of European colonialism (with the American variety encompassing Cuba, the Philippines, and Hawaii) gave sanction to a racial hierarchy in which the place of each race was justified variously by reference to "natural selection," "the survival of the fittest," the supposed genetic transmission of necessary superior acquired characteristics (i.e., Lamarckianism), and monogenism or polygenism.(1) Of course, not all statements concerned with race developed all these ideas, but in the writings of Josiah Nott, George R. Gliddon, Samuel Morton in anthropology, and F. H. Giddings, W. G. Sumner, Charles H. Cooley, Lester Ward, Albion Small, and E. A. Ross in sociology, these ideas about race play a central role; Frazier has observed that the statements on race by these American "founders" of these two disciplines amounted to little more than acceptance and rationalization of the racial status quo that found most Black people trapped in debt peonage in the South.(2)

The second period, from the era of the wars to the beginnings of the Southern civil rights movements, was dominated by the work of Robert E. Park, in which social-psychological constructs (e.g., "social distance," "marginal man," "attitudes") were embedded in a cyclical theory of racial contact (competition → conflict → accommodation → assimilation).(3) Park and his adherents (among whom were Louis Wirth, Rose Hum Lee, Emory S. Bogardus, Charles S. Johnson, Bertram W. Doyle, Horace Cayton, Jitsuichi Masuoka, E. C. Hughes, and E. F. Frazier)(4) focused the inquiry not on race but on race relations as the massive migration of Black folk from the rural South registered its effects on urban and industrial life. Park's theory is static, assimilationist, and ultimately grounded in individualistic moralism since "personal relations and personal friendships are the great moral solvents ... [u]nder [which] all distinctions of class, caste, and even race, are dissolved...,"(5) but it represented a hesitant advance over the explicitly racist notions of the earlier period.

The third period, from the time of the Montgomery bus boycott to the present, has witnessed the emergence of non-traditional theories of race relations which challenge the old assumption of assimilation (e.g., as does the colonial thesis) and the unquestioned acceptance of the capitalist social order (e.g., as does the Marxist thesis). Traditional theories themselves often have been refurbished, as in the move away from an all encompassing assimilationism to a more modest cultural pluralism (or, to illustrate, from Park's cycle to Milton Gordon's "structural pluralism"). Undoubtedly the single most important cause for these changes in traditional theory and for the emergence of rival theories was the tumultuous periods of the 1960s, characterized by the urban rebellion.

The four models of race relations which have been discussed may be related to the above periodization. The ethnic group model dates from the first period, and its propositions (especially those concerning assimilation) were formed in the wake of the tremendous tide of European immigration in the late nineteenth and early twentieth centuries.(6) Though instances of the use of caste and Marxist class analysis existed as sub-currents in this first period, the most influential statements on race relations from these two perspectives were made in the second period.(7) And similarly, precursors of the colonial model may be found in the earlier periods, but its most pertinent application has been made in the last period outlined.(8)

Race Relations and Social Change: A Synopsis of the Four Models

As suggested in the Introduction, the models discussed in the previous chapters may be located on a polar continuum, according to the tendency of their overall interpretation to be coherent with recognized perspectives, dominant or non-dominant. (See Chart 5.1.) This overall interpretation itself will be outlined for each model below.

One pole is represented by the ethnic group model on the right; it is clearly in line with the dominant perspective on race relations as they concern politics, history, and social science in general. The other pole is the Marxist model which is generally responsive to views which are non-dominant. Occupying intermediary positions, from left to right, are the colonial model which politically tends to be left-of-center and closer to the Marxist model, and the caste model, which occupies a right-of-center position in proximity to the major presuppositions of the ethnic group model.

A synopsis of our overall interpretation of models follows. They are reviewed in the order of their presentation in earlier chapters.

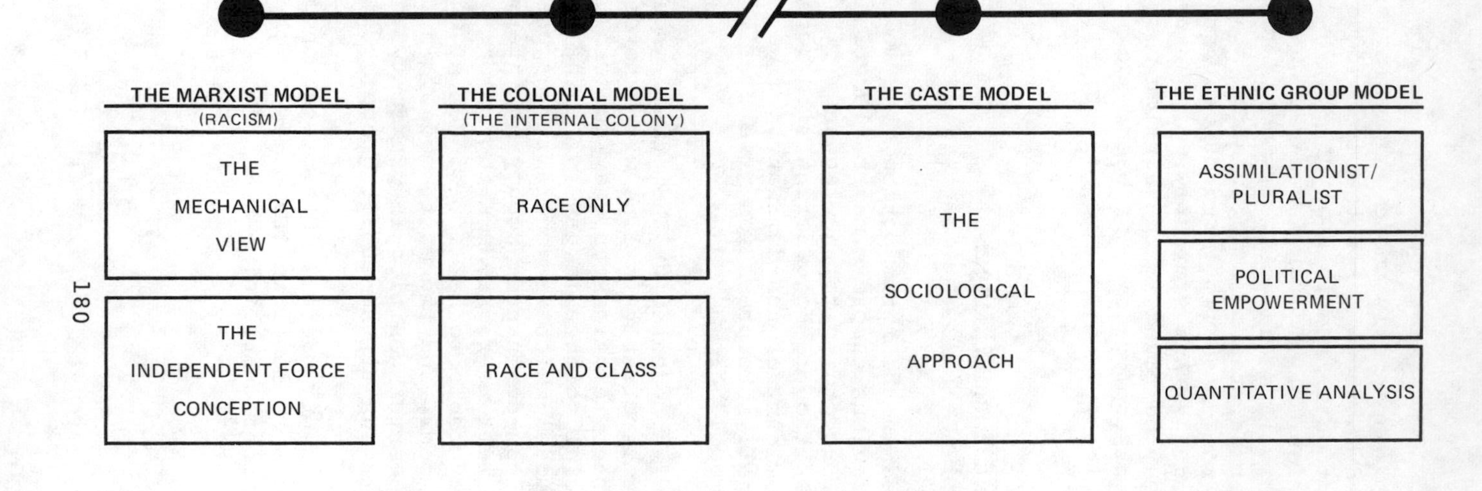

CHART 5·1: A SOCIO-POLITICAL CONTINUUM OF THE FOUR PRINCIPAL RACE RELATIONS MODELS, SHOWING SUB-GROUPS AND THEORETICAL DISJUNCTURE.

The Ethnic Group Model: The Dominant Perspective from the Right

Three subdivisions of this model were reviewed above: the quantitative approach (presented in various aspects by the Duncans, and the Taeubers); the approach to political empowerment, traditional versus non-traditional routes (Patterson versus Carmichael and Hamilton); and, the assimilationist/pluralist view which identifies value consensus, assimilation, the American Creed, and presumed internal group weakness as its central subject matter (Gordon, Banfield, Moynihan and Glazer).

The mode of consciousness which is generally ascribed to the ethnic group by these writers is either assimilationist or pluralist. In the social context of modernity, assimilation or pluralism are said to resonate with the social philosophy of modern industrial society though the precise nature of the workings of industrialization are rarely critically reviewed. Hence, exploitation is generally not discussed, nor its possible relation to other social forces (i.e., exclusion, conflict, power).

Since assimilation provides the terms of social interaction, the heterogeneous groups in society judge themselves by these terms. They may endorse these terms (Moynihan) or redefine the form of the terms, but not their substance (pluralism -- Gordon). In either case, exclusion serves to promote "fellowfeeling" and community and its negative side is neglected. Power is dispersed throughout the social order and only a group's internal strength or weakness limits its exercise and attainment of power. When groups conflict, they do so over their relative share of the society's valued attributes and not over the definition of the attributes themselves since their allegiance to a consensual social order precludes the latter possibility. Even when divergent routes to political empowerment are entertained (as with Carmichael and Hamilton), the basic goals of that empowerment are presented as congruous with the general values of the society (e.g., constant economic growth, capitalist economic relations, private enterprise, etc.).

Therefore, in general, the ethnic group model holds ameliorative social change to be a function of the ethnic group's ability to employ traditional routes to social advancement, reputedly used by all previous groups. These traditional routes concentrate on gradual reform proposed within the ambit of social and philosophical liberalism.

The Caste Model: A Perspective from Right-of-Center

Appearing more as an elaborate sociological analogy than as a coherent body of formal propositions, the caste model is the least theoretically integrated of the four viewpoints reviewed here. The use of the term "caste" as an exclusively historical descriptive modifier has been noted elsewhere. Though more recent treatments of the caste model have attempted to place the model on a more secure basis, they are not without their own ambiguities.

The mode of consciousness attributed to the caste is assimilationist: its members share a consensual moral code with other castes in caste society. But the central problem with this assertion, and with the model itself, concerns the determination by comparative method of whether or not the term caste is interchangeable between India and the U.S. South, c. 1930-49, and beyond. In the absence of this information, the analogy is suspect.

As in the ethnic group model, the historical context for "caste relations" is modern industrial society (specifically its Southern agricultural sector) but this political economy is not critically reviewed. In neither model is exploitation discussed since reciprocal political rights (ethnic group model) and mutual religio-social obligations (caste model) apparently inhibit society's members from "feeling" exploited. Power in the caste system is dispersed, though castes are arranged hierarchically, and one aspect of power, its moral basis, is prominently outlined. Exclusion is seen as a largely negative phenomenon, and though its unintended consequences are recognized, this feature of exclusion only contributes to the psychological and cultural pathology of caste subordinates. Conflict, then, is homeostatic, tending to involve a complicated system of repressed aggressions and rivalries, compensating gains, and etiquette between castes.

Given a traditional caste society, in which a system of mutual obligations and prerogatives defines all social interaction of castes, purposive social action toward mobility (such as through political parties, labor unions, or government agency) contradicts the caste principles of dharma, reincarnation, and caste loyalty. Large-scale, intergenerational mobility does not appear to be a possibility in a caste system; smaller kinds of changes occur. Thus, when caste advocates, like Myrdal, look to a modern political economy to generate liberalizing changes in caste relations they are shifting the ground of analysis to an external factor as the cause of ameliorative social change. This may be read as an admission of the inability to explain social change in a modern industrial order via pre-capitalist, agricultural, caste social principles.

The Colonial Model: A Perspective from Left-of-Center

As with the two models already discussed, there are notable differences of interpretation within the colonial paradigm. A fundamental difference, which divides the model into two camps, concerns the basis for definition of the "internal colony": the first camp (Prager, Blauner) tends to identify it by the salience of its racial characteristics while the second camp (Allen, Jackson, Ofari, Brown) cites the confluence of racial characteristics and class position. This difference in group definition also influences the mode of consciousness which is attributed to the "internal colony": those who see its identity as primarily racial ascribe to it a quest for cultural identity that suggests a legitimation of the cultural pluralism that is often espoused by ethnic analysts (e.g., Gordon, Moynihan and Glazer). Those who base the definition of the internal colony on race and class generally attribute to those colonies a mode of consciousness that is nationalistic, either latent or manifest.

The internal or domestic colony is situated within the historical context of twentieth-century industrial society, though its links to earlier, more classical forms of colonialism are not unnoticed. But, the differences already noted mean that this context is approached equivocally, sometimes (camp one) as merely the most recent setting in which an old battle for dignity and identity is waged, and at other times (camp two), as an imposing obstacle in the path of that struggle. However, the capitalist political economy is judged to be hierarchical and marked by social inequality. Hence, power is hierarchical, unevenly distributed, and monopolized, but the unintended consequences of power also promote its latent accumulation. Exclusion, then, not only appears as negative, as an expression of the power of the dominators, in the form of institutional racism -- and this is the only viewpoint among the four models reviewed here which consistently raises the theme of institutional racism -- but also contradictorily, its unintended consequence is the generation of opposition to exclusion. This opposition is founded on a culture which the oppressed construct "behind the veil." Thus, conflict between oppressor and oppressed is not limited to quarrels over the distribution of valued attributes within routinized channels, but always potentially invokes the ultimate question of alternate, competing conceptions of social order itself; this contest of world views is the basis for the culture conflict that characterizes colonial relations. Exploitation under capitalism, as can be seen by earlier remarks, is generally evaluated as an important influence on colonial race relations, but sometimes (camp one) it is regarded as a first cause that now operates in a separate sphere of social reality while another view (camp two) considers it a primary and continuing cause of racial oppression.

Consistent with the two camps in the model, which diverge on the definition of the internal colony and its relation to the capitalist political economy, plans for social change also diverge. Though self-determination is an agreed-upon goal, the first camp appears to equate this with a revitalized cultural identity that emerges from a successful culture conflict. The second camp does not underestimate the importance of cultural identity but in its view a victorious struggle for self-determination and cultural autonomy can only be guaranteed as the oppressed are eventually drawn into a struggle against capitalism itself.

The Marxist Model: The Non-Dominant View from the Left

Though many camps within Marxist social analysis can be distinguished, two prominent lines of thought within the Marxist tradition have been discerned in regards to race relations theory. A generally older line of interpretation (Cox, Perlo) understands racial prejudice to be a manipulable ideological quantum, generated by capitalist exploitation and used by ruling class deliberately to divide the working class. Racial prejudice, then, represents false consciousness. Another more recent line of thought (Baran and Sweezy, Boggs) holds that racial prejudice, though grounded in capitalism's exploitative social relations of production, has now acquired a dynamic of its own, capable of directing social action.

The mode of consciousness attributed to that segment of the working class (in Boggs' term, the "underclass") which suffers racial prejudice is assimilationist, in the case of the older perspective, and nationalist, in the more recent one. In the older perspective, racial consciousness is an ideology that falsely mediates praxis and consciousness; it prevents white and black workers from seeing their common anti-capitalist interests. The newer perspective does not deny this view but emphasizes instead that racial consciousness is not exclusively a possession of the ruling class and that, as an ideology, its ability to direct social action has had the direct effect of stimulating an ideological response, _viz._, nationalism, among the victims of racist abuse against their racial oppressors; the class question itself is mediated by this reality.

Both lines of thought discuss black/white race relations within the context of a capitalist political economy and agree that modern racial prejudice has its beginnings in the evolution of this particular social order. Further, since capitalist society is hierarchical and distributively unequal, power (whether economic, political, or social) is represented as being hierarchically distributed and unevenly monopolized by dominant social classes as a subtractive element. Exclusion, then, is an expression of their power to penalize and stigmatize a portion of the working class, the better to be able to divide it; but, the dialectical relation of exclusion to the elaboration of subordinate group norms, values, and traditions in opposition to that exclusion is often unexamined, even when recognized. As a result, the culture of struggle created by the subordinate group is overlooked. Consequently, though conflict is treated as a disjunctive phenomenon, the attention paid to its manifestation in visible periods of (usually labor) unrest tends to miss other, sometimes less visible, evidences of profound value dissensus (as in revolutionary black nationalism) as the basis for disintegrative social conflict.

Finally, the Marxist statements on race relations examined here place social change within the context of a class-divided society based on capitalism. The basis for eliminating all forms of social inequality is a revolution predicated on class struggle. But there is disagreement as to how racism, as a particular form of inequality under capitalism, is to be transcended: one program calls for workers to unite in adherence to a colorless (or, raceless) formulation of the class struggle; another program avers the necessity of recognizing the historical particularity of the class struggle in the United States by confronting the contradictory nature of racism (i.e., it is both a source of oppression and division within working class, but it is also the stimulant of an oppositional ideology and group life among the oppressed) and defeating its ultimate cause, the capitalist political economy itself.

The Quest for Theoretical Synthesis: Representative Statements

Banton, van den Berghe, Rex, Schermerhorn, and Kinloch each have produced synthetic statements on race relations.(9) We will not provide an exhaustive review of these statements but rather a selective evaluation as regards four points deemed most important for the conceptualization of race relations. (As throughout this essay, we primarily focus on black/white relations.) These points are: the normative-descriptive dimension; the structural dimension; the assessment of subordination; and, the assessment of culture and ideology.

The first, *the normative-descriptive dimension*, refers to the orientation of the theoretical statement as regards the principles chosen to explain phenomena (normative) and the methods by which this explanation is supported (descriptive). Hypothetically, a wide range of choices is possible for both aspects of this dimension and it is possible that a statement may be acceptable in one aspect but not in the other. The second, *the structural dimension*, concerns the representation of the structural features of race relations that the statement conveys; two structural features of especial interest are exclusion and exploitation. The third, *the assessment of subordination*, asks how does the statement account for the behavior, the culture, and the institutions of racially subordinate groups. And the last, *the assessment of culture and ideology*, asks how does the statement explain the genesis and operation of racism as an ideology and as an influence on culture.

The most significant questions about the first dimension do not involve the methodological features of a theoretical statement on race relations, but its normative aspect, i.e., the value presuppositions which the theorist invokes to substantiate the explanation.(10)

It is usually readily admitted that the research efforts of theorists concerned with race relations, while creatively employing the case study method, survey techniques, and increasingly specialized statistical methods such as multiple classification analysis, are subject to much needed improvement.(11) But, the interpretation of data in this field is still very much dependent on the debates over value presuppositions which are largely unresolved.

Perhaps the single most important debate about value orientations centers on the question of order versus conflict theories of behavior and social problems. Horton argues persuasively that all theories of behavior and social problems are normative in that they define and explain these phenomena from "socially situated value positions."(12) And since race relations are often the subject of problematic inquiry, the importance of this observation is manifest.

Attempting to bridge the gap between structural-functional, or order, theories and conflict theories of social phenomena, van den Berghe offers a proposed synthesis.(13) His review of "cautious" and "sophisticated" functional analysis (as practiced by, for example, Kingsley Davis, Robert K. Merton, and Talcott Parsons) leads him to enumerate its basic postulates as follows: holism stressing interrelated parts; multiple causation; dynamic equilibrium; tendency of dysfunctions to be absorbed; gradualism; three primary sources of change -- exogenous factors, growth through differentiation, and invention or innovation; and, social integration predicated on value consensus.(14) While he is willing to accept the first two postulates as valid, he uncovers a number of logical and empirical errors concerning the last five points. Grouping them together as pertaining to either the concepts "consensus" or "dynamic equilibrium," he demonstrates that there is no necessary direct link between consensus and equilibrium, and that the minimization of change implied by adjustment, and the inability to analyze endogenous or malintegrative change, are serious weaknesses of functionalism.(15)

Turning to "the Hegelian-Marxian dialectic," van den Berghe scores both Hegel's idealism and Marx's economic determinism as untenable, and rejects the implication that the dialectical process is the only source of change or that polarization is inherent in conflict. Relieved of these elements, he presents the dialectic in its minimum acceptable form as positing that change is ubiquitous and endogenous, and that it often arises from the contradiction of two or more "factors" (here, understood as values, ideologies, roles, institutions, or groups). This "minimum dialectic approach" is to be applied to the analysis of values, institutionalized principles, and group conflicts.(16)

Van den Berghe proposes a synthesis of these two theoretical positions by reformulating them so that their objectionable features are dropped, permitting them to be combined into "an expanded equilibrium model" which includes the possibility of at least two cycles of change, one integrative and the other malintegrative. Basically, dialectics is to be rendered an augmentative theoretical principle in the refined analysis of system dynamics. The synthesis is possible, he asserts, because it is argued that the two theories are _complementary_ and reconcilable, as shown by their convergence or overlap on the points of holism, the dual role of consensus and conflict as each capable of producing the other, an evolutionary perspective on social change, and an equilibrium view of society common to both theories.(17)

Schermerhorn is very receptive to van den Berghe's proposed synthesis, adding that one should be able to choose between conflict theory and order theory as the situation demands. This method of choice of normative theoretical framework he dubs "mechanical allocation."(18) Banton seems to agree with Schermerhorn's suggestion, but he (Banton) offers transaction theory as the framework most likely to encompass the consensual and often neglected coercive elements of social reality, and race relations in particular.(19) Rex dissents from the proposed synthesis and its _ad hoc_ use because, for him, race relations theory can be properly concerned only with those situations which possess three defining characteristics, one of which is the inherency of conflict (the other two being structural distinctiveness expressed by ascriptive role allocation and the existence of a justificatory ideology of discrimination).(20) Kinloch's attempt to refurbish Park's race relations cycle by adding the notion of colonialism (broadly defined by him as a social structure in which a particular elite subordinates an indigenous population, defines certain physical characteristics negatively, and imports other race groups for purposes of economic exploitation) to it and by retaining the idea that industrialization by itself promotes social change toward inevitable assimilation, would also appear to dissent from the proposed synthesis. Within the cycle, conflict will tend to be homeostatic and not disjunctive.(21)

In light of the summary above of the proposed synthesis and several reactions to it, the first observation to be made is that van den Berghe does not really resolve the issue at hand. And Schermerhorn's compromise of "mechanical allocation" merely continues to skirt the issue. By jettisoning Marx's critique of political economy and labeling it determinism, van den Berghe avoids any analysis of the epistemological foundations upon which use of the dialectical method in Marx is based.(22) Since, according to this method, order and conflict are <u>dialectical</u>, and not complementary, and are subsumed under the general cosmological law of the inherency of motion exhibited by matter, it is these epistemological assumptions which must be examined.(23)

Admittedly, the determination of the dominance of one state or the other (i.e., order or conflict) at a given point in time is an empirical question. But, if a normative synthesis is attempted without an examination of the interpenetration of opposites and the inherency of motion exhibited by matter, and other epistemological domain assumptions which are explicated in a corpus of political economic thought stemming from Marx, then that synthesis cannot be regarded as successful.(24) Van den Berghe's real accomplishment is not a genuine synthesis but a rather shallowly disguised effort to strengthen functional theory through the addition of a suitably housebroken and depoliticized dialectic. Other theoretical statements on race relations encounter similar difficulties with respect to their normative frameworks.(25)

The structural dimension of a theoretical statement on race relations should state the manner in which social structures such as the job market, the state, primary and secondary group life, public and private sector enterprises and agencies, etc., affect the content, status, and direction of race relations. A focus on the treatment of the basic concepts such as exclusion in its negative or barrier function and exploitation may serve to explicate this dimension; in particular, the notion of institutional racism will receive attention as a derivative of exclusion.

The proposition advanced by Rex that ascriptive role allocation always forms a part of genuine race relations situations may be seen as an effort to articulate the concept of exclusion and it is an important contribution toward a conceptualization of institutional racism.(26) However, exploitation remains a shadowy entity in Rex's analysis, though it is considered a primary determinant of disjunctive conflict in typically colonial cases.(27) It is not defined, and the question of differential rates of exploitation among various segments of a multi-racial proletariat in metropolitan countries is not contemplated. Schermerhorn's "degree of enclosure" is meant as an expression of the exclusion of subordinate groups from society-wide institutions and associations, but he addresses it primarily to an explication of plural societies and offers only a reformulation of van den Berghe's ideal-type of competitive race relations as "maximal racism" as an approach to institutional racism. He also speaks of "vertical racism" where racism is considered a justificatory ideology of socioeconomic position and acts to rank subordinate and dominant groups accordingly.(28) Exploitation is nowhere defined by Schermerhorn, and seems to be subsumed piecemeal under the various "intergroup sequences" (e.g., annexation, colonization, migration, etc.) which he outlines.(29) Banton, in criticizing Bogardus' work on social distance, offers some insights on exclusion that may be useful in postulating institutional racism, *viz.*, that social distance may result from types of role relationships and from the lack of common interests or experiences.(30) On the other hand, exploitation receives only brief mention and is treated as a commonsense substantive denoting a putative negative social (though not necessarily economic) relationship.(31)

In van den Berghe's analysis, exclusion emerges as a "calculated, invidious device of racial subordination" once race relations move from the paternalistic ideal type to the competitive ideal type, i.e., from Gemeinschaft pre-industrial societies (e.g., colonial Brazil) to Gesellschaft industrial ones (e.g., the United States).(32) But this imposition of exclusionary mechanisms is pictured as being chiefly the conscious product of a "ruling group," and social and cultural forces are largely left out of the account.(33) The transition from paternalistic to competitive ideal type race relations also apparently is responsible for a change in the manner of exploitation, but this is not spelled out.(34) Kinloch gives an exposition of institutional racism centering on the racist manner in which the functions of control, socialization, and provision of physical facilities may be executed, and he presents a propositional inventory for testing its existence.(35) Exploitation receives attention as the chief force behind the rationalization of social inequality through racial ideologies, but exploitation is not defined, and the interaction of economic and non-economic forces is left implicit.(36)

From the above review of the five synthetic statements under consideration, it is clear that exclusion occupies a central place in race relations theory because it expresses a major defining characteristic of race relations situations and because its existence and maintenance in such situations may have a basis (or bases) outside the sphere of race *per se*. However, when one of these possible bases, exploitation, is examined, a less clear exposition results: exploitation is conceded to be of importance, but it would appear that the term "exploitation" is subject to two meanings. First, it has a recognizable coinage as a concept of economic analysis expressly developed by nineteenth-century political economy, especially in the work of Marx.(37) In this first sense, exploitation is a technical term capable of precise, scientific measurement. A more frequent usage gives the term a common-sense meaning which denotes a putative, negative social relationship, sometimes but not necessarily encompassing economic relations. This second meaning attributed to the term appears to enjoy as much currency as the first in the statements reviewed above. What remains to be done is to integrate the two meanings of the term with a specification of the relationship between exploitation and exclusion in various social settings.

The third evaluative criterion, the assessment of subordination, is related to the structural dimension of exclusion in its positive aspect and has particular relevance for the subject of Black culture. It is axiomatic that no theoretical statement on race relations which denies the validity and integrity of Afro-American culture can be deemed acceptable.

Among the synthetic statements being reviewed, we find van den Berghe's assertion that acculturation of the "overwhelming majority of the population" to dominant culture combined with the "virtually complete deculturation" of Afro-Americans makes for the existence of social pluralism as regards this group and others, but not cultural pluralism. Cultural differences between whites and Afro-Americans are attributed to "cultural 'drift'" among the latter.(38) Kinloch's insistent focus on the dominant elite, and especially its values, as the controlling factor in race relations situations reduces subordinate group behavior in general to a reaction-formation and Black group life in particular to a culture-less void filled only by pathology and imitation of white norms. Racial nationalism becomes simply a reaction to the denial of the American Creed; it affirms nothing within Black people themselves.(39) Schermerhorn expresses agreement with van den Berghe's judgment on this matter, except that in a footnote he is willing to concede that "centrifugal goals" (i.e., nationalism as an expression of culture) were never completely unrepresented among Black people.(40)

A rather straightforward mimetic model of Black culture is presented by Banton, in which the copying of white norms, the destruction of the African past, and unresolved psychological dilemmas create a problematic environment for the much-sought assimilation.(41) Rex takes a position that is somewhat inconsistent since he holds that Afro-Americans (more than most metropolitan minorities) are part and parcel of the country's "social and cultural system" which is based on the "ultimate value system" of the Bill of Rights, at the same time that he acknowledges the revolutionary potential of Black nationalist ideologies and social movements.(42)

None of the above statements constitutes the basis for a satisfactory approach to Black culture. Valentine has argued that models of Black culture are generally of three kinds: deficit, in which pathology, and incomplete mimetic reaction-formation are the principal explanatory modes; difference, in which linguistic uniqueness, the assumption of static unitary culture, and the culture-of-poverty thesis are offered as explanation; and, bi-cultural, in which Afro-American culture, conceived as structurally variable, interacts with the dominant culture as "intertwined or simultaneously available repertoires."(43) As a fourth alternative, a dialectical model of Afro-American culture may be postulated in which the African heritage, the struggle against racial oppression, and the Afro-American experience combine and interact, and express themselves historically through a dialectical relationship of production, social relations of production, and culture (especially, cultural institutions) that engenders bi-culturalism, tempered by social class divisions.(44) Most of the statements from the race relations theorists cited above are easily recognizable as variants of the deficit model; only Schermerhorn and Rex seem vaguely sensitive to the possibilities of a bi-cultural paradigm. A more suitable vehicle for comprehending the effects of exclusion in this positive sense (i.e., as an unintended producer of cultural life among racial subordinates) is available in a dialectically conceived bi-cultural model of Afro-American culture.

The last evaluative criterion chosen in order to

gauge the effectiveness of the synthetic statements under review concerns the analysis of the ideational content of racism (i.e., racism as an ideology) and its interaction with culture. Early studies of racism were dominated by the field of social psychology so that the ideational content of racism, focused almost exclusively on the individual, was often set adrift theoretically with only weak moorings to other important spheres (e.g., group, political, economic) of social analysis.(45) Conversely, other interpretations pursue a reductionist scheme in which the ideational content of racism is typically rendered a surrogate expression of economic motives.(46) These two poles may be regarded as the Scylla and Charybdis of race relations theory on this question.

Van den Berghe, though disdainful of a vulgar Marxist analysis, gives a good imitation of one by maintaining that racism, defined as a "set of beliefs," is "a fairly superficial symptom of much more widespread and basic problems (i.e., economic ones)." Though these beliefs are capable of generating conflict when confronted by the dominant (though unfulfilled) values of the democratic tradition, this conflict occurs only within the confines of a social order that is held together by "political coercion" and "economic interdependence." That is, the ideational content of racism has influence only under the push of these last two factors; racism is an "epiphenomenon."(47)

Schermerhorn holds that racism (in the United States), "a complex of ideas," is a product of the intergroup sequence (i.e., the historical contact and subsequent interaction of distinct peoples) of slavery. The ideational content of racism does not concern culture ("norms and values") but rather structure (a "set of crystallized social relationships...") since conflict centers on structural matters like segregation. The degree of structural pluralism (in this case, enforced exclusion), and with it, one assumes, the amount of antagonistic race feeling, will apparently fluctuate according to some "self-regulating principle" derived from economic change.(48)

In Kinloch's formulation, racism as an ideology develops as a result of a negative contact situation dominated by a colonial elite. Its intensity and pervasiveness are determined by the degree to which the society is colonial (using his definition of the term as indicated earlier). Racism, once entrenched, becomes institutional, comprising "a social system in which race is the major criterion of role assignment, role rewards, and socialization...." However, industrialization promotes status inconsistency among racial subordinates causing them to challenge the racial status quo. A new form of "intergroup accommodation" then emerges; the ideational content of racism and its interaction with culture thus depends on the structural phenomena of industrialization and economic development.(49)

Defining racism as a doctrine, Banton notes that a "social structure of domination" provides the context in which it functions. This structure contains "positive incentives" to work and co-operation because the frequent use of force invites marginal effectiveness. Thus, though the overall effect of the structure of domination is to secure subordinate-superordinate relations, nonetheless, there are sufficient "cross-cutting ties" within it that racial frictions are often eased by common social class interest. Rules of etiquette, sexual prohibition, and irrational beliefs all are included in the structure of domination. Under the impress of industrialization and urbanization, social change promotes discontinuities in social life, especially as between work and leisure. These discontinuities manifest themselves in situationally inconsistent behavior that is harmonized by a "cultural clothing" that smoothes over contradictions. Urbanization compartmentalizes social life, leading to discontinuities in contrast to the continuous fabric of the structure of domination which Banton identifies with race relations in the rural South. Social relations become less personal and more inflexible and categoric as the social context undergoes the transformation from unurbanized non-industrial to urban industrial; the ideational content of racism becomes more categoric and inflexible, too, and may exacerbate class differences.(50)

Rex considers the ideational content of racism to be a "derivation" (he borrows the term from Pareto) that people use to justify their actions. The derivation is expressed as a "typification" (he borrows the term from Berger and Luckman) that is created through the intersubjective sharing of language, whose use always involves an implicit moral code. Language is used to distinguish physical and social objects, and in the latter case "particularistic" and "classificatory" modes of ascription determine the rights and roles which belong or are granted to the object. In relatively large, complex societies, social objects will tend to be distinguished in a classificatory (i.e., roles and rights are assigned specific to non-kin group relations) way, while a particularistic (i.e., roles and rights assigned to specific kin group relations) mode will prevail in simpler societies.

When the relations between distinguishable groups in complex societies involve conflict and economic competition for survival between them, psychological aggression, and verbalized conflict attitudes, Rex asserts that the operation of the classificatory mode of ascription is most likely to result in everyday (i.e., mundane, common as opposed to explicitly theoretical or philosophical) racism. On the other hand, explicit theories of racism (the product of a small coterie of intellectuals), represent the systematic articulation of legitimating ideas. Such legitimations most commonly draw their substance from the normative realms of social life of religion, culture, history, ideology, science, and social science. Everyday racism finds its most important and effective outlet to ordinary citizens through the media and, together with intellectual racism, constitutes "a kind of hierarchy of beliefs and attitudes." Depending on the kinds of linkages between the various levels in this hierarchy, Rex argues that it may be possible to determine not only the influence of explicit racist theories in the society, but also the extent to which the very structure of the society's thinking is itself racist. These explicit theories are essentially deterministic in nature and though biogenetic arguments have been typical historically, functional equivalents such as cultural chauvinism and religious bias must also be taken into account -- all presume an invariable relation between identified groups and their "evaluated qualities."(51)

Most assessments of the ideational component of racism and its interaction with culture may be grouped under one of two approaches: epiphenomenal-reductionist, or interactive. The first group tends to see racist ideas and their expression in culture as mere illustrations of the workings of more basic (usually economic) processes. In the second view, the underlying determinative power of economic and structural processes is not denied, but to it is added the notion that ideas _of themselves_, when codified as theories (explicit or implicit) or cultural traditions, may become social forces and exert a semi-autonomous power, to direct social life; the intellectual record of a society is thus its history of the reciprocal contact between these two spheres.(52) This interaction produces "representations," collective distillations of the thought of an epoch, which may obscure or clarify (make "opaque" or "transparent") true social relations. As ideology, these representations have a mixed character, partly reflecting truth and partly reflecting error, and with the emergence of the separation of mental labor from physical labor in human history "[b]y virtue of their link with 'reality' -- a reality transposed and interpreted -- ideologies _can affect reality by imposing rules and limitations on actually living men_" (emphasis added).(53) Of the two approaches, the second is clearly more suited for analyzing the complex interaction of ideas and the sociocultural milieu.

Accordingly, the schemes of van den Berghe and Schermerhorn may be rejected, the first because the argument is economic determinist and, therefore, severely limited in its ability to deal with non-economic phenomena, and the second because a similar economic automation with laissez-faire undertones seems to be at work, resulting in the explicit omission of cultural concerns. Both presentations are one-sided, though Schermerhorn's is not as reductionist as that of van den Berghe.

Banton and Rex are much more successful in dealing

with the question of interaction as it concerns the ideology of racism because they offer theoretical constructs designed to consider the complex, interactive relationship of ideology (or ideas) to social structure. Kinloch's scheme, especially in its focus on institutional racism, is helpful, but it is hampered by the assumption of economic automatism, i.e., that economic change toward industrialization and urbanization necessarily promotes significant change in race relations, whether such change is ameliorative or not.(54) Banton and Rex more appropriately leave this matter open, and Rex in particular must be credited with developing a theoretical scheme which is sensitive to the myriad possibilities stemming from the interaction of a given ideological phenomenon and its sociocultural milieu.(55)

The Guidelines for Synthesis

From this brief critical exposition of several leading theoretical statements, the tasks necessary for synthesis can be glimpsed. The subject of Afro-American culture continues to demand careful thought so that outdated and spurious generalizations may be avoided. A dialectical, bicultural model of Afro-American culture most effectively encompasses the social psychological and socioeconomic factors which must comprise a successful treatment of this phenomenon. Often, the question of Black culture is tied to another issue reviewed above, viz., the normative-descriptive dimension of race relations theories, as when the denial of Black culture is held to invalidate the uniqueness of the religious and political ideologies which it frequently sustains.(56) Following Rex's assertion that all genuine race relations situations contain an inherent element of conflict, we propose that the most suitable normative framework for race relations theory is a conflict framework, specifically of the Marxist type. Finally, the work of Rex, Banton, and Kinloch provides useful approaches to the ideological component of racism -- e.g., Banton's "structure of domination" and "discontinuities," Rex's "classificatory ascription" and "mundane vs. intellectual racism" -- and to the subject of institutional racism as a fundamental item in the structural dimension of race relations theories and situations -- e.g., Kinloch's holistic definition, and Rex's "ascriptive role allocation."

A satisfactory model of race relations should be able to raise important questions about relevant social situations, to answer some of these questions, and to suggest others which further illuminate the understanding of problems at hand. John Rex, whose work has already been cited, proposed that race relations theory should concentrate primarily on those situations which possess the following three characteristics: the interaction of two or more distinct groups forced to live together by economic or political conditions; a high degree of conflict between the groups in which "ascriptive criteria" are used to mark social boundaries and to assign roles; and, the use of a "deterministic theory" -- such a theory may take a religious, cultural, scientific, historical, or sociological form -- that seeks to legitimate the subordinate position of certain groups by attributing their status and roles to supposed innate characteristics.(57)

Rex's criteria suggest the kind of questions that a successful model of race relations must address: How do the circumstances of contact between the groups influence their initial and subsequent interaction? What part do the different characteristics (physical or cultural, real or perceived) of the groups play in their interaction, especially over time? How does exclusion function between and in the groups? What forms does conflict take, what influences its disposition, and what are its possible outcomes? What kind of justification has arisen to legitimate the racial status quo, how has it changed, and what relation does it bear to the structural features of the society? And, how does the overall social context act to influence relations between the groups and the internal socioeconomic and cultural state of each group itself?

Thus, from the standpoint being argued here, the ethnic and caste models of race relations must be judged the least acceptable or suitable. The colonial and Marxist models are the most suitable, but independently they do not explain as much about American race relations as they might if satisfactorily combined. A summary of the principal weaknesses and strengths of each model will explain this assessment.

The caste model can be traced to an elaborate analogy with pre-colonial India. As indicated earlier, this analogy was often left unsupported by relevant ethnographic and sociological data.(58) Consequently, while rich in descriptive treatment of a certain epoch in Black-white relations (the early twentieth-century South), the model is poor in its ability to provide a national framework in which to view these relations. Related to this point is this model's inability to explain change outside of a Southern rural agricultural background as the locus of Black-white relations shifted urban and northward, unless reference is made to "the South going North."(59) The model does not provide an assessment of the links between the interacting groups and the overall society since its regional focus tends to preclude this. And, the portrayal of Black culture never leaves the realm of cultural pathology, thus being quite one-sided and biased. In sum, though this model (and especially its descriptive noun and adjectives, e.g., caste, caste-like, etc.) certainly will continue to inspire evocative usage, no meaningful theoretical advances can be expected from it.

Undoubtedly, the single most popular vantage point from which U.S. race relations are viewed is the ethnic model. Until very recently, it was the reigning orthodoxy.(60) Rooted in liberal socio-political theory, the model places assimilation as its final goal and then looks to understand the obstacles or advantages which may affect this goal as it surveys major groups in society. A later refinement of the model (M. Gordon's) allows for "cultural pluralism" by limiting the sphere of assimilation to all non-primary group (i.e., non-kin, or not intimately social) contact across ethnic lines while preserving a sense of allegiance to the larger society. This allegiance, whether presented in the cultural pluralist or assimilationist variants of the model, is reputedly based on a social and ethical consensus which pervades all of American society. Proponents of the model often engage in the quantitative analysis of selected features (e.g., voting behavior, degree of residential segregation, occupational status, etc.) of group life, and negative comparisons lead to the assertion of the internal weaknesses of certain groups (cf. Moynihan and Glazer's work critiqued in Chapter 1). The proponents are often joined by critics who emphasize non-traditional routes to political empowerment but who do not venture beyond the threshold provided by liberal assumptions and formulas; these critics (e.g., Carmichael and Hamilton) merely raise, in rather candid form, some of the more perplexing aspects of the ethnic group model when it is applied to U.S. race relations.

Chief among these perplexities is the question of race (or color) itself, and by extension, that of institutional racism. Theorists of this perspective sometimes are not sure that race is a characteristic of ethnic groups (e.g., Moynihan and Glazer's 2nd ed. 1970 preface, pp. x, xiii), or that it has decisive influence in certain areas of inter-ethnic contact (e.g., the Duncans' 1968 American Sociological Review piece), or that institutional racism needs to be accounted for at all (e.g., M. Gordon's book, 1964). Such uncertainty and obfuscation about one of the central issues of race relations study must be reckoned a serious weakness of this model.

Compounding this inadequacy is the fact that the model also does not provide a tenable representation of the links between the interacting groups and the larger social context, especially as regards economic analysis. Such notions as it does offer concerning this subject -- notions such as the "little business man/ethnic community tradition" (Moynihan and Glazer) -- are easily refuted not only by ideological foes but by presumably impartial government sources as well.(61)

Finally, as with the caste model, the ethnic group model tends to view Black culture as a form of social pathology. Whether it is the notion of inability to defer gratification or the alleged absence of a business tradition and stable family unit, proponents of this model most often tend to argue that the handicap of counterproductive cultural norms bears a great deal of the responsibility for Black social degradation and racial tension. These arguments themselves have been subjected to withering and successful criticism, but more important is the fact that they divert attention away from the connection between the family unit, the culture of the ethnic group, and the wider social context, especially as regards the influences the latter may have on ethnic groups and their (i.e., the groups') interaction.(62)

It is precisely this wider social context, and the interaction of social groups with it and with each other, that is at the heart of the concerns of the Marxist model. American society as a whole is its typical focus, especially as regards its economic and related activities. The principal strength of this model is that, unlike the others (with exceptions among adherents of the colonial model), it is willing to engage in criticism of the very foundations of modern capitalist society. Indeed, some of its assertions about the effect of economic development on race relations are routinely accepted and repeated by non-Marxist scholars in the field.(63) And by virtue of its economic analysis, only the Marxist model attempts to locate the race dilemma squarely within the context of the development of American capitalism.(64)

But too often, proponents of the model are unable to translate successfully their economic insights into perceptive commentary on and understanding of the racial difficulties which embroil the American work experience. The notion of "false consciousness" too often was used simply to evade the necessity of confronting the reality of racism as a social force in American life. Similarly, because exclusion based on racial distinctions is not often properly understood, its aspects such as Black culture and Black nationalism are usually portrayed unsympathetically. With the development, however, of a divergence within the model on the interpretation of racism as an ideology, it is possible that the generally more advanced "independent force" conception may supplant the older mechanical approach among those who favor a Marxist perspective on race relations.

Within the colonial model there is also a divergence on the definition of the "internal colony" which bears on the interpretation of racism as an ideology. Proponents of this model who tend to define the "internal colony" by race only, rather than by race and class, also view racism as a social ideology largely detached from current economic motives. Others (e.g., Allen) disagree, defining the internal colony by race and class, and arguing that economic motives have not only a past connection (usually conceded) but a present impress on racism as an ideology under capitalism.

A key point in this disagreement centers on whether or not the socioeconomic experience of Black people has subjected them to exploitation of the type described in Marxist political economic theory. A noteworthy debate between a proponent of the colonial model, William K. Tabb, and his critic, Donald J. Harris, is instructive.(65) Harris reviews Tabb's presentation of the colonial model and finds that it lacks a firm basis in an examination of "the internal logic and laws of capitalism," especially as regards the term "exploitation."(66) Rejecting the conventional neo-classical economic definition of the term, Harris offers one based on Marx's discovery of the unequal exchange between capital and labor for the commodity, labor-time.(67) Using this definition, Harris argues that the existence of spatial separation (ghettoes), task segregation (restriction from, and confinement to, certain types of work), and social oppression (educational and cultural discrimination) are not sufficient to prove the existence of exploitation, or its particular form which is relevant to the colonial case, super-exploitation. For Harris, only the verification of differences in the ability of white and Black labor to enforce the rules of exchange -- or the intervention of an intermediary such as the state, to the disadvantage of Black workers -- would constitute proof of the latter phenomenon.(68)

Failing such proof, Harris maintains that the ghetto is best seen as part of the sphere of the "petty-capitalists" who seek to rationally obtain profits and fend off the intrusions of the more powerful "corporate capitalists."(69) These latter often seek to penetrate the petty-capitalist sphere when competition requires, and may initiate changes (e.g., tokenism, extension of credit to Black entrepreneurs, raiding of skilled ghetto labor force, etc.) which are in direct contradiction to the interests of the overwhelmingly white petty-capitalist class.(70) However, since the opportunities for investment in the ghetto are themselves limited by the standards of the corporate sphere, the ghetto continues to fester and the work experience of Black people is conditioned by racial discrimination which acts as "a convenient mechanism for rationing the total amount of available jobs" (emphasis in the original); the mechanism is actuated by the size of the reserve army of unemployed.(71) Thus, since "...American blacks are, and have always been, organically linked with American capitalism from its very beginning...," Harris proposes that a correct theoretical formulation of this situation is needed though he does not propose to consider the validity of "the colonial analogy" as a political strategy and tactic.(72)

Tabb counters that it is precisely the validity of the colonial analogy to the political and social struggles of the ghetto which has given it great value.(73) Further, correcting Harris's Marxian definition of exploitation so it is based properly on the sale of labor-power and not labor-time, Tabb notes that Harris has two significant problems in his critique: no theory is presented to account for the special oppression of Black people, and the colonial analogy stands implicitly accepted by reason of no better alternative being presented.(74) Both points turn on the fact that Harris has not successfully explained racism, especially since his treatment seems to suggest that this phenomenon will be ended by the development of monopoly capitalism.(75)

Tabb argues that Harris has not reckoned with the different spheres of corporate interest, some of which do have a stake in the maintenance of a "low cost labor pool."(76) At any rate, Tabb scores the "overly narrow" definition of exploitation which Harris uses. Tabb notes that by confining the investigation to labor market experience, "only the tip of the iceberg" of Black social oppression is seen, and that the further effect of this definition is to make discrimination appear as a "deus ex machina" unaccounted for by the analysis.(77) This is especially so since Harris neglects the role of the state in the perpetuation of Black exploitation and oppression.(78) In Tabb's estimation, Harris himself does not present a Marxist alternative to the colonial anology by reason of the omissions in his analysis, the most crucial being the failure to investigate the role of consciousness as a product/producer of economic and social relations.(79)

However, Tabb does concede that his earlier work did not adequately state the interaction of spatial and class relations which form the ghetto. He now prefers to analyze the Black experience as a "colonial analogy," and not a colonial model because essentially this perspective is "best viewed as a sub-category of a general class analysis."(80) But, racism must be understood as an "autonomous force" and the spatial existence of the ghetto holds strategic importance which demands attention.(81)

The debate between Tabb and Harris points to the greatest strength of the colonial model: its ability to capture the feeling-tone of oppression and exploitation as experienced by the majority of the racially subordinate group. And the phenomenon of racism is a major factor in that experience. Both these aspects of the model stem from its treatment of exclusion, in which this phenomenon is accorded a special role as the purveyor of discriminatory practice and ideology. Further, the origins of exclusion are usually sought in the social relations established prior to the appearance of the capital-wage labor relation.(82)

The subject of exclusion is not, however, an unalloyed gain attributable to the colonial model since the treatment of exclusion in its positive aspect -- as the group life and traditions of the colonized -- is not always successful. The limitations and difficulties of its discussion of the culture of the oppressed have already been indicated.(83) These problems often lead to the formulation of essentially utopian schemes for the decolonization of race relations.(84)

We can conclude, then, that the path toward an overall, synthetic view of U.S. Black/white race relations seems clear. It lies in the joining of economic analysis derived from the Marxist tradition with the socio-psychological and cultural insights gained from the colonial perspective. No other path is open.

Many unresolved issues and problems remain; some of them have been illustrated in the two earlier chapters which dealt with these models.(85) In the works of Boggs, Allen, and Tabb herein reviewed the emergence of a successful synthetic theoretical statement is glimpsed.

Notes

1. See Marvin Harris, The Rise of Anthropological Theory (New York: Thomas Y. Crowell and Co., 1968), pp. 89-93, 108-141; Michael Banton, Race Relations (New York: Basic Books, 1967), pp. 18-54; and George W. Stocking, Jr., "American Scientists and Race Theory: 1890-1915," Ph.D. dissertation, University of Pennsylvania, 1960, pp. 324-363.

2. E. F. Frazier, "Sociological Theory and Race Relations," American Sociological Review, 12:3 (June 1947), p. 268. The periodization discussed in this section leans heavily on this article.

3. R. E. Park, Race and Culture, ed. by E. C. Hughes et al. (Glencoe, Illinois: The Free Press, 1950), p. 150.

4. The list has been compiled from: Stanford M. Lyman, "The Race Relations Cycle of Robert E. Park," Pacific Sociological Review, 11:1 (Spring 1968), pp. 18-19; J. Bracey, A. Meier, E. Rudwick, eds., The Black Sociologists: The First Half Century (Belmont, California: Wadsworth Publishing Co., 1971), pp. 1-12; and, Park, Race and Culture.

5. See Frazier, p. 270; the quoted phrase by Park is from his Race and Culture cited in Lyman, p. 17.

6. See Milton M. Gordon, Assimilation in American Life (New York: Oxford University Press, 1964), Ch. 4, esp. pp. 96-114.

7. In 1875, Alexander Crummel, the noted Black advocate of African repatriation, denounced racial injustice as "the tyranny of caste," cited in Bracey, et al., eds., Black Nationalism in America (New York: Bobbs-Merrill Co., 1970), p. 130. And Joseph Weydemeyer, a pioneer American Marxist, condemned "both black and white slavery" after Lincoln's election in 1860; see Philip S. Foner, Organized Labor and the Black Worker, 1619-1973 (New York: International Publishers, 1974),

p. 12. But neither of these illustrations represents the coherence and exposition of the major statements of Warner and Myrdal for caste, or of Debs and Cox for Marxist class analysis.

8. Here, DuBois' "nation within a nation" thesis, advanced in the 1930s, may be recalled; see W. E. B. DuBois, "A Negro Nation Within the Nation?," Current History, 42 (June 1935), pp. 265-270.

9. Michael Banton, Race Relations (New York: Basic Books, 1967); Pierre van den Berghe, Race and Racism (New York: John Wiley and Sons, 1967); John Rex, Race Relations in Sociological Theory (New York: Schocken Books, 1970); Richard A. Schermerhorn, Comparative Ethnic Relations: A Framework for Theory and Research (New York: Random House, 1970); and Graham C. Kinloch, The Dynamics of Race Relations: A Sociological Analysis (New York: McGraw-Hill, 1974).

10. The action of value presuppositions on the social scientist's work is examined by Max Weber, "'Objectivity' in Social Science and Social Policy," in M. Weber, Methodology of the Social Sciences, trans. and ed. by E. A. Shils and H. A. Finch (Glencoe, Illinois: The Free Press, 1949), p. 76.

11. Schermerhorn, pp. 6-12. "Multiple classification analysis" is discussed in Andrew Greeley, "Political Participation among Ethnic Groups...," American Journal of Sociology, 80 (1974), pt. 1, pp. 170-204.

12. John Horton, "Order and Conflict Theories of Social Problems as Competing Ideologies," American Journal of Sociology, 71:6 (May 1966), pp. 701-713; the quote is from p. 702.

13. Pierre L. van den Berghe, "Dialectic and Functionalism: Toward a Theoretical Synthesis," American Sociological Review, 28:5 (October 1963), pp. 695-705.

14. P. L. van den Berghe, "Dialectic and Functionalism," p. 696.

15. P. L. van den Berghe, "Dialectic and Functionalism," pp. 696-698.

16. P. L. van den Berghe, "Dialectic and Functionalism," pp. 699-700.

17. P. L. van den Berghe, "Dialectic and Functionalism," pp. 698, 701-704.

18. Schermerhorn, p. 52. Following Schermerhorn's principle of "mechanical allocation," Barth and Noel construct a typology of "conceptual frameworks" -- designated "race cycle," "consensus," "interdependence," and "conflict" -- that may be selected in sequence to explain the phenomena of race relations as they pass through the stages of "emergence," "persistence," "adaptation," and "change." But their combination of frameworks does not amount to a synthesis because it is essentially Park's cycle with accreted elements from other theories, and because crucial normative issues -- e.g., the epistemological assumptions and political economic critique of conflict theory -- are left unexamined. See Ernest A. T. Barth and Donald L. Noel, "Conceptual Frameworks for the Analysis of Race Relations: An Evaluation," Social Forces, 50 (March 1972), pp. 333-348.

19. Banton, pp. 63-64, 67. Transaction theory, according to Banton, holds that human actors enter into relations based on the calculation of rewards and punishments; groups form as a reaction to the stimuli provided by these exchanges.

20. Rex, pp. 27, 117, 132.

21. Kinloch, pp. 6, 9, 121, 123.

22. The essentials of the dialectical method may be grasped in Maurice Cornforth, Materialism and the Dialectical Method (New York: International Publishers, 1975) (originally 1953); its epistemological assumptions are presented in the context of polemical discussion by V. I. Lenin, Materialism and Empiro-Criticism (Peking, China: Foreign Language Press, 1972) (originally 1908), esp. Chs. 1, 2, and 3. Finally, as an illustration of

Marx's use of the dialectical method, see "Estranged Labour," "Critique of the Hegelian Dialectic...," and "The German Ideology (part I)," in Robert C. Tucker, ed., The Marx-Engels Reader (New York: W. W. Norton, 1972), pp. 56-67, pp. 83-103, pp. 111-164; note especially the use of paradox in the first essay cited.

Cornforth notes that Lenin scoffed at the idea that the triad (thesis-antithesis-synthesis), which van den Berghe uses to justify his assertion that Marxism employs an equilibrium model of society, was the basis of the dialectical method (Cornforth, p. 78). However, of a more serious nature is the tendency of certain writers to rend the integrated fabric of Marxist thought, as if its economics and sociology were blithely separable from its politics. In addition to van den Berghe (and Schermerhorn, p. 43) as an example of this tendency, the critical discussion of Dahrendorf by Hazelrigg, in which the latter makes this separation, may be cited; see Lawrence E. Hazelrigg, "Class, Property, and Authority: Dahrendorf's Critique of Marx's Theory of Class," Social Forces, 50 (June 1972), pp. 473-487, esp. pp. 473-474. Conversely, the importance of understanding Marxist thought holistically is emphasized by Henri Lefebvre, The Sociology of Marx (New York: Random House, 1968).

23. See V. I. Lenin, Materialism and Empiro-Criticism, Ch. 3.

24. See, for a discussion of this point in the dialectical method, Mao Tse-Tung, "On Contradiction," in Four Essays on Philosophy (Peking, China: Foreign Language Press, 1968), pp. 23-78.

25. For example, Lieberson takes Park's cycle as his starting point, but modifies it by outlining two possible sequences: one in which the dominant group migrates to an area and establishes its rule over indigenous groups, and the other in which the dominant group, after establishing itself, imports other racial and ethnic groups for subordinate positions. The two "contact situations" lead, respectively, to increased probabilities of war and nationalism in the former case (called "migrant superordination") and to lessened

conflict, strong consensual bonds, and assimilation (dubbed, confusingly, "indigenous superordination"; Lieberson redefines "indigenous" to include colonizers) in the latter. When the equation of U.S. experience with the latter case is made, the dilemmas of Lieberson's normative framework stand clearly revealed, e.g., how is the position of Black folks, as unassimilated, to be explained by his theory? See Stanley Lieberson, "A Societal Theory of Race and Ethnic Relations," _American Sociological Review_, 26 (1961), pp. 902-910. Similarly, Coleman's application of the concept of "developmental change" (i.e., gradualism assisted by social engineers) to race relations rests on the assumption that "general values and goals" provide a "stable element" in planning ameliorative change -- an order normative framework; see A. Lee Coleman, "Race Relations and Developmental Change," _Social Forces_, 46:1 (September 1967), pp. 1-8. And Himes' discussion from a functionalist perspective adopts an order normative framework to explain race relations involving Black people and whites as the homeostatic working of racial conflict to promote "ultimate values," avoiding questions of the origins of racial oppression, disjunctive conflict, and the connections between racial conflict and the sources which perpetuate racial oppression; see Joseph S. Himes, "The Functions of Racial Conflict," _Social Forces_, 50 (September 1971), pp. 53-60.

26. Rex, pp. 25, 38, 117-118, 138.

27. Rex, pp. 53, 56, 122, 130.

28. Schermerhorn, pp. 15, 74, 103, 125, 126.

29. Schermerhorn, pp. 45, 92-121, 122-163. It is worthy of note that Schermerhorn's failure to discuss exploitation reveals itself in his assertion that the economic ties developed between racial subordinates and the dominant group in a classical colonial situation are "symbiotic." Since symbiosis normally involves a _mutually beneficial_ exchange between living organisms, it would seem that the term "parasitic" is more appropriate to a social situation in which exploitative economic interest guides the colonizer (ibid., pp. 26, 55).

30. Banton, pp. 315-318, 325-328.

31. Banton, pp. 141, 145, 153, 159, 166.

32. Van den Berghe, Race and Racism, pp. 32, 33, 37, 89.

33. Van den Berghe, Race and Racism, pp. 93-94, 130, 145.

34. Van den Berghe, Race and Racism, pp. 16-17, 93, 123, 128.

35. Kinloch, pp. 214-216, 227.

36. Kinloch, pp. 12, 41, 50, 84-85, 125, 216.

37. Marx defined the degree of exploitation under capitalism as the rate of surplus value expressed in the ratio of surplus labor to necessary labor, where the value of labor is known. See K. Marx, Capital, vol. 1, trans. by S. Moore and E. Aveling, ed. by F. Engels (New York: Charles H. Kerr and Co., 1906), pp. 240-241.

38. Van den Berghe, Race and Racism, pp. 22, 36, 82-83, 94, 113-115; the quoted phrases are from pp. 83 and 113.

39. Kinloch, pp. 88, 138, 143-144, 177-178.

40. Schermerhorn, pp. 71, 84, 89, 208, 215, 227-228; the quoted phrase appears on p. 89, n. 11.

41. Banton, pp. 141, 346-348, 357-367; as an illustration of the burdensome pressures under which the Black psyche strains, Banton (pp. 345, 358) cites the Watts rebellion as a sign of chaotic despair and hopelessness. A contrary view has been offered that, far from being an act of despair, the spontaneous tumult was an act of political defiance by a community fed up with white (especially police) domination and governmental non-responsiveness; see Bayard Rustin, "The 'Watts Manifesto' and the McCone Report," Commentary, 41 (March 1966), pp. 29-35.

42. Rex, pp. 77, 112-113, 150; the quoted phrases are found on pp. 113 and 150.

43. Charles A. Valentine, "Deficit, Difference, and Bi-cultural Models of Afro-American Behavior," Harvard Educational Review, 41:2 (May 1971), pp. 137-157; the quote is found on p. 141.

44. Blauner (Racial Oppression in America, 1972, pp. 124-161) has attempted an implicit bi-cultural model of Black culture. His statement, however, does not include the notion of dialectics, which I have added and which I discuss in Ch. 2 as "the processual interaction method of culture study," i.e., production, social relations of production, etc., are to be conceived of as spheres of human activity which interact developmentally to create social life. Here, I am applying this idea specifically to the concept of Black culture. A review of competing theories of Black culture, together with a preliminary analysis of its institutions and history, may be found in Robert Staples, Introduction to Black Sociology (New York: McGraw-Hill, 1976), esp. Chs. 3 and 4.

45. Cf. Schermerhorn, pp. 9-10; and Kinloch, pp. 65-68.

46. Cf. Rex, pp. 1-2.

47. Van den Berghe, Race and Racism, pp. 11, 15, 93, 126, 130, 138-139; the quotes are from pp. 11, 93, 130, and 139.

48. Schermerhorn, pp. 73, 80, 84, 107, 143, 186, 215; the quotes are from pp. 73, 80, and 186.

49. Kinloch, pp. 54, 108, 121, 122, 123, 203-205, 214; the quotes are taken from pp. 122 and 214. There is a curious disjuncture in Kinloch's theoretical presentation: the point of the entire book seems to be to emphasize the importance of structural phenomena in race relations over and above those that are only psychological or social-psychological. Yet, when the project of decolonization (and, one presumes, the diminution and

eradication of racism) of society is set forth, the most pressing task is held to be the need to humanize the values of the dominant elite (ibid., pp. 217-218). One possible explanation for this puzzling conclusion is that adopting Park's cycle but refurbishing it as a "colonial sequence" (ibid., p. 203) allows Kinloch to picture exploitation as ultimately dependent on a society's wishes (ibid., p. 218) and at the same time to believe that the realization of the 'American Dream' will wipe out racism (ibid.) as assimilation is eventually attained.

50. Banton, pp. 8, 153-162, 335-336, 342, 356; the quoted phrases appear on pp. 153, 154, 155, and 356.

51. Rex, pp. 136-161; quotes appear on pp. 137, 139, 142, 151, 156, and 159. The works by Pareto and Berger and Luckmann which Rex refers to are: Vilfredo Pareto, Mind and Society, 1935; and Peter Berger and Thomas Luckmann, The Social Construction of Reality, 1966.

52. The semi-autonomous nature of ideas, especially when they are systematized as ideology, is argued in Peter Berger and Thomas Luckmann, The Social Construction of Reality (Garden City, New York: Doubleday, 1966), pp. 1-92. A classic argument on this point, in which the author associates the semi-autonomous power of ideas with the mediations which guide social action at certain stages of historical development, is K. Marx, "On the Jewish Question," in Robert C. Tucker, ed., The Marx-Engels Reader, pp. 24-51, esp. p. 30.

53. Henri Lefebvre, The Sociology of Marx, Ch. 3, "Ideology and the Sociology of Knowledge," pp. 59-88; "representations," "opaque," and "transparent" are introduced on p. 60, while the long quote is taken from p. 80.

54. A most penetrating rebuttal of this assumption is given by Herbert Blumer, "Industrialization and Race Relations," in Guy Hunter, ed., Industrialization and Race Relations: A Symposium (New York: Oxford University Press, 1965), pp. 220-253. Blumer's main point is that

the *a priori* theoretical judgment that the prerequisites of the industrial system (e.g., secular reason, contractual relations, impersonal markets, physical and social mobility, etc.) will inevitably disrupt and improve traditional race patterns is not warranted given certain empirical evidence (e.g., the textile industry in the U.S. South). This evidence, he argues, demonstrates that industrialization *conforms* to pre-existing racial norms, rather than changing them; when these norms do change, it is most likely the result of non-economic (usually political and social) factors.

55. For example, when Rex discusses the future of the Afro-American rebellion, begun in the 1960s, he envisions either its success in promoting assimilation or separation, or its role in sustaining still further conflict. A writer under the influence of the economic automatism assumption probably would have been more inclined to interpret this phenomenon as simply part of the process of assimilation, fueled by economic improvement (ibid., p. 112).

56. The tying together of these two issues -- Black culture and related religious or political ideologies -- such that both are denied uniqueness, distorted, or rendered pathological is best illustrated by the Kerner Commission Report's assertion that Black nationalism ("militancy") is only a disguised, impotent plea for inclusion into American society. See *Report of the National Advisory Commission on Civil Disorders*, 1968, pp. 111-113.

57. Rex, pp. 159-160.

58. Gerald D. Berreman, some of whose writing was reviewed in Ch. 2, has continued to pursue the caste model for U.S. race relations, attempting to document it with comparative ethnographic findings. See Gerald D. Berreman, *Caste in the Modern World* (Morristown, New Jersey: General Learning Press, 1973).

59. See Moynihan and Glazer, *Beyond the Melting Pot*, 2nd ed., 1970, pp. xxiii-xxiv. Though not formal adherents of this model, these authors invoke the notion

mentioned when they explain recent (c. 1965) tensions in Northern racial matters.

60. Outside sociology, in the field of history, the most visible adherent of the ethnic group model is Oscar Handlin, in whose works the trials and tribulations of European immigration are recounted. Handlin, in one of his pieces, considers the difference between this process and the experience of Third World groups in this country and rejects economic explanations, settling instead on a vaguely defined combination of social psychological and material factors; see Oscar Handlin, <u>Race and Nationality in American Life</u> (Boston: Little, Brown, 1957), esp. pp. 1-28, 51-67.

61. The decline of small business in America has long been noted, though Moynihan and Glazer cite it as a tradition of prime importance for those ethnic groups which have successfully integrated. The reality of American business today is economic concentration and monopoly, a fact documented in 1964 by the <u>Statistical Abstract of the United States</u> (1964), published by the U.S. Department of Commerce, Bureau of the Census, as quoted in F. Lundberg, <u>The Rich and the Super Rich</u> (New York: Lyle Stuart, 1968), pp. 295-298.

62. For contrary views of the Black family and its competencies as a socialization agent and cultural resource, see William Ryan, <u>Blaming the Victim</u>, rev. ed. (New York: Random House, 1976), Ch. 3; Herbert G. Gutman, <u>The Black Family in Slavery and Freedom: 1750-1925</u> (New York: Random House, 1977); Andrew Billingsley, <u>Black Families in White America</u> (Englewood Cliffs, New Jersey: Prentice-Hall, 1968); and Robert Staples, <u>op. cit.</u>, Ch. 5.

63. The notion of the tight labor market, essentially derived from Marx's principle of the reserve army of labor, is an example. Marx held that pressure on wage levels is maintained (downward pressure, that is) by "relative surplus population" so that surplus value may be realized from the difference between the value of labor power expended and the value of the commodity produced. This means that unemployment will tend to rise

as capital accumulation proceeds, unless measures are taken to check joblessness. Liberal pundits on race relations often hold that only a tight labor market, in which workers are scarce and jobs plentiful, can promise the alleviation of discrimination; racism, it is assumed, succumbs before economic expansion and success. For illustration, see the arguments on this point by the following liberal authors: Eli Ginzberg, The Negro Potential (New York: Harper and Row, 1964), p. 39; Eli Ginzberg and Alfred S. Eichner, The Troublesome Presence (New York: Free Press, 1964), p. 335; and James Tobin, "On Improving the Economic Status of the Negro," Daedalus, 94 (Fall, 1965), p. 895 -- all cited in Sidney Willhelm, Who Needs the Negro? (Garden City, New York: Doubleday, 1970), pp. 161-162. On Marx's formulation of the principle of the reserve army of labor and its effect on the process of capital accumulation, see Paul M. Sweezy, The Theory of Capitalist Development (New York: Monthly Review Press, 1942), pp. 85, 87-92.

64. A thought-provoking piece, representative of this attempt, is Harold M. Baron, "Racial Domination in Advanced Capitalism: A Theory of Nationalism and Divisions in the Labor Market," in Richard C. Edwards, Michael Reich, and David M. Gordon, eds., Labor Market Segmentation (Lexington, Massachusetts: D. C. Heath, 1975), pp. 173-216.

65. The debate appears as the following articles in the Review of Black Political Economy (RBPE): Donald J. Harris, "The Black Ghetto as 'Internal Colony': A Theoretical Critique and Alternative Formulation," RBPE, 2:4 (Summer 1972), pp. 3-33; and William K. Tabb, "Marxian Exploitation and Domestic Colonialism: A Reply to Donald J. Harris," RBPE, 4:4 (Summer 1974), pp. 69-87. Harris' critique was inspired by Tabb's book, The Political Economy of the Black Ghetto (New York: Norton, 1970).

66. Harris, p. 9.

67. Harris, p. 10.

68. Harris, pp. 9-12.

69. Harris, pp. 15-21.

70. Harris, pp. 21-22.

71. Harris, pp. 11, 23-25, 27. The quote is taken from p. 25.

72. Harris, pp. 30; 33, n. 23.

73. Tabb, "A Reply," p. 84.

74. Tabb, "A Reply," pp. 72, 80-81.

75. Tabb, "A Reply," pp. 70, 74.

76. Tabb, "A Reply," p. 73.

77. Tabb, "A Reply," pp. 72, 73, 77.

78. Tabb, "A Reply," pp. 77-78.

79. Tabb, "A Reply," p. 80.

80. Tabb, "A Reply," pp. 80, 85-86.

81. Tabb, "A Reply," pp. 83-85, 86.

82. Tabb alludes to this when he notes that Harris maintains that the corporate sphere of capital does not invest in the ghetto because Black people are poor, without giving an explanation for the basis and origin of that poverty ("A Reply," p. 79). Similarly, Rex observes that the solution to the problem of explaining via Marxist analysis the racism and racial privilege of white workers, without use of the "false consciousness" notion, is to introduce "a secondary hypothesis" that conflict positions had been previously determined on non-economic criteria as to who should occupy inferior work roles; John Rex, Race Relations and Sociological Theory, pp. 16, 132. Blumer's conclusion that in the presence of a "firmly established racial order" industrialism merely conforms to the racial code, changing its form but not disturbing its overall content, provides non-partisan support for the manner of

investigation of exclusion typically pursued by proponents of the colonial model; Herbert Blumer, op. cit., esp. pp. 232-233, 236-237, 240-245.

83. See Ch. 3 of the present work.

84. A prime example of the dangers of utopianism is the argument by Adolph L. Reed, Jr., that since Black people are a nationality whose culture and self-determination have been denied, they must seek to acquire power through building a primary industrial base in a monopolized economy; Adolph L. Reed, Jr., "Marxism and Nationalism in Afro-America; Introduction: A Note on Black Intellectuals," Social Theory and Practice, 1:4 (Fall 1971), pp. 1-39, esp. pp. 30-32.

85. One of the key issues, as pointed out in Ch. 4, is the correct statement of the relation between economic and non-economic factors in a given social or historical situation and of the directional tendencies of this dialectic. For race relations theory, the concept of consciousness, as derived from the Marxist tradition, holds promise for establishing linkages between these factors. E. J. Hobsbawm's observation that forms of class consciousness arise within classes during the course of economic development, and that some are harmonious with socioeconomic reality while others are not, would seem to be applicable broadly to the problem of explaining dialectically (i.e., contradictorily) racism's uses and persistence under capitalism; see E. J. Hobsbawm, "Class Consciousness in History," in Istvan Meszaros, ed., Aspects of History and Class Consciousness (London: Routledge and Kegan Paul, 1971), pp. 5-21, esp. pp. 11-13.

A Selected Bibliography

Ackerman, Frank, and Andrew Zimbalist. "Capitalism and Inequality in the United States." In The Capitalist System: A Radical Analysis of American Society. Eds. Richard C. Edwards, Michael Reich, and Thomas E. Weisskopf. 2nd ed. Englewood Cliffs, New Jersey: Prentice-Hall, 1978, pp. 297-307.

Allen, Robert L. Black Awakening in Capitalist America: An Analytic History. New York: Doubleday, 1969.

----------. Reluctant Reformers: Racism and Social Reform Movements in the United States. New York: Doubleday, 1974.

Aronowitz, Stanley. False Promises: The Shaping of American Working Class Consciousness. New York: McGraw-Hill, 1973.

Bailey, Harry A., Jr. "Negro Interest Group Strategies." Urban Affairs Quarterly, 4:1 (September 1968), pp. 27-38.

Balbus, Isaac D. "The Concept of Interest in Pluralist and Marxian Analysis." Politics and Society, 1:2 (February 1972), pp. 151-177.

Banfield, Edward C. The Unheavenly City Revisited. Boston: Little, Brown, 1974.

Banton, Michael. Race Relations. New York: Basic Books, 1967.

Baran, Paul A., and Paul M. Sweezy. Monopoly Capital: An Essay on the American Economic and Social Order. New York: Monthly Review Press, 1966.

Baron, Harold M. "The Web of Urban Racism." In Institutional Racism in America. Eds. L. Knowles and K. Prewitt. Englewood Cliffs, New Jersey: Prentice-Hall, 1969, pp. 134-176.

----------. "The Demand for Black Labor: Historical Notes on the Political Economy of Racism." Radical America, 5 (March-April 1971), pp. 1-46.

----------. "Racial Domination in Advanced Capitalism: A Theory of Nationalism and Divisions in the Labor Market." In Labor Market Segmentation. Eds. Richard C. Edwards, Michael Reich, and David M. Gordon. Lexington, Massachusetts: D. C. Heath, 1975, pp. 173-216.

Barth, Ernest A. T., and Donald L. Noel. "Conceptual Framework for the Analysis of Race Relations: An Evaluation." Social Forces, 50 (March 1972), pp. 333-348.

Berreman, Gerald D. "Caste in India and the United States." American Journal of Sociology, 66 (1960-1961), pp. 120-127.

----------. Caste in the Modern World. Morristown, New Jersey: General Learning Press, 1973.

Blauner, Robert. Racial Oppression in America. New York: Harper and Row, 1972.

Blumer, Herbert. "Industrialization and Race Relations." In Industrialization and Race Relations: A Symposium. Ed. Guy Hunter. New York: Oxford University Press, 1965, pp. 220-253.

Boggs, James. The American Revolution: Pages from a Negro Worker's Notebook. New York: Monthly Review Press, 1963.

----------. Racism and the Class Struggle: Further Pages from a Black Worker's Notebook. New York: Monthly Review Press, 1970.

Carmichael, Stokely, and Charles V. Hamilton. Black Power: The Politics of Liberation in America. New York: Random House, 1967.

Cox, Oliver C. Caste, Class, and Race: A Study in

Social Dynamics. New York: Monthly Review Press, 1959 (originally 1948).

Cruse, Harold. The Crisis of the Negro Intellectual. New York: William Morrow, 1967.

Dahl, Robert A. "Power." International Encyclopedia of the Social Sciences. 1968 ed.

Dewey, John. Liberalism and Social Action. New York: G. P. Putnam and Sons, 1935.

Dollard, John. Caste and Class in a Southern Town. 3rd ed. Garden City, New York: Doubleday, 1957 (originally published 1937).

Drake, J. G. St. Clair, and Horace R. Cayton. Black Metropolis. Rev. and enl. ed., 2 vols. New York: Harper and Row, 1962 (originally 1945).

DuBois, W. E. B. "Marxism and the Negro Problem." Crisis, 40 (May 1933), pp. 103-104, 118.

----------. "Segregation in the North." Crisis, 41 (April 1934), pp. 115-117.

----------. "A Negro Nation Within the Nation." Current History, 42 (June 1935), pp. 265-270.

----------. The Souls of Black Folk. New York: Johnson Reprint Corp., 1968 (originally published Chicago: A. C. McClurg and Co., 1903).

Duncan, Beverly, and Otis D. Duncan. "Minorities and the Process of Stratification." American Sociological Review, 33 (1968), pp. 356-364.

Ellison, Ralph. Shadow and Act. New York: Random House, 1964.

Fanon, Frantz. The Wretched of the Earth. Trans. Constance Farrington. New York: Grove Press, 1968.

Fineberg, S. A. "The Common Goal: The Single Society,"

Crisis, 78 (1971), pp. 16-19.

Flores, Guillermo. "Race and Culture in the Internal Colony: Keeping the Chicano in His Place." In Structures of Dependency. Eds. F. Bonilla and R. Girling. Stanford, California: Stanford University Press, 1973, pp. 189-223.

Forsythe, Dennis. "Radical Sociology and Blacks." In The Death of White Sociology. Ed. Joyce A. Ladner. New York: Random House, 1973, pp. 226-233.

Frazier, E. F. "Sociological Theory and Race Relations." American Sociological Review, 12:3 (June 1947), pp. 265-271.

Gait, Edward A. "Caste." Encyclopedia of Religion and Ethics. Vol. 3. New York: Charles Scribner's Sons, 1925, pp. 230-239.

Gellner, Ernest A. "Model (Theoretical Model)." Dictionary of Social Sciences. Eds. J. Gould and W. L. Kolb. New York: Crowell-Collier, 1964, p. 435.

Gerth, H. H., and C. Wright Mills. From Max Weber: Essays in Sociology. New York: Oxford University Press, 1946.

Girvetz, Harry K. From Wealth to Welfare: The Evolution of Liberalism. Stanford, California: Stanford University Press, 1950.

Gordon, Milton M. Assimilation in American Life: The Role of Race, Religion, and National Origins. New York: Oxford University Press, 1964.

Gouldner, Alvin W. The Coming Crisis of Western Sociology. New York: Basic Books, 1970.

Greeley, Andrew. "Political Participation Among Ethnic Groups in the United States: A Preliminary Reconnaissance." American Journal of Sociology, 80 (1974), pt. 1, pp. 170-204.

Hare, Nathan. "The Sociological Study of Racial Conflict." Phylon, 33 (1974), pp. 27-32.

Harris, Donald J. "The Black Ghetto as 'Internal Colony': A Theoretical Critique and Alternative Formulation." Review of Black Political Economy, 2:4 (Summer 1972), pp. 3-33.

Harris, Marvin. "Caste, Class, and Minority." Social Forces, 37 (March 1959), pp. 248-254.

----------. "Race." International Encyclopedia of the Social Sciences. 1968 ed.

----------. The Rise of Anthropological Theory: A History of Theories of Culture. New York: Thomas Y. Crowell, 1968.

Horton, John. "Order and Conflict Theories of Social Problems as Competing Ideologies." American Journal of Sociology, 71:6 (May 1966), pp. 701-713.

Hunt, E. K. Property and Prophets: The Evolution of Economic Institutions and Ideologies. New York: Harper and Row, 1972.

Inden, Ronald B., and McKim Marriott. "Caste Systems." Encyclopedia Britannica: Macropedia. 1974 ed.

Introduction to Afro-American Studies. 4th ed., 2 vols. Chicago: Peoples College Press, 1977.

Jackson, George. Soledad Brother: The Prison Letters of George Jackson. New York: Bantam Books, 1970.

----------. Blood In My Eye. New York: Random House, 1972.

Kaiser, Ernest. "Racial Dialectics: The Aptheker-Myrdal School Controversy." Phylon, 9 (1948), pp. 295-302.

Kantrowitz, Nathan. "Ethnic and Racial Segregation in the New York Metropolis, 1960." American Journal of Sociology, 64 (1968), pp. 685-695.

Kaplan, H. Roy. American Minorities and Economic Opportunity. Itasca, Illinois: F. E. Peacock, 1977.

Katznelson, Ira, and Mark Kesselman. The Politics of Power: A Critical Introduction to American Government. New York: Harcourt, Brace, Jovanovich, 1975.

Kerner, Otto, et al. Report of the National Advisory Commission on Civil Disorders. Washington, D.C.: U.S. Government Printing Office, 1968.

Kinloch, Graham C. The Dynamics of Race Relations: A Sociological Analysis. New York: McGraw-Hill, 1974.

Knoke, David, and Richard B. Felson. "Ethnic Stratification and Political Cleavage in the United States, 1952-68." American Journal of Sociology, 80 (1974), pt. 1, pp. 630-642.

Knowles, Louis L., and Kenneth Prewitt, eds. Institutional Racism in America. Englewood Cliffs, New Jersey: Prentice-Hall, 1969.

Kroeber, A. L., and Clyde Kluckhohn. Culture: A Critical Review of Concepts and Definitions. New York: Random House, 1952.

Kuhn, Thomas S. The Structure of Scientific Revolutions. 2nd ed., enl. Chicago: University of Chicago Press, 1970.

Leach, E. R. "Introduction: What Should We Mean By Caste?" In Cambridge Papers in Social Anthropology, No. 2: Aspects of Caste in South India, Ceylon and North-West Pakistan. Ed. E. R. Leach. Cambridge, England: Cambridge University Press, 1969, pp. 1-10.

Lefebvre, Henri. The Sociology of Marx. New York: Random House, 1968.

Lenin, V. I. Imperialism, the Highest Stage of Capitalism. Peking, China: Foreign Language Press, 1970.

----------. "The Socialist Revolution and the Right of Nations to Self-Determination." In Lenin on the National and Colonial Questions. Peking, China: Foreign Language Press, 1970, pp. 1-19.

Lieberson, Stanley, and Glenn V. Fuguitt. "Negro-White Occupational Difference in the Absence of Discrimination." American Journal of Sociology, 73 (1967-68), pp. 188-200.

Lundberg, Ferdinand. The Rich and the Super Rich. New York: Lyle Stuart, 1968.

Lyman, Stanford M. "The Race Relations Cycle of Robert E. Park." Pacific Sociological Review, 11 (Spring 1968), pp. 16-22.

Marx, Karl. Capital. Vol. 1. Trans. Samuel Moore and Edward Aveling. Ed. Frederick Engels. New York: Charles H. Kerr and Co., 1906 (originally published 1867).

----------. "On Class." In Structured Social Inequality. Ed. Celia S. Heller. New York: Macmillan, 1969, pp. 14-23. (Originally appeared in Capital, Manifesto of the Communist Party, The German Ideology, and The Poverty of Philosophy.)

Montagu, Ashley. Man's Most Dangerous Myth: The Fallacy of Race. 5th ed. New York: Oxford University Press, 1974.

Moynihan, Daniel P., and Nathan Glazer. Beyond the Melting Pot: The Negroes, Perto Ricans, Jews, Italians, and Irish of New York City. 2nd ed. Cambridge, Massachusetts: The M.I.T. Press, 1970 (originally published 1963).

Myrdal, Gunnar. An American Dilemma: The Negro Problem and Modern Democracy. 20th anniversary ed., 2 vols. New York: Random House, 1962 (originally 1944).

O'Dell, J. H. "Colonialism and the Negro American Experience." Freedomways, 6 (1966), pp. 296-308.

----------. "A Special Variety of Colonialism." Freedomways, 7 (1967), pp. 7-15.

----------. "The July Rebellions and the 'Military State.'" Freedomways, 7 (1967), pp. 288-301.

----------. "The Contours of the 'Black Revolution' in the 1970s." Freedomways, 10 (1970), pp. 104-114.

Ofari, Earl. The Myth of Black Capitalism. New York: Monthly Review Press, 1970.

----------. "Marxism, Nationalism, and Black Liberation." Monthly Review, 22 (March 1971), pp. 18-33.

Park, Robert E. Race and Culture. Ed. E. C. Hughes. Glencoe, Illinois: The Free Press, 1950.

Park, Robert E., and Ernest W. Burgess. Introduction to the Science of Sociology. 3rd. ed. rev. Ed. Morris Janowitz. Chicago: University of Chicago Press, 1969.

Parsons, Talcott. The Social System. Glencoe, Illinois: The Free Press, 1951.

----------. "Full Citizenship for the Negro American?" In The Negro American. Eds. T. Parsons and Kenneth Clark. New York: Beacon Press, 1966, pp. 709-754.

Patterson, Beeman C. "Political Action of Negroes in Los Angeles: A Case Study in the Attainment of Councilmanic Representation." Phylon, 30 (1969), pp. 170-183.

Perlo, Victor. Economics of Racism, U.S.A.: Roots of Black Inequality. New York: International Publishers, 1975.

Photiadis, John D., and Jeanne Biggar. "Religiosity, Education, and Ethnic Distance." American Journal of Sociology, 67 (1961-62), pp. 666-672.

Prager, Jeffrey. "White Racial Privilege and Social Change: An Examination of Theories of Racism." Berkeley Journal of Sociology, 18 (1972/73), pp. 117-150.

Record, Wilson. The Negro and the Communist Party. New York: Atheneum, 1951.

Reich, Michael. "The Economics of Racism." In Problems in Political Economy: An Urban Perspective. Ed. David M. Gordon. Lexington, Massachusetts: D. C. Heath, 1971, pp. 107-113.

Schermerhorn, Richard A. Comparative Ethnic Relations: A Framework for Theory and Research. New York: Random House, 1970.

Spero, Sterling D., and Abram L. Harris. The Black Worker: The Negro and the Labor Movement. New York: Atheneum, 1972 (originally published 1931).

Staples, Robert. "Race and Colonialism: The Domestic Case in Theory and Practice." The Black Scholar, 7 (June 1976), pp. 37-48.

Stolzman, James, and Herbert Gamberg. "Marxist Class Analysis versus Stratification Analysis as General Approaches to Social Inequality." Berkeley Journal of Sociology, 18 (1973/74), pp. 104-127.

Sweezy, Paul M. The Theory of Capitalist Development: Principles of Marxian Political Economy. New York: Monthly Review Press, 1942.

Tabb, William K. "Marxian Exploitation and Domestic Colonialism: A Reply to Donald J. Harris." Review of Black Political Economy, 4:4 (Summer 1974), pp. 69-87.

Taeuber, Alma F., and Karl E. Taeuber. "The Negro as an Immigrant Group: Recent Trends in Racial and Ethnic Segregation in Chicago." American Journal of

Sociology, 69 (1963-64), pp. 374-382.

Turner, James, and W. Eric Perkins. "Towards a Critique of Social Science." The Black Scholar, 7 (April 1976), pp. 2-11.

Turner, Jonathan H. The Structure of Sociological Theory. Homewood, Illinois: The Dorsey Press, 1974.

U.S. Bureau of the Census, Current Population Reports, Special Studies. Series P-23, No. 54. "The Social and Economic Status of the Black Population in the United States, 1974." Washington, D.C.: U.S. Government Printing Office, 1975.

U.S. Civil Rights Commission Report. "Social Indicators of Equality for Minorities and Women." Washington, D.C.: U.S. Government Printing Office, August 1978.

Valentine, Charles A. Culture and Poverty: Critique and Counter-proposals. Chicago: University of Chicago Press, 1968.

----------. "Deficit, Difference, and Bi-cultural Models of Afro-American Behavior." Harvard Educational Review, 41:2 (May 1971), pp. 137-157.

van den Berghe, Pierre L. "The Dynamics of Racial Prejudice: An Ideal Type Dichotomy." Social Forces, 37 (December 1958), pp. 138-141.

----------. "Dialectic and Functionalism: Toward a Theoretical Synthesis." American Sociological Review, 28:5 (October 1963), pp. 695-705.

----------. Race and Racism. New York: John Wiley and Sons, 1967.

Warner, W. Lloyd. "American Caste and Class." American Journal of Sociology, 42 (September 1936), pp. 234-237.

Warner, W. Lloyd, and Allison Davis. "A Comparative Study of American Caste." In Race Relations and

The Race Problem: A Definition and An Analysis. Ed. Edgar T. Thompson. Durham, North Carolina: Duke University Press, 1939, pp. 219-245.

Wolff, Robert P. The Poverty of Liberalism. Boston: Beacon Press, 1968.

Wright, Erik Olin. "On Class Boundaries in Advanced Capitalist Societies." Studies on the Left, 1976, pp. 3-42.

Wright, M. Frank. "The National Question: A Marxist Critique." The Black Scholar (February 1974), pp. 43-53.

Index